Applying to Graduate School in Psychology

DATE DUE

Applying to Graduate School in Psychology

Advice From Successful Students and Prominent Psychologists

Edited by **Amanda C. Kracen and Ian J. Wallace**

American Psychological Association
Washington, DC

In memory of Elizabeth A. Fries, Ph.D.,
an exemplary scholar and mentor who is missed dearly

Dedicated to our partners
Ronan Wallace and Claire Valderrama

Contents

Contributors

Héctor Y. Adamés, BA, is a 5th-year clinical psychology doctoral candidate at Wright State University in Dayton, Ohio. Before graduate school, Mr. Adamés earned a BA from Montclair State University and worked as a mental health specialist at the University of Medicine and Dentistry of New Jersey. His clinical and research interests include Latino mental health, trauma, and professional training. He is a predoctoral fellow at Boston University School of Medicine Center for Multicultural Training in Psychology and an active member of the National Latino/a Psychological Association and the American Psychological Association of Graduate Students. He has received numerous awards, including the National Latino/a Psychological Association's 2006 Distinguished Student Service Award and the Wright State University School of Professional Psychology's 2005 Jimmy Johnson Scholar Award.

Roy F. Baumeister, PhD, received his doctorate in social psychology from Princeton University in 1978. He is the Francis Eppes Eminent Scholar and the director of the Social Psychology Program at Florida State University in Tallahassee. The Institute for Scientific Information recently ranked him among the most frequently cited psychologists in the world. He has roughly 350 publications, including 20 books and, most recently, a textbook, *Social Psychology and Human Nature*. Dr. Baumeister's research focuses on self and identity, the need to belong, self-control, decision making, emotion, social rejection, free will, aggression, sexuality, and power. In his spare time, he composes and plays music, and he enjoys windsurfing and kitesurfing. He lives with his wife and daughter by a small lake in northern Florida.

is interested in how the cortisol rhythms of married couples are affected by daily hassles and in how "risky" family environments affect adult health through biological and behavioral pathways. She has won several awards for her work, including the Psi Chi–American Psychological Association's (APA's) Edwin B. Newman Graduate Research Award, the National Science Foundation Graduate Research Fellowship, and a Student Research Award from APA's Division 12 (Society of Clinical Psychology), Section IV (Clinical Psychology of Women).

Robert J. Sternberg, PhD, earned his doctorate in psychology from Stanford University. He is the dean of the School of Arts and Sciences at Tufts University in Medford, Massachusetts, as well as the director of the Center for the Psychology of Abilities, Competencies, and Expertise (PACE Center) in Somerville, Massachusetts. Dr. Sternberg is an internationally renowned scientist who researches intelligence, creativity, thinking styles, learning disabilities, and love. He has authored more than 1,100 books and articles and has won roughly two dozen awards for his scholarship. In recognition of his contributions in psychology, he has been awarded eight honorary doctorates. He is a past president of the American Psychological Association (APA) and has served on the boards of directors of the APA, American Psychological Foundation, and Eastern Psychological Association. He is the 2007–2008 president of the Eastern Psychological Association.

Melba J. T. Vasquez, PhD, earned a doctorate in counseling psychology from the University of Texas. She is in independent practice in Austin, Texas, and publishes in the areas of ethics, ethnic minority psychology, psychology of women, training and supervision, and counseling and psychotherapy. She is coauthor, with Kenneth S. Pope, of *Ethics in Psychotherapy & Counseling: A Practical Guide* (3rd ed., 2007) and *How to Survive and Thrive as a Therapist: Information, Ideas, and Resources for Psychologists in Practice* (American Psychological Association [APA], 2005). She cofounded the National Multicultural Conference and Summit and serves as a member-at-large on the APA's board of directors (2007–2009). Dr. Vasquez is a fellow of the APA and holds the diplomate of the American Board of Professional Psychology. She is a past president of the Texas Psychological Association and of APA Divisions 35 (Society for the Psychology of Women) and 17 (Society of Counseling Psychology).

Foreword

For many students, getting into graduate school is a milestone. The graduate school experience undoubtedly has an important impact on one's personal and professional life. Some students set their sights on graduate school before they begin their undergraduate education and use their freshman year to forge their plans for making themselves competitive applicants. Other students begin to entertain the idea of going to graduate school in their senior year or even years after graduation. Most students, however, begin to solidify their professional goals and make their plans for graduate school in their sophomore or junior year. Regardless of when students begin to focus on their graduate school goals, they have many questions about the graduate school application process—a process that can be frightening, exciting, appealing, anxiety-provoking, complex, competitive, and time-consuming. This was certainly true for me when I applied to graduate schools more than 36 years ago. During my 29 years of teaching at James Madison University, I saw the application process become even more complex and competitive and engender even more questions and anxiety about what students need to do to be competitive candidates. Now, in my role as executive director of Psi Chi, when I talk with students about applying to graduate school, I hear the same anxious questions I heard when I was teaching.

Fortunately for today's students, the editors have put together an excellent book that is uniquely suited to answer students' questions about the realities of preparing for, applying to, and making decisions about graduate school. *Applying to Graduate School in Psychology: Advice From Suc-*

cessful Students and Prominent Psychologists is an engaging and refreshing collection of stories in which students share the joys and challenges of applying to graduate school and provide wise advice about every stage of the application process. The graduate student authors have done an excellent job of capturing the concerns and feelings of students and the finest nuances of what the application process is like for students, because they *are* students who recently navigated this difficult path themselves. They understand what it is like to be a graduate school applicant in today's highly competitive, expensive, and diversified educational environment. The authors represent diverse cultures, educational experiences, stages of life, financial means, professional interests, and career goals. Their experiences can generalize to most undergraduates or graduates seeking admission to graduate school.

Unlike most books that provide detailed lists and timetables of what students should do to prepare for graduate school and craft the ultimate application, this book goes beyond the lists and timetables. It offers inspirational, realistic, and often humorous personal stories about what the experience is really like and how best to prepare for it. Don't be misled by the conversational, mentoring voice used by the contributors. The chapters are filled with excellent practical tips and strategies on (a) setting up your undergraduate program or your employment so you will have the courses and experiences valued by graduate schools; (b) selecting potential programs that are good matches for your interests, abilities, and finances; (c) preparing graduate school applications that are tailored to each school and will make you stand out among applicants; (d) preparing for and conducting an impressive interview; and (e) selecting the right school for you. The student contributors speak to the readers as only peers can do. Students and recent graduates will be able to identify with them, and for that reason, the advice will be even more meaningful and powerful.

Though having the student perspective in each chapter is one of the most valuable qualities of this book, the essays by contemporary leaders in psychology are equally valuable. The professional perspectives and experiences of these psychologists offer important insights into the graduate application process, the graduate school experience, and the life of a professional psychologist that can otherwise only be gained by thoughtful reflection on successful, productive careers in the field. These seasoned, respected psychologists serve as inspirational role models for students who are trying to look beyond the graduate school application process and beginning to contemplate what their lives might be like as psychologists.

Applying to Graduate School in Psychology is a unique blend of success stories of contemporary students looking forward to their professional careers and thoughtful reflections by some of psychology's most eminent teachers and scholars. Whether you are a student or recent graduate beginning the graduate school application process or a teacher and faculty advisor working with undergraduate students, this book is one you must read. For graduate school applicants, it provides helpful, practical advice for the application process in a supportive and encouraging manner. For teachers and advisors, as well as being a delightful romp down memory lane, the book provides useful ideas and suggestions to pass along to students who have questions about applying to graduate school. For students and teachers alike, once you start reading this book you will have a difficult time putting it down, and when you are finished you will have a list of invaluable suggestions for getting into graduate school. May you make the most of what this excellent resource has to offer.

Virginia Andreoli Mathie, PhD
Executive Director
Psi Chi

Preface

n the 1st month of graduate school in psychology, while nursing beers on a late summer afternoon when we probably should have been studying, we had one of those get-to-know-you conversations that are typical between new classmates. Our experiences applying to graduate school became the topic of conversation. We both agreed that the application process had been an expensive and challenging, although rewarding, endeavor. We also agreed that no book answered many of the questions we had when applying to graduate school. We had wanted a student-written book that shared information, in addition to details, on how students got admitted to graduate school, what paths they took to get there, and what advice they had for applicants. In essence, we wanted to hear the real stories of successful students. In this ideal book, we also wanted to hear from famous psychologists who had gone through the application process, attended graduate school themselves, and had since been involved with the teaching and training of graduate students. As we wondered how we could help make the application process less mysterious and less challenging for people seeking admission to graduate school, we tossed around the idea of developing a new book.

A few months later, the book development began in earnest and the project took off. We have been working together for a few years now, and it has been fantastic to watch this book take shape and grow from an idea into a collection of stories and resources. We believe it fills a gap for applicants who search for a comprehensive understanding of the application process. Our aim has been to create a book that mentors you, the reader, through each step and consideration in the application process. Nine chapters written by graduate students illustrate the application process from a peer perspective, while contributions from nine eminent psychologists provide unique perspectives on relevant topics. We hope this book achieves our original intent: to help you better understand, through our stories and suggestions, how to successfully apply and get accepted to graduate school in psychology.

Needless to say, we could not have developed this book without help and support from many others. In particular, this book would not exist without such stellar student contributors. Thank you, Héctor Y. Adamés, Alison B. Breland, Frank J. Corigliano, Christina M. Grange, Hayal Z. Kaçkar, Sangeet S. Khemlani, Kristine M. Molina, and Darby E. Saxbe, for staying committed through revision after revision and e-mail after e-mail. In addition, aware of how incredibly busy they are, we thank the prominent psychologists for writing their essays. Drs. Roy F. Baumeister, Clara E. Hill, Gerald P. Koocher, Elizabeth F. Loftus, David G. Myers, Hector F. Myers, James O. Prochaska, Robert J. Sternberg, and Melba J. T. Vasquez, we believe that your experience, wisdom, and passion will inspire students to join the community of psychologists. We are also grateful to Dr. Virginia Andreoli Mathie of Psi Chi for penning the foreword and infusing it with her enthusiasm for psychology. We are indebted to our graduate school mentors, Drs. Steve Danish, Elizabeth Fries, and Kathy Ingram, who supported this project and provided encouragement along the way, even when they probably thought we should have been working on our dissertations. Furthermore, we owe many thanks to Dr. Everett Worthington, for sharing his expertise and helping us stay the course when our enthusiasm lagged. Karen Muehl was a godsend for editing, so we thank her for providing an astute perspective. We also wish to thank Linda McCarter, Lansing Hays, Emily Leonard, and Devon Bourexis, of the Books Department of the American Psychological Association, for their feedback, guidance, and encouragement.

Finally, we want to acknowledge our appreciation for one another as coeditors. We came together as individuals to collaborate on this book—enriching it, we hope, with our different strengths and perspectives—and have emerged as colleagues and friends. At a personal level, we are indebted to the many people who have helped us reach our academic achievements thus far. Amanda thanks Drs. Katie Baird, Melanie Bean, Jeni Burnette, Jean Corcoran, and Marilyn Stern, for their personal and professional support, and is incredibly grateful to Irene Gonzalez as well as her family: Scott, Laurel, Elizabeth, Chris, Ahya, and, of course, Ronan. Ian is thankful for his coworkers at The Life Skills Center, including Tanya Forneris, Lisa Harmon, Kristyn Hoy, Nile Wagley, Alice Westerberg, Katy Wilder Schaff, and especially his friends and family for their support throughout this project.

Applying to
Graduate School
in Psychology

Introduction

f you are applying—or even considering applying—to graduate school in psychology, you need this book. It is like no other. As graduate students ourselves, this is the book we wanted when we applied to graduate school. It is a useful resource if you are intent on getting accepted to a graduate program and want information beyond just the logistics of applying. Reading it will inform you about the many nuances of graduate school and the application process. We hope that by being more informed, you will increase the likelihood of getting accepted to a graduate program, especially your top choice.

Applying to Graduate School in Psychology: Advice From Successful Students and Prominent Psychologists is unique indeed. Of course, like other available books, this one provides concrete information to help you prepare for each step of the application process. However, it also offers additional distinctive features.

1. Chapters authored by graduate students. We believe the experience of applying needs to be explained by those who know it best: the students. Having recently entered graduate school, we can share the finer details of the application process and mentor readers through the process. Therefore, in this book you will find the perspectives of nine diverse students who share personal accounts of their journeys to graduate school and their experiences of the application process.

2. Essays written by famous psychologists. This book features essays penned by nine prominent psychologists. They have made major contributions to the field and to our society—and they are human too. Each of them attended graduate school and likely experienced what you might be feeling now: uncertainty and apprehension about the graduate school journey ahead. Because they care about students and are passionate about psychology, they share insights, advice, and the lessons they learned. Their essays are intended to help you develop a more complete understanding of the field and navigate your own path to graduate school.

3. An insider's view of getting into graduate school. Many of the students and psychologists who contributed to this book currently serve on admissions committees or have done so previously. They are intimately acquainted with the issues related to getting into graduate school. Thus, we encouraged the contributors to "tell it like it is" because otherwise, who will? Therefore, this book provides unwritten rules of applying that we wish we had known but nobody told us. For instance, it addresses what exactly you should bring with you on an interview (see chap. 7) and explains a good strategy for accepting an offer (see chap. 8).

4. A thorough discussion of relevant issues. This book examines the important issues that you need to understand to make better choices and decisions regarding graduate school in psychology. Few books provide such an in-depth review of the factors that will affect you. The contributors go beyond standard information and generalizations to fully explore issues, such as what life is like as a graduate student (chap. 2) and the financial considerations of a career in psychology (chap. 3).

5. Personal tales of contributors. One message in this book is that there is neither a perfect applicant who gets into graduate school in psychology nor a perfect path leading you there. The array of personal stories highlights the ups and downs the contributors experienced when contemplating and applying to graduate school. Reading their tales will help you better envision the application process, which often seems intimidating, overwhelming, and even scary. We hope that by learning about how the contributors successfully got into graduate school, you will see that it is possible and then apply their strategies yourself.

This book is for people considering graduate school in psychology and those who advise and mentor potential applicants. One of the difficulties of developing a book like this is that our audience is very diverse. First, let us say that we are delighted by this! We are thrilled that people from all walks of life consider graduate school in psychology; the field will become richer and more representative of our greater society as our professional community diversifies. Throughout this book, the contributors try to be as inclusive as possible of all readers, and make special efforts to address the concerns of underrepresented applicants, such as minority populations, mature adults returning to education, foreign students, and students with children.

Readers also have diverse professional interests. Thus, an aim of this book is to address the remarkable variety of psychology graduate school structures and emphases. As such, this book is appropriate for people interested in different graduate degrees (e.g., PhD, PsyD, EdD, MA, MS) and various careers in psychology. It is applicable if you are considering any of the subfields offered in psychology, such as clinical, counseling, school, experimental, and so on.

The student contributors, including ourselves, were selected because we successfully applied to graduate school, are committed to helping new students pursue graduate studies, and represent the diversity of the field. All of us were students (representing PhD, PsyD, and EdD programs) when we wrote our chapters, and three of us had previously completed terminal master's degree programs. We attend schools located in the western, midwestern, southern, and northeast regions of the United States, where we are studying different subfields (e.g., clinical, counseling, educational, experimental psychology) and have unique career interests and goals. When writing, we were at different stages of our studies, from 1st- to 5th-year students. We also represent various demographic characteristics; we differ in the areas of gender, age, socioeconomic status, sexual orientation, and disability status. We are African American, Asian American, Caucasian, and Latino. A few writers are first-generation college students, and one writer is an international student. In sum, because we student contributors are a motley crew, readers will have the opportunity to hear about a broad range of perspectives and experiences.

The prominent psychologists who contributed essays to this book are some of the most famous living psychologists in the United States and are enthusiastic about psychology as a career choice. Drs. Roy F. Baumeister, Clara E. Hill, Gerald P. Koocher, Elizabeth F. Loftus, David G. Myers, Hector F. Myers, James O. Prochaska, Robert J. Sternberg, and Melba J. T. Vasquez are devoted to mentoring students. They represent the diversity of the field, too, as can be seen in the differences in their gender, age, ethnicity, and career interests and paths.

This book contains chapters, essays, a list of recommended resources, and a glossary. The chapters and essays are presented in an order that mirrors the application process, starting from exploring the field of psychology to making final decisions about schools and future plans. Each chapter covers an important issue or a distinct step in the process of applying. Within the chapters, the contributors do three things. First, because it is helpful to get to know a person before receiving suggestions and advice from that person, each student contributor shares some of his or her story with you. Second, each student contributor examines the topic of the chapter in a straightforward manner, sharing insight from within the trenches of graduate school. Finally, each chapter closes with personal tips from the author. These are points that may not specifically fit in any one chapter but that we wished someone had told us before we applied.

Each chapter is followed by an essay on a related topic that is written by a prominent psychologist. Some essays are visionary, some are practi-

Héctor Y. Adamés

An Overview
of the Field
# of Psychology

1

From: Dominican Republic; raised in Passaic, NJ
Area of study: Clinical Psychology, Wright State University, Dayton, OH
Previous degree(s): BA in psychology from Montclair State University, Montclair, NJ
Career before graduate school: Mental health specialist at a medical center
Number of graduate schools applied to: 10
Age when started this graduate program: 25
Professional interests: Latino mental health, trauma, and professional training in psychology
Career aspirations: Continue delivering clinical services and conducting research

Starting in elementary school, many of us likely were asked, "What do you want to be when you grow up?" As a child, you might have felt confused about the answer to this question; nonetheless, you might have said you wanted to be a doctor, rock star, firefighter, dancer, or baseball player. Many years later, you may still be experiencing confusion when considering psychology as a career choice. For instance, do you feel lost while thinking about the various graduate school options available? Do

I would like to thank Leon D. VandeCreek, PhD, ABPP, and Janette Rodríguez-Varela, MA, for their assistance and editorial contributions to this chapter, as well as Elizabeth L. Haines, PhD, for her mentorship.

plex and demanding process. I was angry and frustrated by having to consider all these demographic and cultural factors when applying to graduate school. Nonetheless, I knew I had to acknowledge and respect my anger, allowing it to fuel my desire to contribute to our society and to my communities.

When researching doctoral programs online, I looked for ones in which topics and courses on diversity and multiculturalism were evident in the curriculum and the mission statement. I also sought a program in which faculty members and the student body represented various demographic groups. I wanted a program that specializes in training ethnic minority psychologists to deliver psychological assessment and treat disenfranchised ethnic communities and individuals with multiple identities (e.g., lesbian, gay, bisexual, transgendered, physically challenged, multiracial, or economically disadvantaged individuals). I consequently realized I was interested in attending a program where I not only felt welcomed and would be well trained but also knew the importance and saliency of multiculturalism was understood. Reflecting on my needs, career aspirations, and motivations helped me find a suitable program. I was thrilled to be accepted to the PsyD program at Wright State University because it was an ideal fit and met my needs. Pursuing higher education has been an exciting endeavor, and I'm slowly realizing what I want to be when I grow up.

The Why, Who, and What of Psychology

To pursue graduate study in psychology and to find your niche within the field, it is helpful to discuss three important questions: (a) Why choose a career in psychology? (b) Who chooses a career in psychology? and (c) What can be done with a graduate degree in psychology? The intent of this chapter is not to be prescriptive but rather to stimulate your own critical thinking and decision making as you ponder your future. I invite you to start considering whether psychology is the field for you.

WHY CHOOSE A CAREER IN PSYCHOLOGY?

As a discipline, psychology focuses on the thoughts, feelings, and behaviors of humans. It traverses numerous areas of investigation, from psycholinguistics to sports psychology to psychopharmacology, which makes it interesting and rewarding—and a popular undergraduate major. People often explain that they chose to study psychology because they want to help people. For many, helping people means being a counselor or therapist and working directly with clients and patients. Others in the field may help people in different ways: by (a) conducting a major research study, (b) lecturing undergraduate psychology students, or (c) delivering performance-enhancing workshops to corporations. Psychology allows professionals to help people in many ways.

Each of us has unique motives to choose psychology as a career. Understanding your personal reasons allows you to be more focused when applying for a graduate degree in psychology and can help you stay connected to your bigger goals in life. Knowing why I chose psychology as a career has allowed me to navigate through higher education with more direction and enthusiasm. Besides my goal of helping people, I am motivated to study psychology by three additional factors, which I think are common to many other people too. The first is intellectual stimulation: The field of psychology suits my curious nature. I enjoy learning and am excited that as a psychology trainee I get to write and talk about ideas with my colleagues. Second, I get bored easily, so a career in psychology provides me with the flexibility to do a number of diverse activities. For instance, with a doctoral degree, I hope to teach at the college level, provide training and consultation to businesses, and conduct therapy and assessments. Third, an advanced degree in psychology will provide me with a platform from which I can create systemic changes for the betterment of ethnic minorities and disenfranchised individuals. I hope to create change through training, teaching, role-modeling, and taking on leadership positions—all of which give me a sense of purpose and meaning.

Additional benefits motivate students to earn a graduate degree in psychology. Many students anticipate the prestige associated with an advanced degree. Another benefit of higher education is increased employability, because a master's or doctoral degree frequently opens up additional job opportunities. Also, students often pursue graduate degrees in psychology for monetary reasons. Although there is little hope that many of us will be pulling in Dr. Phil's annual income, higher education is associated with higher incomes. For instance, with regard to comparable positions, people with doctoral degrees in psychology typically earn more than do those with master's degrees (Pate, Frincke, & Kohout, 2005).

WHO CHOOSES PSYCHOLOGY AS A CAREER?

If you come to graduate school, you will join over 40,000 full-time students who attend about 2,000 psychology graduate programs (Norcross, Kohout, & Wicherski, 2005). The field of psychology is composed of a heterogeneous group of people. I see this diversity among my peers in graduate school, among my professors, and at the national conferences I attend. It is important to examine and understand the demographics of the field because if you come to graduate school, these are the people from whom you will learn, work with in the future, and probably befriend. You need to ask yourself, Will I be comfortable in this field? The answer to this question clearly has implications for your career decisions and graduate school selection.

The field of psychology is becoming more racially diverse. According to research summarized by the American Psychological Association (APA), the percentage of people of color in higher education and the workforce has doubled over the past 3 decades (APA, 2003a). The most recent statistics reported by APA (2006a) show that its 2005 general membership was 68% White, 2% Hispanic or Latino, 2% Asian, and 2% Black. Less than 1% of members reported American Indian or multiethnic race, and 26% did not specify a category. In addition, APA (2004) reported that students who enrolled in graduate psychology programs in 2002 were 80% White and 20% people of color, specifically 7% Black, 6% Hispanic or Latino, 5% Asian, 1% Native American, and 1% multiracial.

The gender distribution in psychology is similarly shifting. Until recently, men dominated the field, yet women now make up the majority of APA members, students, and new graduates (APA, 2003b). In fact, in 2005 women constituted 53% of APA membership (APA, 2006a), and the most recent figures for newly enrolled master's and doctoral students show that 75% and 70%, respectively, are women (Pate, 2001).

There is also diversity in the field regarding age and sexual orientation. According to APA (2007, Table 1) data on people who earned doctoral degrees in 2005, the average age of respondents was 35 years. The majority of people, 58%, were in their 30s, 22% were under age 30, and 20% were age 40 and older. In addition, 6% of individuals identified as gay, lesbian, or bisexual.

As I mentioned earlier, I was attracted to my current program because of its commitment to diversity, which I feel is represented in the program's students and faculty. For instance, some faculty members and peers of mine are openly gay or lesbian. Other students have visible physical disabilities. Many are international students, with the largest group from India. Despite these differences, however, the racial and ethnic composition of our students and faculty is relatively homogenous. My program seems to be representative of the previously noted statistics, which indicate a disproportionately low number of ethnic minorities in psychology graduate programs. Therefore, I have found it empowering to read literature on the experience of other Latino/as pursuing advanced degrees. This effort reflects my motto for approaching life: ¡Sí se puede! or Yes, you can! If you are a member of a minority group, I encourage you to seek out mentors who can support you. In addition, you may find it helpful and inspiring to read articles and books regarding the experiences and challenges faced by members of your group. A few books you might consult are listed under Recommended Resources at the end of this volume.

WHAT CAN BE DONE WITH A GRADUATE DEGREE IN PSYCHOLOGY?

Individuals with a graduate degree in psychology are employed in a variety of settings and do different types of work. The amazing range of employment options is a hallmark of psychology as a field, in contrast to the stereotypical images presented in the media of what people in psychology do (Does a patient lying on a couch for therapy come to mind?). Although some of us do therapy, many others in the field do other types of work that contribute to understanding and promoting the emotional, physical, and mental health functioning of both unwell and healthy human beings. As Dr. Koocher suggests in the essay at the end of this chapter, graduate training in psychology will provide you with knowledge and skills that can be used in an array of settings and with a variety of individuals and organizations. Therefore, with so many options open to you, I urge you to consider whether you might enjoy pursuing some of the common paths that are available to those with a graduate degree in psychology.

First, a popular career option for individuals with graduate degrees in psychology is a position in academia. These individuals are employed at different types of educational institutions, including universities, colleges, community colleges, and professional schools. Faculty members are usually involved in some or all of the following tasks: teaching, research, writing, administration, mentoring, and clinical supervision. Often they are pretty busy juggling many of these tasks in the span of a single day. For instance, I have a professor who has an interesting career. In addition to teaching, he writes prolifically about ethics, consults frequently with lawyers about ethical violations, and serves as the director of a psychological assessment clinic. In general, people who pursue an academic career enjoy numerous benefits, such as autonomy, flexibility, intellectual stimulation, and, for many, a 9-month contract.

A second popular path in the field of psychology is clinical practice, which broadly refers to providing therapy, assessment, or both, to clients and patients. Therapy, also known as counseling or psychotherapy, can take many forms; however, it is usually a relationship between a therapist and a client or patient that is dedicated to alleviating distress and enhancing well-being. With professional training, clinicians can also administer and interpret assessments (e.g., emotional, personality, intelligence, neuropsychological) to gain insight about how to help clients and patients. Clinicians may serve children or adults and work with them

TABLE 1.1

Primary Employment Settings of Doctoral and Master's Degree Recipients in Psychology

Setting	Doctoral degree[a]	Master's degree[b]
University and 4-year colleges	24	13
Medical school	4	—
Other academic settings	3	—
Schools and other educational settings	11	25
Independent practice	8	3
Hospitals	14	19
Other human service settings	11	20
Managed care settings	7	—
Business, government, or other settings	19	20
Not specified	1	—

Note. The values represent percentages and may not total 100% because of rounding. Dashes were inserted where data were not available. Data from American Psychological Association (2007) and Singleton, Tate, and Kohout (2003). [a]Doctoral degree recipients in 2005. [b]Master's degree recipients in 2001 and 2002.

remarks in his essay, students may one day even pursue careers dedicated to extraterrestrial psychology!

Now that you are familiar with some psychology careers, it helps to see what people in the field are actually doing. Table 1.1 provides a list of the settings in which recent doctoral and master's degree recipients are employed. This table illustrates the broad possibilities that are open to those with graduate degrees in psychology. The variety of possible job settings, compared with other professions, is one of the reasons I pursued a doctoral degree. I want to work in a few different settings, and my degree should allow me to enjoy flexibility during my career.

Training in Psychology Graduate Programs

I've always been amazed at the variety of different training possibilities in psychology graduate programs. There are different degrees, subfields, and training models offered in psychology—there are a lot of choices!

DEGREES

The master of arts (MA), master of science (MS), doctor of psychology (PsyD), and doctor of philosophy (PhD) are the most common degrees granted in psychology. Prospective graduate students pursue a certain degree on the basis of personal and professional reasons. To make such a decision, applicants weigh their professional interests and career goals, financial costs, and demands on their time. Because this is a major decision, let me share some more information about the degrees.

Master's degrees typically take 2 years to complete and prepare recipients for work in the field or further graduate study. Students can enroll in a terminal master's degree program or complete this degree as an intermediate step on their way to earning a doctoral degree. In my case, I enrolled in a terminal master's degree program, which I used as a stepping stone to a doctorate. Although there is great variability, the major distinction between the degrees is that an MA frequently focuses less on research competencies than does an MS. The training and graduation requirements tend to reflect the differences. The MA is more likely to require a comprehensive examination and offer a thesis as an option, whereas the MS is more likely to require students to complete a thesis.

A doctoral degree is the highest degree that can be obtained in psychology and generally takes anywhere from 4 to 7 years to earn. This degree prepares students for a wider range of job opportunities. In particular, a doctorate is the preferred degree for faculty members at colleges and universities. It is also viewed as the entry-level degree in the field for individuals who offer licensed, independent clinical services. To complicate matters, there are two major types of doctoral degrees in psychology: the PhD and the PsyD. The former is considered to be the research degree, whereas the latter is a newer degree that focuses on the practice of psychology and is a professional degree. Approximately 75% of all doctoral students in psychology earn PhDs (APA, 2007, Table 9).

Finally, other degrees offered in related fields provide specialized training in psychology. For example, a doctor of education (EdD) degree is offered in a department of education and usually focuses on educational, school, or counseling psychology. Another option is a combined degree in which students become qualified in two fields. If, for instance, you are interested in the fields of law and psychology, some joint programs grant a juris doctor (JD) degree and either a PhD or a PsyD. These combined JD–PhD and JD–PsyD programs offer interdisciplinary training, so the two fields are integrated and complementary. As you can see, besides the familiar ones, there are other unique degrees to investigate when you are deciding to study psychology.

SUBFIELDS OF PSYCHOLOGY

By now, you probably realize the variety in the field of psychology. APA officially recognizes 54 different divisions, each representing a specialty interest in psychology (for a complete listing of APA Divisions, see http://

www.apa.org/about/division.html). Therefore, you probably won't be surprised to learn that you select from among numerous subfields when pursuing a graduate degree. According to *Graduate Study in Psychology* (APA, 2008), psychology doctoral students who graduated in 2005–2006 earned degrees in the following subfields: clinical (46%); school or educational (9%); counseling (7%); developmental (4%); cognitive (4%); experimental (3%); social and personality (4%); industrial/organizational (3%); child and adolescent (2%); neuroscience, physiological, or psychobiology (3%); health (2%); and other (12%).

One of the struggles faced by those considering graduate school is finding out about the intricacies of subfields. I cannot elaborate on each of them here, but let me share some suggestions for ascertaining more information. I found that it helped to read information on trusted Web sites (see Recommended Resources for suggestions). Next, I searched topics related to graduate training on PsycNET (http://www.apa.org/psycinfo), a database of peer-reviewed literature in psychology, which informed me about the history of psychology subfields. Last, I talked with professors, mentors, and graduate students in person and online. I joined multiple electronic mailing lists, particularly those of APA divisions. To my surprise, people were more than willing to provide information about their training programs and share their personal experiences.

Overall, the homework I did made me more knowledgeable about the subfields, especially the distinctions between clinical and counseling psychology. The differences are subtle and often not always fully understood by prospective applicants. Thus, let me try to clarify the issue. Norcross, Sayette, Mayne, Karg, and Turkson (1998) reviewed the literature regarding the differences between clinical and counseling psychology graduate programs. They argued that the distinctions between the subfields are less pronounced than they were in past decades, yet identified five remaining distinguishing characteristics. Graduate programs in clinical psychology outnumber those in counseling psychology. Clinical programs are typically located in psychology departments whereas counseling programs are frequently housed in schools of education. Clinical psychologists generally study and help people with psychopathology and conduct more projective assessments. However, counseling psychologists focus their efforts on healthier people who struggle with problems of living and adjustment over the life span, and they conduct more career assessments. Clinical psychologists more frequently report behavioral or psychodynamic theoretical orientations, whereas their counseling psychology counterparts more often endorse a person-centered approach to therapy. Finally, although qualified to work in both settings, clinical psychologists are more likely to work at hospitals, whereas counseling psychologists are more likely to work at university counseling centers. As I mentioned, however, the differences between the subfields are diminishing, and they currently seem quite similar.

TRAINING MODELS

If you are considering clinical, counseling, or school psychology doctoral programs, it is important to understand the two widely recognized training models: Boulder and Vail. The models arose out of national conferences that focused on training and were held in Boulder, Colorado, in 1949 and Vail, Colorado, in 1973 (Donn, Routh, & Lunt, 2000). They differ in how much they emphasize research, and the distinction is reflected in their training goals. The Boulder model, also known as the scientist–practitioner model, seeks to train students to develop clinical skills *and* independently conduct research. Programs that award a PhD degree typically follow the Boulder model. In contrast, the Vail model, referred to as the practitioner–scholar model, trains students to develop clinical skills and be consumers of research (Norcross, Castle, Sayette, & Mayne, 2004). Students in this model primarily learn to deliver clinical services that are informed by research; they typically devote less attention to developing research skills. Students who graduate from a doctoral program adhering to the Vail model usually earn a PsyD degree. I personally chose a program adhering to the Vail model because it prepares me to use scientific knowledge to work with clients and patients. This training allows me to better exercise the passion I have for applied clinical work. However, you'll be disappointed if you are hoping to earn a doctoral degree from an accredited program and escape a statistics class. As Norcross and Castle (2002, ¶8) wrote, "PsyD programs require some research and statistics courses; you simply cannot avoid research sophistication in any APA-accredited program."

Although the Boulder and Vail training models each have a specific focus, individual graduate programs vary considerably. Some PhD programs have become fairly practice oriented, whereas some PsyD programs have developed a stronger research focus. Whichever route you consider, you will want to investigate the balance of research and clinical training at each program you are interested in.

PHD OR PSYD?

Individuals pursuing a clinically oriented doctoral degree in psychology have two choices: PhD or PsyD. At the current time, 60% of all clinical doctoral students earn a PhD, while the remainder receive a PsyD (APA, 2007, Table 9). In addition to separate training models, other differences exist between the PhD and PsyD degrees. So that you can make an informed choice when deciding which degree to earn in graduate school, it is critical to know the facts.

Of all the APA-accredited clinical doctoral programs, PhD programs are more selective than PsyD programs; the former accept about 10% of applicants whereas the latter grant admission to about 40% of applicants

(Norcross, Kohout, & Wicherski, 2005). This trend rings true for nonaccredited programs too. PhD programs enroll smaller classes of students each year, with an average size of 9 or 10 students; in contrast, PsyD programs typically range in size from 15 to 49 students (Norcross et al., 2004). Students who attend a PhD program are more likely to receive financial assistance than are university-based PsyD students, and even more likely than those at freestanding private-school PsyD programs (Norcross et al., 2004).

Brace yourself as I discuss debt because it can be frightening. Data from recent graduates show that PhD students incurred a median debt of $50,000 (Wicherski & Kohout, 2005), whereas PsyD students carried a median debt of $100,000 (APA, 2007, Table 9). You should also know that there is considerably less variety among the theoretical orientations of faculty members at PhD programs than among faculty at PsyD programs (Norcross et al., 2004). Another difference between the degrees is the number of years to completion. On average, the PhD degree requires 6 years, compared with 5 years for the PsyD (Norcross et al., 2004).

In the past, some psychologists viewed the variation between the degrees as deficiencies of PsyD training programs. As a PsyD student, I am aware of a number of misconceptions associated with the Vail model. For instance, people have told me, "It will be very difficult for you to find a job with a PsyD" and "PsyD students do not even have to complete a dissertation." In fact, these statements are untrue. Research indicates that few differences exist in employment opportunities (Hershey, Kopplin, & Cornell, 1991). Also, Donn and colleagues (2000) stated in an article on the history of psychology training that "Many, if not most, PsyD programs actually do require students to carry out a dissertation as part of their training, albeit ones with a different focus than the traditional PhD dissertation" (p. 425).

In general, I believe it is imperative to recognize that the PhD and PsyD degrees offer *different* training experiences to students with *different* interests. Each degree possesses unique strengths and serves a function in the field of psychology. I am thankful that times appear to be changing and both degrees are becoming equally valued for their contributions to the field. A sign of this recognition came in 1996 when Dorothy Cantor became the first president of APA to hold a PsyD.

ACCREDITATION

When asking professionals and current graduate students about clinically oriented doctoral programs, you are likely to hear about accreditation, a designation relevant only to clinical, counseling, and school psychology doctoral programs and internships (accreditation does not apply to experimental doctoral programs and master's degree programs). The accrediting organization in the United States is APA, and the comparable organization in Canada is the Canadian Psychological Association (CPA). An accredited program meets comprehensive standards for a quality education and guarantees that it has demonstrated the ability to provide students with a basic standard of training (APA, n.d.). The designation serves as a form of quality assurance. In addition, after graduating from an accredited program, students usually find it easier to get an internship and a job and are eligible for licensure. Attending an accredited program just makes life much easier nearly every step of the way.

To determine whether a graduate program is accredited, you can consult the latest edition of APA's book *Graduate Study in Psychology* or check the APA's Office of Program Consultation and Accreditation Web site (http://www.apa.org/ed/accreditation) and CPA's Accreditation Web site (http://www.cpa.ca/psychologyincanada/canadianuniversities/cpaaccreditedprograms). They provide lists of the accreditation status of PhD and PsyD programs. If a program is not accredited, it can mean several things. It may be uninterested in obtaining accreditation, it may have been unsuccessful in attaining accreditation, it may have lost its accreditation, or it may be a new program that is in the initial stages of applying for accreditation. I suggest that you ask programs about their accreditation status and intentions. I wanted to attend an accredited program not only because it ensures I am receiving quality training that is overseen by an organization independent of my doctoral program but also because it increases my prospects for career choices and mobility.

ACCEPTANCE RATES

So how tough is it to get into a graduate program in psychology? To tell you the truth, it can be difficult, but rates vary dramatically by degree and subfield. Let me share data regarding acceptance rates for students applying for the 2003 academic year, as summarized by Norcross, Kohout, and Wicherski (2005). The average acceptance rate for master's degree programs in psychology is 57%, with neuroscience being the most competitive (32%) and quantitative being the least competitive (73%). The acceptance rate for master's clinical degrees is 53%. However, doctoral programs are typically more competitive. The average acceptance rate for all doctoral programs in psychology is 27%. I'll get to clinical psychology programs in a moment, but it is useful to know that acceptance rates for the other subfields range from 19% (social psychology, personality psychology) to 50% (educational psychology). For clinical psychology doctoral programs, the acceptance rates for all programs are 21%. As noted previously, accredited clinical psychology PhD programs accept about 10% of applicants whereas accredited PsyD programs offer admission to 40% of applicants. At nonaccredited clinical psychology programs, 20% and 60% of PhD and PsyD applicants, respectively, are accepted.

Costs of Graduate School and Salary Expectations

Any discussion of graduate school in psychology requires a look at the costs involved and the salaries that can be expected. Here, I briefly outline some key figures to consider and refer you to chapter 3 of this volume for a more in-depth description of finances. Often, the major expense of graduate education is tuition. In general, in-state students pay less than do out-of-state students, and private schools tend to be more expensive than public schools. According to Norcross, Kohout, and Wicherski (2005), approximate median tuition costs for the academic year of 2003–2004 for in-state and out-of-state residents in master's degree programs were $3,200 and $8,300, respectively. Corresponding costs for in-state and out-of-state residents in doctoral degree programs were $6,300 and $14,100, respectively.

Looking at the potential costs of graduate school caused me a lot of stress; I had no idea whether I could afford it. However, my worries subsided after I learned about funding opportunities that are often available for graduate students (see chap. 3, this volume). In my case, I was fully funded for 2 years, which means that I received a monthly stipend and my tuition was fully paid. That said, I still carry some debt, which is common for graduate students. The majority of doctoral graduate students in psychology (68%) report being in debt because of their graduate studies; unfortunately, of those in debt, 35% report owing $75,000 or more (APA, 2006b).

At this point, I wish I could tell you that people in the field of psychology earn impressive salaries; however, don't get your hopes up. Much like many areas of psychology, income varies significantly within the field. Recent master's degree graduates from 2001 and 2002 earned an average salary between $29,000 and $48,000 a year (Singleton, Tate, & Kohout, 2003, Table 11). Individuals with doctoral degrees tend to have higher salaries. Doctoral degree recipients in 2005 earned starting salaries that ranged from about $40,000 to $80,000 (APA, 2007, Table 11). Various factors, such as psychology subfield, job setting, and years of experience, impact the income you can expect to earn. I was disappointed when I learned about salary expectations for psychologists. Although I consider these average salaries to be solid and respectable, they are lower than what I expected in return for investing 5 to 6 years in higher education. My dreams for a Bentley have been dashed, but I do love the work that I do and the profession I am entering.

Conclusion

Although I'm admittedly biased, psychology as a profession has a lot to offer. By reading this book, you are educating yourself about the many options available to you, and by reading this chapter, I hope you have gained a better overview of the field of psychology. I also hope that my passion for psychology is contagious and that you are inspired to consider graduate school. If you choose this path, I encourage you to be proactive throughout the application process: Do your homework, become informed, and contemplate your long-term career goals. These steps will better prepare you for the arduous yet exciting process of graduate training in psychology. Remember, ¡Sí se puede!

Practical Tips

1. **Psychology is what you do, not who you are.** During the application process, strive to keep a healthy balance between work and play. Permit yourself to step away from the applications and enjoy your hobbies. Balance is important for your overall wellness and creativity.

2. **Know yourself.** It is important to be introspective as you consider earning a degree in psychology. Graduate school can be a long journey of many years; knowing what motivates you will enable you to persevere when obstacles arise.

3. **Network and ask questions.** Find people who already have achieved career goals similar to the ones you are seeking, and ask them how they got to where they are. People enjoy sharing their stories. You may be surprised at what you can learn!

4. **List your interests.** When I was deliberating between research-oriented and clinically oriented degrees, I made a list of the career opportunities I might enjoy. Next, I organized them into two categories: those that required a license (e.g., clinical work) and those that did not (e.g., research, teaching, consulting, advocacy). The list helped me see where my interests fell and which type of degree was more appropriate for me.

References

American Psychological Association. (2008). *Graduate study in psychology*. Washington, DC: Author.

American Psychological Association, Center for Psychology Workforce Analysis and Research. (2003a, April). *Demographic shifts in psychology: People of color.* Retrieved June 25, 2007, from http://research.apa.org/general08.html

American Psychological Association, Center for Psychology Workforce Analysis and Research. (2003b). *Demographic shifts in psychology: Women.* Retrieved June 25, 2007, from http://research.apa.org/demoshifts.html

American Psychological Association, Center for Psychology Workforce Analysis and Research. (2004). *Race/ethnicity of newly enrolled students in doctoral-level departments of psychology: 2002–03.* Retrieved August 3, 2006, from http://research.apa.org/race03.html

American Psychological Association, Center for Psychology Workforce Analysis and Research. (2006a). *Demographic characteristics of APA members by membership status, 2005.* Retrieved November 7, 2006, from http://research.apa.org/profile2005t1.pdf

American Psychological Association, Graduate Education. (2006b). *Level of cumulative debt related to graduate education: 2003 doctorate recipients.* Retrieved February 21, 2007, from http://www.apa.org/ed/graduate/cumuldebt.html

American Psychological Association, Center for Psychology Workforce Analysis and Research. (2007, June). *2005 Doctorate Employment Survey—List of tables.* Retrieved July 4, 2007, from http://research.apa.org/des05tables.html

American Psychological Association, Office of Program Consultation and Accreditation. (n.d.). *Guidelines and principles for accreditation of programs in professional psychology.* Retrieved February 10, 2007, from http://www.apa.org/ed/gp2000.html

Breckler, S. J. (2006, April). Embracing the many applications of psychology. *Monitor on Psychology, 37,* 24.

Donn, E. J., Routh, D., & Lunt, I. (2000). From Leipzig to Luxembourg (via Boulder and Vail): A history of clinical psychology training in Europe and the United States. *Professional Psychology: Research and Practice, 31,* 423–428.

Hershey, J. M., Kopplin, D. A., & Cornell, J. E. (1991). Doctors of psychology: Their career experiences and attitudes toward degree and training. *Professional Psychology: Research and Practice, 22,* 351–356.

Norcross, J. C., & Castle, P. H. (2002). *Appreciating the PsyD: The facts.* Retrieved November 4, 2006, from http://www.psichi.org/pubs/articles/article_171.asp

Norcross, J. C., Castle, P. H., Sayette, M. A., & Mayne, T. J. (2004). The PsyD: Heterogeneity in practitioner training. *Professional Psychology: Research and Practice, 35,* 412–419.

Norcross, J. C., Kohout, J. L., & Wicherski, M. (2005). Graduate study in psychology: 1971 to 2004. *American Psychologist, 60,* 959–975.

Norcross, J. C., Sayette, M. A., Mayne, T. J., Karg, R. S., & Turkson, M. A. (1998). Selecting a doctoral program in professional psychology: Some comparisons among PhD counseling, PhD clinical, and PsyD clinical psychology programs. *Professional Psychology: Research and Practice, 29,* 609–614.

Pate, W. E., II. (2001). *Analyses of data from Graduate Study in Psychology: 1999–2000.* Retrieved November 10, 2006, from http://research.apa.org/grad00contents.html

Pate, W. E., II., Frincke, J. L., & Kohout, J. L. (2005, May). *Report of the 2003 APA Salary Survey.* Retrieved February 12, 2007, from http://research.apa.org/03salary/homepage.html

Singleton, D., Tate, A. C., & Kohout, J. L. (2003, June). *2002 Master's, Specialist's, and Related Degrees Employment Survey.* Retrieved June 25, 2007, from http://research.apa.org/mes2002contents.html

Wicherski, M., & Kohout, J. (2005, August). *2003 Doctorate Employment Survey.* Retrieved June 25, 2007, from http://research.apa.org/des03.html

Essay 1
A Snapshot of Psychology: The Personal and Professional Benefits I've Enjoyed
Gerald P. Koocher

I cannot imagine a more enabling academic background than psychology for a wide range of career and life opportunities that extend well beyond traditional views of the psychologist's job description. Therefore, I feel grateful for a near disastrous encounter with a physical chemistry course that helped convince me to change my undergraduate major to psychology at Boston University. Since starting high school, I had thought of myself as headed toward a career as a research scientist in organic chemistry, although I loved working with children as a summer camp counselor for a local YMCA. Early in 1965, when my less than stellar grades in "p-chem" crystallized a choice of changing majors or leaving college for a tour with the military in Viet Nam, a wise friend asked whether I had ever considered a major that involved working with kids. I had not, and my initial encounter with Psych 101 (i.e., sitting among 1,200 students in a lecture hall listening to a diffident faculty member lecture in a monotone, followed by occasional "discussion section" meetings with a distinctly unhelpful graduate student) gave no hint of a promising career. Still, I signed up for some smaller classes in developmental, personality theory, and abnormal psychology; grew enthusiastic about a career in psychology; and soon realized I'd need a doctorate for the path I hoped to follow.

Graduate school can be a demanding as well as a rewarding experience. Although I didn't realize it at the time, my graduate training in psychology provided a fantastically generalizable set of skills. I'd never heard of the Boulder model and did not fully understand what *scientist–practitioner* actually meant until years later. In graduate school I learned the fundamentals of a scientific approach to assessment, treatment of psychopathology, etiology of normal and abnormal behavior, and scientific writing. I also learned group dynamics, observational skills, health care professionalism, and critical thinking, while having the opportunity to do clinical work, teach, and conduct research. I also learned by example what behaviors characterized those faculty and peers I regarded as successful and those who seemed inconsistent, inept, or totally clueless. I vowed not to repeat the slip-ups I observed in others and often succeeded while making new missteps of my own creation.

Shortly after completing my internship and postdoc at Boston's Children's Hospital and Harvard Medical School, I accepted a clinical faculty position. I promptly became a member of the Massachusetts Psychological Association and the American Psychological Association. At the time this seemed the thing to do: Affiliate with the organizations of the profession I'd just joined. These memberships turned out to have a powerfully beneficial effect on my career. First, I learned very quickly about critical issues facing the profession on both the local and the national levels. An individual who is busy making a go of a career cannot keep abreast of everything. Therefore, the publications I received and the meetings I attended through my affiliations kept me current and alerted to the most pressing issues affecting my work. Next, I got involved. I volunteered to work on activities that interested me and soon became involved in organizational leadership. A major benefit of having psychological skills included the ability to actually effect change through involvement in these organizations by advocating for legislation, planning conferences, and creating study groups. Along the way, I came into contact with many wonderful colleagues who shared interests, values, and societal goals. Although there are more within-differences than between-differences, psychologists tend to be interesting, dynamic individuals. A major perk of being a psychologist is having fascinating colleagues.

As my career progressed, I learned to remain mindful of the fact that all people, no matter how impressive their social position or accomplishments, have the same fundamental needs, follow the same behavioral principles and patterns, and fall prey to the same human foibles. I also learned that sometimes I could apply these principles with great skill and success in my personal life, such as when attempting to teach new vocabulary or stunts to my four pet parrots. I also learned that sophisticated psychological knowledge does not always translate to effective intervention or immunity to emotional distress. The first lesson was when my daughter demonstrated, more than 2 decades ago, that Nate Azrin's *Toilet Training in Less Than a Day* does not work well for every child. Later I learned, more painfully, that my years of work with families of children with terminal illness could not protect me or blunt the pain of losing a much-loved child of a dear friend to cancer in the very hospital unit where I served as the consulting psychologist.

One of the advantages of being a psychologist is not being bored. Throughout my career, I have enjoyed being involved in many different activities, including the various components of clinical services, research, teaching, and administration. Each activity benefited from my study of psychology. I have treated patients, conducted research, taught courses, supervised clinical cases, applied for and won competitive research grants, wrote articles and books, and managed an academic department. Successes (and sometimes failures) in each of these activities were invariably linked to behavioral observation, assessment, analysis, and intervention, all skills that I have honed as a psychologist.

Training in psychology also affects personal growth and development; it can help you become a better person. For instance, my training as a psychologist has taught me self-reflection and fostered a desire for growth along with an ability to recognize when my education had grown stale or when I needed new skills. This type of professional "observing ego" becomes increasingly important as you realize that the half-life of the knowledge you acquire in graduate school runs 6 to 8 years. The heavy emphasis on psychodynamic theory and projective techniques I experienced in the 1970s remains conceptually useful, but today's practitioners absolutely must have a firm grasp of cognitive and behavioral intervention approaches, actuarial-based assessment strategies, multicultural issues, and the evidence-based practice debate. The prevailing theories and techniques will continue to evolve and thus, as psychologists, we will continue to grow and learn.

In addition to keeping up with psychology, you will find that career growth requires broadening your perspective. For instance, I began taking courses aimed at acquiring skills I never imagined I might need during my days as an undergraduate or graduate student. These included microeconomics and the insurance industry, negotiation, decision analysis, and financial management. Acquiring these management tools also generated a sense of confidence and an interest in climbing the administrative ladder, leading me to accept a job as an academic dean at Simmons College. I now find myself overseeing graduate and undergraduate programs in health care administration, nursing, nutrition, and physical therapy. My work as a pediatric psychologist and as a hospital-based internship program administrator prepared me well to work with other health professionals, and my foundational skills as a psychologist have also served me very well. With our varied skills and burning curiosity, psychologists have the capability of succeeding in many roles.

When the college president offered me the dean position, he asked, "What will you miss most about leaving hospital work?"

I replied, "The day-to-day work with sick kids."

He responded with a grin, "Have you met the undergraduate faculty?"

In my roles as dean and senior academic administrator, my training as a psychologist is invaluable. On a daily basis I must help resolve disputes; motivate people to change their behavior; deal with emotional distress and acting-out behavior (on the part of students *and* faculty); and help others to consider and address issues related to optimizing learning, refining evaluation methods, and recognizing biases and valuing individual differences.

As a budding psychologist, you will have many opportunities not available to previous generations of psychologists because of scientific advancement and social change. Keep in mind that most of what we know as professional psychology today began as recently as World War II. Previous generations would not have thought of discussing personal problems with people outside the family. Psychology has long accounted for a substantial number of undergraduate college majors, and seeking help or consultation from psychological experts has become well-accepted in Western society. Therefore, after you earn a graduate degree in psychology, many of you will provide diagnostic assessments and psychotherapy, but you might also write prescriptions for medication; develop new treatments for medical and mental illnesses; develop community prevention programs; run medical centers, social agencies, corporations, and universities; start entrepreneurial businesses; help resolve tensions in family-run businesses; enhance law enforcement and national security; consult to a range of industries; and improve the quality of human life in many areas. Within 2 decades some of you might even practice extraterrestrial psychology!

The background needed to address all of these exciting issues, activities, and client populations begins with psychology, particularly the scientific principles that govern behavior, cognition, emotion, learning, motivation, normality, and disorder. Psychology provides the key. The skills I acquired during my education and training as a psychologist have proved far more valuable than I had ever imagined. I encourage you to follow your passion and seek out the best graduate school experience for you. Being a psychologist has brought me countless personal and professional benefits (too many to list here), and I wish you the same. Therefore, I leave you with seven basic principles as you pass through graduate school and into your career:

1. Get past worrying about whether you're good enough. Every other beginning graduate student has the same worries; if not, they're too egotistical to bother with.

2. Join the American Psychological Association of Graduate Students (plus the American Psychological Association and your state psychological association after graduation) because networking with your peers will always pay off.

3. Don't worry about specializing too early in your career. You'll have plenty of time to hone your expertise after completing your degree, and new opportunities in areas you have never thought of will present themselves.

4. Find good mentors and earn their support. Ask your peers which faculty or supervisors prioritize their students, remain available, and get them through the program. Forget about high-profile but temperamental faculty. The headaches probably will not be worth the prestige you imagine you might acquire by working with them.

5. If your doctoral program requires a dissertation or final project, pick a topic that interests you but can be carried out easily. Get your degree done and earn your license as quickly as you can meet the requirements. Save your exotic or grandiose projects for the rest of your career.

6. Understand traditional career paths but eschew constraints of convention. Look around and reflect on how your knowledge and experience generalize to new opportunities.

7. Consider strategic alliances with other professionals (e.g., architects, corporate executives, government officials, engineers, physicians, software designers), thinking beyond traditional mental health practice.

Hayal Z. Kaçkar

Life as a Psychology Graduate Student

2

From: Istanbul, Turkey

Area of study: Educational Psychology, Northern Illinois University, DeKalb

Previous degree(s): BA in English language and literature from Bogazici University, Istanbul, Turkey; MS Ed in educational psychology from Northern Illinois University, DeKalb

Career before graduate school: Middle and high school English teacher

Number of graduate schools applied to: 1

Age when started this graduate program: 28

Professional interests: The role of adolescents' family, community, and school contexts in fostering their social, moral, and educational development

Career aspirations: Become a university professor who teaches and does research

The life of a graduate student is unique. Therefore, before you commit to spending years of your life in graduate school, it is important to consider how you feel about the experiences that may lie ahead. Graduate school is an important undertaking, with responsibilities and pressures that will affect not only your academic life but also your personal life. The experience can also be deeply rewarding. In this chapter, I hope to give you an honest account of the requirements, as well as the drawbacks and the

I would like to thank Amanda C. Kracen, Ian J. Wallace, Darby E. Saxbe, and the anonymous reviewers for their help and contributions in the preparation of this chapter.

joys, of graduate study. As a native of Turkey, I also share my perspective as an international student who is living and studying in the United States.

I was born, raised, and spent the first 25 years of my life in Istanbul, Turkey. I came to the United States in 2001 to pursue a master's degree in educational psychology. My interest in psychology began in high school and is intertwined with my love of the arts. I was a literature major in high school and, as a hobby, I loved to watch European movies. Yet, what I enjoyed most was not watching a story's plot develop but observing and analyzing the psychological backgrounds and portraits of the characters.

After high school, I studied English language and literature at Bogazici University, where I was a mediocre student without a definitive career path (in fact, my college professors would probably be surprised to see me pursuing a doctoral degree and aspiring to become a professor!). Although I was enthusiastic about studying literature, I somehow knew that it was not my true calling; yet, I did not know what was. In many ways, I guess I was the typical college student whom Dr. Loftus describes in her essay at the end of this chapter—I had no idea what I wanted to do with the rest of my life.

To explore different career options, I enrolled in a teaching certification program at Istanbul University. Upon graduation, I found a job and taught English for 3 years at a private middle and high school; the experience brought me one step closer to finding my professional niche. As a teacher, I was committed to making a difference in my students' lives. I took every opportunity to listen to and talk with them. I tried to understand their individual characteristics and how their unique developmental experiences outside of school affected their learning and behavior in the classroom. During breaks between classes, instead of going with my fellow teachers to the lounge, I would often sit with my students in the classroom or hang out with them in the corridors, observing how they interacted during unstructured activities. They helped me realize that to be a better teacher I needed to learn more about the psychological foundations of teaching and learning as well as adolescent behavior, development, and education.

While I was contemplating more effective ways of teaching, my younger sister, whose lifelong dream had been to get a master's degree in the United States, was accepted to a graduate program at Northern Illinois University (NIU). Lacking my sister's courage, confidence, and determination to study abroad, I had never considered leaving my country, my family, and my job. However, when she was accepted to NIU, I was inspired. I quit my job and moved with her to America to look for graduate programs that might suit me.

In 2001, after getting settled in Illinois, I scheduled an appointment with a faculty member from NIU's Department of Leadership, Educational Psychology, and Foundations (LEPF) to inquire about the master's program requirements and my eligibility for applying. At first I was concerned that I would not be accepted because my undergraduate degree was not in education or psychology, which the LEPF program preferred. I was also dreading taking the Graduate Record Examinations (GRE) because as a literature major I had not solved a mathematical problem in 10 years. However, talking with an LEPF faculty member convinced me that the educational psychology program would be a great fit because it was an opportunity to explore the questions I had about adolescents' educational development.

Because I missed the deadlines for applying for the fall semester, I started taking classes as a student-at-large in the spring semester. I also enrolled in a 2-month GRE preparation course, took the exam, and earned a satisfactory score. The test wasn't as hard as I had anticipated after all. I also took the Test of English as a Foreign Language (TOEFL), which was less distressing because I had a good command of the English language and had taken it several times before. Once each part of my application was complete, I submitted my one and only application to graduate school in psychology to NIU. I was overjoyed to be admitted to the master's program, with an assistantship and tuition waiver to boot. A few years later, though, after earning a master's degree, I felt I still needed to earn a doctoral degree to fully answer the questions I had about teaching. Thus, I applied to NIU once again and was accepted to the doctoral program in educational psychology. As I write this, I have just completed my examination for doctoral candidacy and am now commencing the dissertation process.

Unlike many of my fellow graduate students, I applied to only one master's degree program. I did this for numerous reasons; most important was the convenience and support that living with my sister provided while I completed the degree. In addition, the educational psychology graduate program at NIU was an ideal fit for my professional needs. First, I wanted a program that did not foster competition among students; I would not feel comfortable if my performance was constantly compared with that of other students. Second, I wanted a program in which the faculty members not only were approachable and personable but also placed high demands on and had high expectations of students. It was important for me to work with professors who were not intimidating and who were engaged advisors and mentors. The LEPF program at NIU satisfied both of my criteria. When I entered the program I found it easy to build strong, trusting relationships with the faculty. This process might also have been made easier by the small size of our department, which has about 60 graduate students (both master's and doctoral students) and 8 professors. It was also appealing that, despite their diverse research and teaching interests, the faculty members maintained a high level of collegiality and academic professionalism in their interactions with each other.

While a master's student, I found the environment in the program to be very motivating, which is why I pursued a doctoral degree at NIU. When I applied for the doctoral program, my decision was solely school-related and had nothing to do with my sister because by then she had graduated, gotten married, and moved to New York City. Even though I would have preferred a livelier lifestyle than what is available in DeKalb, Illinois, I was so happy and satisfied with my graduate program that I did not consider applying elsewhere.

It has been an exciting, interesting, and challenging journey from Turkey to the United States, and from being a baffled middle school teacher to a less baffled doctoral candidate in educational psychology. So what's life like as a graduate student in psychology? Although each graduate student has a unique answer, I want to share many of the commonalities to help inform you as you consider this path. Therefore, in this chapter, I discuss many typical aspects of life as a graduate student in psychology, including the lifestyle, the academic responsibilities, the development of a professional identity, and the benefits and struggles of graduate school itself.

The Graduate School Lifestyle

You may have figured out by now that for most people life changes when they enter graduate school. Becoming a graduate student will likely have a significant impact on your self-identity and lifestyle, including how you spend your time, the compromises you may need to make, and how you manage your money. Many students, including myself, find that life starts revolving around your role as a graduate student, particularly if you are enrolled full-time. Therefore, graduate school is not "just school," and for that matter, you are not "just a student." Rather, graduate school is an important choice because it is a professional endeavor; indeed, it is an enormous commitment of time, money, and effort that affects your life and lifestyle.

IDENTITY

When entering graduate school, you add a new identity to your persona—that of a graduate student—which needs to be integrated with your other identities. Most students have jobs, families, friends, and other commitments besides graduate school, so it can be challenging to integrate and prioritize this new role. For instance, a classmate of mine was faced with being a parent, spouse, school principal, and graduate student all at the same time. Her excellent time management skills were crucial to managing the various tasks expected of her each day. Although you might not have as much on your plate, you too may need to effectively balance, or learn to balance, multiple roles and responsibilities to help you succeed as a graduate student.

TIME

Graduate school is not a 9-to-5 endeavor for most students. Your responsibilities as a student typically do not end when you come home from school. It is not uncommon for graduate students to work several evenings a week; you might have papers to write, presentations to prepare, e-mails to respond to, data to analyze, or research to do about a client (e.g., to deliver therapy and/or administer assessments). There is great variability among students and across programs, but most graduate students I know spend more than 40 hours each week on academic responsibilities. Some even work closer to 80 hours a week. On the upside, however, most graduate students enjoy flexible working hours. Of course, you will have duties that are scheduled for you (e.g., classes, assistantships, practicums), but outside of these requirements you can often be independent and choose where and when to work. For instance, I often work from home, where I can multitask—doing my laundry, cooking a meal, and completing my homework at the same time. I also enjoy the freedom, when my schedule allows, to see a movie in the afternoon, go to the dentist, go to the gym, or take a nap (as long as I get my work done, of course).

Because there is always work to do in graduate school, for some people it can be hard to truly get away. Unlike those who have a conventional job with weekends off, graduate students often use parts of their weekends to do work. Long weekends or holidays off from academic responsibilities can be a rare luxury. Although you might physically be away from school, you may still be there mentally. Therefore, sometimes you may need to pack your books along with your swimsuit for a vacation by the sea. Every summer I visit my home country of Turkey for about 3 weeks, and my books occupy almost half the space in my luggage—and half of my time at home. The good thing, however, is that upon returning to school, I'm glad I did some schoolwork in addition to spending time with friends and family.

FINANCES

Graduate school also affects your wallet. The years you spend in graduate school will probably not be the richest (financially, that is) of your life. Instead, expect to accumulate intellectual wealth. Although there is great variation among students, the majority of psychology graduate students incur some debt to finance their education (American Psychological Association, 2008). The financial trade-offs of graduate school vary by program and should be an important consideration when applying.

Some schools offer funding opportunities to students, such as assistantships, fellowships, grants, scholarships, and paid practicums (see chap. 3). However, even with loans and financial support, many students cover living expenses and graduate school costs by working one or possibly multiple jobs. As you can imagine, life gets pretty busy juggling academic responsibilities and paying the bills. Graduate students ideally get jobs in their field. For example, they might teach at local colleges, administer assessments at a prison, manage a research laboratory, or code data. In addition, clinical, counseling, and school psychology doctoral students tell me they look forward to the last year of their degree, when they will be working full-time at a predoctoral internship, because they will earn modest salaries (typically around $20,000).

Most graduate students live on a budget, which is of course influenced by personal values and preferences. Most students I know, for example, share their rent with a roommate to save money. I too have done several small things to conserve money during graduate school. I look in newspapers for student discounts or coupons (e.g., for food and books) and cook many of my meals at home. In addition to these thrifty techniques and occasional financial support from my family, I have been fortunate to have an assistantship. For working 20 hours per week, the assistantship pays me a monthly stipend of about $700 and covers the cost of my tuition during the academic year. Thus, I pay only my student fees each semester. These financial factors, along with the affordability of NIU and the low cost of living in DeKalb, were also important reasons why NIU was a good choice for me.

COMPROMISE

Like every major commitment, graduate school often requires compromises. For instance, you may have to compromise on the time you devote to pursuing hobbies, the distance you live from loved ones, or your immediate financial stability. Among other things, I've had to compromise on where I live while in school. For this native of Istanbul, the biggest and most cosmopolitan city in Turkey, the quiet and monotonous lifestyle in DeKalb was a major adjustment. However, instead of fighting against this low-key lifestyle, I've made it work to my advantage by appreciating the fewer distractions that allow me to concentrate more on my studies. I am now glad that I made this compromise. With this in mind, I encourage you to carefully consider the compromises you may need to make, as they will certainly impact your lifestyle in graduate school.

Academic Aspects of Graduate School

In graduate school, academic requirements and expectations of students extend beyond merely attending classes, doing homework, taking tests, and maintaining an adequate grade point average. Other academic responsibilities often include conducting research, doing clinical work, and fulfilling other degree requirements. In addition, graduate students might be expected to engage in assistantships, scholarly activities, and service to the university and professional organizations. In the sections that follow, I briefly describe each of these academic responsibilities.

CLASSES

Unlike with undergraduate studies, classes in graduate school often are not the main focus of your education. The classes are important in enhancing your knowledge; however, they are only one component of your education, training, and professional socialization in psychology. Students in master's programs who plan to apply to doctoral programs do want to get stellar grades to impress future admissions committees; however, other graduate students are not as concerned about getting straight As because it is just as, if not more, important to get rigorous training in your area of interest. Many doctoral students I know are encouraged by their professors to prioritize research or clinical work over studying for tests. It is more beneficial to a student's professional career to publish a paper or get more clinical training than to get a 98% (vs. an 88%) on the next biopsychology exam. A friend of mine was told by a faculty member, "You are doing too much course work if you are earning all *A*s." The professor encouraged her to devote more time to professional activities.

Although classes often are not the focus of graduate studies, most students do still spend a good deal of time in and preparing for class. Graduate classes differ from undergraduate-level classes. First, they tend to have fewer students than you might have been accustomed to in college. In larger graduate programs (say, 40 students in each cohort), classes probably will be bigger than in smaller programs (say, 3 students in a cohort). For instance, a course that I am now enrolled in has only 4 students, including myself. Second, instruction in graduate-level classes is usually student-centered, that is, it is based on students' active participation, class discussions, presentations, group work, and various other in-class activities. Graduate-level assignments typically involve more reading, writing, and research than did those you had in college. On the upside, however, there are generally fewer tests and quizzes in graduate school, and it is less common to take a formal final exam at the end of a graduate class. Third, students are usually given more autonomy and responsibility regarding their learning. Class projects and papers can be opportunities for students to explore their professional interests. In fact, my first publication originated from a paper I wrote for one of my master's-level courses.

RESEARCH

The amount of research experience required of psychology graduate students varies greatly. It often depends on many factors, including the type of degree and subfield of psychology as well as the individual student's interest in research. Regardless of your passion for research, as Dr. Loftus notes in her essay, it is important to appreciate the scientific process. She asserts that studying science enables students to ask the right questions when attempting to verify claims in their everyday lives. Although I am not training to be an experimental psychologist, I enjoy research. I am involved in a great deal of quasi-experimental research in educational psychology, and I've come to realize that asking the right questions is perhaps the most important thing I learned from my research experiences.

So how involved might you be in research while in graduate school? In graduate psychology programs in which there is less emphasis on conducting research, faculty members focus on developing good consumers of research. In this case, students may be required to take only a research class or two. They might learn about the scientific process, how to evaluate a study and its findings, and how to apply research results to the practice of psychology. If interested, students can get involved with faculty research or develop their own study.

In contrast, students in graduate programs that prioritize and require research are much more likely to be immersed in research activities on a daily or weekly basis. As opposed to being consumers, they are trained to be active researchers. Students tend to take more classes in statistics and research methodology. They learn to review the literature, develop hypotheses, and collect, analyze, and interpret data using appropriate techniques. Students are typically involved in the research of at least one faculty member and frequently work with a few professors to diversify their experience. At a more advanced level, students learn to write grant proposals for research funding, manage complex research projects, oversee research labs and undergraduate research assistants, actively publish and present results, and ultimately develop their own research program. As you see, many students are kept quite busy doing research.

CLINICAL WORK

Clinical, counseling, and school psychology programs are known for training students to practice psychology. Therefore, students devote significant time to learning psychotherapy and assessment skills. Like many others, you too may be eagerly anticipating seeing patients or clients.

Clinical training commences with students taking classes, usually in theory and skill development. Later, they become trainee therapists in a variety of settings. Many programs provide practicum experiences at the university counseling center or at an on-site community clinic as well as at outside treatment facilities. For example, as a student you may spend your first 2 years in graduate school working at a clinic closely affiliated with the psychology department and then choose a practicum placement for your 3rd and 4th years that reflects a personal interest, such as working at a hospital, a school, or a specialty clinic (e.g., treating substance abuse or eating disorders).

Students are trained during practicum experiences to deliver therapy and administer assessments with actual clients. Students can thereby develop their clinical skills and prepare to practice as clinicians after graduate school. While a trainee, you may enjoy learning to conduct individual therapy, facilitate group therapy, and deliver and interpret a variety of assessments (e.g., personality, mood, intelligence, neuropsychological). Although the average number of clients seen by students varies greatly, you might expect to see approximately three to eight clients per week. Students are supervised by licensed clinicians (who are often faculty members). To help you improve, your supervisor may watch recorded sessions or observe you through a one-way mirror. Although I hear being observed really takes some getting used to, my friends in counseling psychology say that it is incredibly valuable for their learning. You can also expect to take part in individual and group supervision, in which you typically discuss clients, clinical issues, and your growth as a clinician.

The amount of time in an average week that students devote to clinical work varies by program. For instance, students in PsyD or other programs that are very clinically focused might spend the majority of their time working with clients and receiving supervision. In contrast, students in more research-oriented clinical, counseling, or school programs may spend fewer hours per week doing clinical work. Although hours vary, students do need adequate clinical hours if they are working toward licensure at the master's level or applying for a predoctoral internship. Doctoral students average about 750 hours of direct client contact and 350 hours of supervision by the time they apply for a clinical predoctoral internship, which is typically their 5th or 6th year of graduate school (Association of Psychology Postdoctoral and Internship Centers, 2007).

OTHER DEGREE REQUIREMENTS

In addition to my classes and research, many other tasks keep me busy on a daily basis. NIU, like all other psychology programs, has other requirements I must complete to earn a degree. These requirements exist to assess the competency of students and ensure they graduate with the skills needed to be a professional in the field. Typical degree requirements include the completion of one or more of the following: thesis, dissertation, or final project; preliminary exams (also known as comprehensive or candidacy examinations or "comps," for short); and a clinical predoctoral internship. A complete list of requirements for a specific graduate program can usually be found in its official student handbook, which is sometimes available online.

As you might expect, requirements vary by degree and program. For instance, in some master's programs in psychology students are required to take a comprehensive examination when they complete course work, whereas in other programs, the oral defense of a thesis or final project fulfills the comprehensive examination requirement. Students in a master's program do not write a dissertation or complete a clinical predoctoral internship, requirements that are reserved for lucky doctoral students.

In general, doctoral students have more requirements than do master's degree students. The infamous requirement is the dissertation or final project, which often takes a year or more to complete. Most doctoral programs also require preliminary or comprehensive exams; the format of these exams varies significantly. They can sometimes be a traditional test, or they might be an oral or take-home exam. Other programs use professional assessments of student performance, such as a portfolio evaluation of work or the submission of an article to an academic journal. Finally, those earning a clinically oriented doctoral degree must complete a clinical predoctoral internship; it is usually in the final year of the degree program when they put their clinical skills to practice. Needless to say, daily life as an intern is very different than daily life as a graduate student at an academic institution. During the intern year, students are focused on doing clinical work in a professional setting, as the year is considered to be the culmination of clinical training.

Although these requirements might sound weighty, they can all be done one at a time. As I write this, I have just completed my comprehensive examination (i.e., a portfolio defense) and am now commencing the dissertation process. My dissertation will be taking up a good portion of my time and attention, and although it can feel overwhelming, I'm also very excited to conduct my own research on adolescent development and community service.

ASSISTANTSHIPS

An assistantship is a job that provides graduate students with financial assistance (e.g., a stipend, tuition waiver, or both) in exchange for research, teaching, or administrative work provided to the department, the university, or an outside agency. Assistantships are typically part-time jobs (10–20 hours per week) throughout an academic or calendar year. Research assistants (RAs) usually assist faculty members with their research activities. For instance, they may write literature reviews; consent participants to a study; review grant proposals; and collect, enter, and analyze data. Teaching assistants (TAs) may assist a professor with teaching a course by preparing class materials, grading student work, proctoring tests, and even lecturing occasionally. Other TAs, often more experienced graduate students, are given full responsibility for teaching an undergraduate or graduate course. A third type of graduate assistantship requires administrative work. Administrative graduate assistants are usually employed in university offices and do a variety of tasks. Depending on their role, their duties may include advising undergraduates on academic decisions, developing health promotion projects, or writing organizational reports. An administrative graduate assistant might also serve as an assistant to the psychology program director and help with the admission of new students. Because assistantship decisions are often not made until weeks or even days before the start of the academic year, you may consider expressing a preference to your future advisor during the summer before you start graduate school.

My experience working as both an RA and a TA in our department has been very rewarding. As an international student attending school on a student visa, I am not allowed to work off campus; therefore, I have appreciated the financial support of my assistantships. I am currently both an RA and a TA. As an RA, I have reviewed and summarized articles, books, and chapters for a literature review; collected, coded, analyzed, and displayed data; and collaborated on papers for publication, conference presentations, and grants. My research assistantship has been a good opportunity not only to put the research skills I learned in classes into practice but also to learn new skills from my experienced professors. My teaching assistantship has also been a tremendous learning experience. As a TA, I have been responsible for teaching my own undergraduate and master's-level adolescent development courses for several semesters. I have used the feedback I receive from my students, and the faculty who occasionally observe my class, to refine my teaching skills and be a more effective teacher in the future.

SCHOLARLY ACTIVITIES

On top of all the requirements I've already outlined are even more to be aware of. As junior colleagues, graduate students are expected and encouraged to take part in professional activities. Graduate students do this in many ways, including reading academic journals, belonging to professional organizations, attending conferences, presenting research, and publishing articles. For instance, I regularly read three journals in my field and belong to two organizations as a student member. I typically attend, if feasible, two conferences each year. A quick hint is this: Often anyone can attend them, so you should consider attending one if possible. I can't stress enough the benefits of going to these conferences. You will be exposed to the latest research and developments in the field and get to network with scholars and students who share your interests. You may also meet the celebrities of the academic world whom you have long admired!

It is an accomplishment for graduate students to present their work at professional conferences. Students and scholars alike apply to present at conferences; they do this by submitting an abstract and having it reviewed by a panel of experts. If the abstract is accepted, they are expected to make a presentation in a specified format (e.g., a poster, lecture, symposium).

Publishing articles in academic journals is also a very prestigious accomplishment, especially for graduate students. Writing academic articles is a task that takes time to learn. Throughout graduate school, I have dedicated consistent effort to developing this skill and have found that collaborating with my professors and peers is very useful. For example, most of my publications would never have been completed without the collaboration with and contributions from my professors.

SERVICE

Graduate students are often involved in service activities within their universities and professional organizations. There are many opportunities to volunteer your time on various university committees, such as those that evaluate faculty for tenure, interview potential faculty members, and review applications of incoming students. Professional organizations are usually happy to have students involved and welcome their participation on committees, task forces, and other working groups. Service within universities and professional organizations is an excellent way to meet new people, network, develop skills, learn the politics of an organization, and foster professional development. I have served on two faculty-search committees for which I reviewed applications and interviewed candidates. The experience was valuable because I learned better interview skills and gained a clearer idea of what to expect from the review process when it is my turn to apply for faculty positions.

Developing a Professional Identity

Socialization into the field of psychology is an aspect of graduate training because it helps a student develop his or her professional identity. Students are socialized into psychology by learning basic knowledge about the field, the ethics governing the profession, professional jargon, and appropriate professional conduct. These aspects gradually become integrated into students' personal identities and, although not concrete, slowly become visible. It is like your hair growing—you don't notice it getting longer until you realize it's time for a haircut.

One point at which I recognized the development of my identity was when I successfully defended my master's thesis. It was the first time I conducted my own research. I was so proud when my committee members shook my hand to congratulate me. It was a rewarding experience that confirmed I had found my niche and was welcomed into the academic community. Others may notice that they are slowly developing into professionals when they successfully complete other milestones that indicate competency (e.g., a client case presentation, a conference presentation, comprehensive exams, published works). In addition, identity development can also be glimpsed at seemingly minor moments such as knowing your stuff during a stimulating class discussion or using professional jargon naturally. You definitely know you are maturing professionally when your partner asks you to stop throwing around terms such as *confidence interval*, *empirically supported treatments*, and *pedagogy*!

I have found that as I move through graduate school, the socialization process helps me feel more independent and capable. I do not need as much support and guidance as I required during my 1st year in graduate school. Like most of my fellow graduate students, as I progress through my education, I seek out more responsibility. In turn, my advisor and other faculty members expect more from me. I am slowly transitioning from a student to a junior colleague, and soon, after graduation, to an early-career professional.

Benefits of Graduate School

Although I just outlined numerous requirements for graduate students, there are also many benefits to graduate school—otherwise we wouldn't make it to graduation! Besides the ultimate reward of earning a degree, students enjoy countless aspects of the graduate school experience. Here I share a few aspects that I have appreciated while a graduate student.

As I previously mentioned, one benefit of graduate school is the independence I have to make decisions, set my own hours, and choose the focus of my career. I really like having flexible work hours and, often, working from home. Another benefit is immersion in an academic community. I find that the graduate school atmosphere is intellectually stimulating; it is characterized by the pursuit of knowledge, the exchanging of ideas, critical thinking, the exploration of diverse perspectives, and growth. If this description excites you, you probably will enjoy being a graduate student. A third benefit of graduate school is the opportunity to become an expert in my field. I am privileged to be spending 5 years training to become an educational psychologist who specializes in adolescent development. With my educational background and training, I look forward to using my talents to improve the science of teaching and learning. I feel very grateful to spend my days pursuing my career.

In graduate school, the rewards keep coming. One major benefit is the relationships that develop with peers and professors, which can last long after graduation. I have made many great friends while in graduate school. We have shared the experience and supported each other along the way. We often get together outside of school to have coffee, do homework, grumble about the trials of graduate school, commemorate birthdays, and celebrate after thesis and dissertation defense meetings. Some friends have also become role models and mentors for me. For example, one such friend was several semesters ahead of me when I started the doctoral program. She was a very successful graduate student and was offered a position as an assistant professor at a university immediately after graduation. She is a great role model who provides useful advice regarding my career path. I hope to follow her lead when it is time to find a job.

Developing trusting relationships with an advisor or other professors can also be very rewarding. On a professional level, they nurture students' development, advocate for them, create opportunities, and write recommendation letters for scholarships or job applications. It is also common for students and professors to collaborate on professional activities after graduation. While working together over the years, many graduate students also develop personal relationships with professors. Most students who have graduated from our program, for example, still frequently call or visit their advisor and other professors. Professors frequently become important parts of students' personal and professional lives.

Struggles of Graduate School

As fulfilling and stimulating as I find life in graduate school, it has its share of frustrations and hardships. Stress is an unavoidable aspect of graduate school, especially because students are usually juggling a full schedule. One specific struggle is that the responsibilities of graduate school can leave a student with limited time and energy to maintain a personal and social life. I, and other students I know, recognize the importance of prioritizing what is most important and, unfortunately, having to make tough decisions about what to neglect. To stay on top of work and meet deadlines, students often sacrifice hobbies, time with family and friends, and, of course, sleep. For example, I frequently have to work late in the evenings while my nonstudent friends are out having fun—definitely a downside of graduate school. That said, I budget my time so I can continue to do a few things that are particularly important to me. I reserve time to regularly see films at the movie theater, read books for pleasure, and visit friends in Chicago. In addition, I have set aside Sunday mornings for a volunteer activity that is dear to my heart— I teach Turkish language and culture to Turkish American children at a Sunday school. It is possible to continue enjoying life outside of graduate school, although in my experience, there is less spontaneity and more time management.

Another struggle is that even your closest family and friends might not understand the demands of graduate school. They may be unable to relate to what you are going through as a graduate student. And to top it off, they may ask annoying questions such as, "So, when will you be done with school?" or "How many more years until you graduate?" Such questions are the last thing you want to hear while you are writing your thesis or dissertation; however, the answers often end up being the only things your friends and family are interested in knowing. What most people fail to recognize is that graduate training takes a long time to complete. A girlfriend of mine whose husband was applying for a doctoral program in psychology jokingly told me that he would finally start his career as she was retiring!

A third struggle you might have is the pressure to be a professional. People often don't understand why I find graduate school stressful and ask, "Why do you worry so much? It's just school!" Well, it really is so much more than school. Graduate school equips students with the knowledge, skills, and experience necessary to become experts in their fields. A doctoral degree, for example, is the highest degree academia can offer; there's no more schooling after that. Thus, the expectation is that by graduation not only should students know their stuff, they should know it well enough to work without the direction of professors. Such ambitious expectations and extensive degree requirements can create a lot of stress.

The constant evaluation of students is another inevitable and stressful part of graduate school. Some evaluation is formal, such as course work, exams, presentations, portfolio assessments, annual evaluations, and teaching observations. For example, those with a teaching assistantship at NIU are observed in class several times by a faculty member. When I first started teaching, I dreaded the very thought of being observed, but there was no way I could escape it. And I'm grateful I couldn't. I was evaluated by a professor whose feedback helped me recognize strengths and areas for improvement. Thus, as anxious as I was about the process, it turned out to be a very useful learning experience that helped me fine-tune my teaching.

Notwithstanding such formal assessments, much of the evaluation in graduate school happens informally. As faculty members train us to be professionals, they expect us to demonstrate appropriate professional behavior. Like a boss in a workplace, faculty members pay attention to individual behavior and form opinions of students. Therefore, they often subtly evaluate things such as professional attire, participation at departmental functions, behavior at holiday parties, e-mail etiquette, and disclosure on social networking Web sites (e.g., Facebook, MySpace). Although most students appreciate the importance of developing a professional identity, the constant attention paid to these issues is another type of evaluation that can feel weighty.

Self-doubt has been a struggle for me in graduate school, and it seems common to many of my peers. Despite enjoying being a student, countless times I thought graduate school was not for me and I wanted to quit everything. When the responsibilities of being a graduate student feel overwhelming, my confidence gets shaken and I doubt myself. At these times I wonder, do I really have the skills to cope with this? Am I competent enough? What do my professors think of me? Am I living up to their expectations? Do I have what it takes to be a true scholar? When I share these thoughts with my fellow graduate students and professors, however, I realize that they all have had similar experiences. I am thankful to have people who can relate to me and provide support. I am always relieved to know that I am not the only student who gets overwhelmed by the demands of graduate school.

In this section, I've outlined some struggles I've encountered that are also common to the typical graduate school experience in psychology. Of course a myriad of other possible challenges, such as academic demands, financial hardship, and strain on relationships, may be applicable to you. It seems obstacles are inevitable on every path, including graduate school, but I am thankful that the benefits of my journey have definitely outweighed the struggles.

Conclusion

I hope the information I've shared about life as a student provides a realistic picture of what to expect if you pursue graduate school in psychology. I have highlighted issues that generalize to most psychology graduate students. Of course, my experiences as a female student from Turkey who is pursuing an EdD in educational psychology are unique to me. Not all of my experiences and suggestions will apply to you. However, I see this as an asset, not a drawback; armed with good information about life in graduate school, you get to anticipate your own path through graduate studies. If you are passionate and self-motivated about it and, as Dr. Loftus eloquently puts it, "want to learn for the sake of learning," then you are likely heading toward some of the most intellectually stimulating and fulfilling years of your life.

Practical Tips

1. **Be inquisitive and think critically.** As Dr. Loftus says, graduate school is a great opportunity for students to develop a researcher's attitude toward life. I also suggest cultivating this mind-set now because in graduate school professors are not likely to merely teach you the facts; instead, they want you to question and test the facts for yourself.
2. **Practice your writing skills.** Most psychology graduate programs require students to do a lot of writing. Because perfecting your writing takes time, start practicing as early as possible when preparing for graduate school. If you are currently a college student, you might consider taking a writing class or a writing-intensive course.
3. **Seek a good mentor or advisor.** Identify potential mentors by networking and reviewing psychology department Web sites for information about professors' professional interests. Consider sending a brief e-mail to potential mentors to gather more information about working with them before you apply. Look for people with whom you share similar academic interests and who would commit their time and attention to working with you.

References

American Psychological Association. (2008). *Graduate study in psychology*. Washington, DC: Author.

Association of Psychology Postdoctoral and Internship Centers. (2007, June 6). Survey of internship applicants, summary of survey results, part 1. Message posted to http://www.appic.org/email/8_3_4_email_match_news.html

Essay 2
Graduate School: Advice
for All Times
Elizabeth F. Loftus

When I was thinking about applying to graduate school, the world was a different place. I spent my undergraduate life at the University of California—Los Angeles (UCLA). It was the 1960s—a period of unrest and turbulence. When I started college, America had 80 million fewer people than it has today. When I started college, the female students were called "girls" rather than "women." When I started college, there was no Internet or Web sites. When I started college, you could walk onto a plane with box cutters and no one would care. When I started college, we all thought Russia was full of communists and was a primary promoter of terrorist attacks, rather than a fellow victim. When I started college, no one had heard of the Beatles.

Like many college students, I had no idea what I wanted to do in life. It was about the same time that one of our modern American heroes, John Glenn Jr., made being an astronaut seem like a good career. He had just orbited three times around the earth, traveling about 81,000 miles in 5 hours, before he splashed into the Atlantic Ocean. He made being an astronaut seem like fun—but there didn't seem to be any girl astronauts, so maybe that wasn't for me. I considered the possibility of becoming a mathematics teacher and briefly flirted with the idea of being a private detective or a stockbroker.

Once I got to UCLA, I spent a lot of time with my two best friends, going to these Friday night things called "beer busts." We spent way too much time drinking beer, flirting with the fraternity boys, and crying on each other's shoulders when one of them broke up with one of us. For the most part, I wasn't thinking about graduate school; I was just worrying about passing calculus and getting a degree in mathematics.

Along the way, a funny thing happened: I discovered psychology. It was all because of an introductory psychology course. The professor (i.e., Allan Parducci) was great. After that course, I gobbled up all the psychology that I could and ended up with sufficient credits for a double major in mathematics and psychology. During my senior year, I heard about a field called mathematical psychology, and that seemed perfect for me. One of my professors told me that Stanford University was *the* place to go for math psych, and they happily accepted my application. I still didn't know exactly what I wanted to do, though.

I wrote about my graduate school years in my book *Witness for the Defense* (Loftus & Ketcham, 1991):

> I'm half-way through my doctoral dissertation—titled "An Analysis of
> the Structural Variables that Determine Problem-solving Difficulty on a
> Computer-Based Teletype"—and to tell the truth, I'm a bit bored with
> the whole thing. Somewhere, at that very moment, in schools
> throughout Santa Clara valley, twelve- and thirteen-year-old kids were
> sitting down at computers, trying to solve increasingly complex word
> problems. I'd take the data, tabulate the answers and make tentative
> conclusions about how adolescents solve problems, which problems
> are more difficult to solve, and why.
>
> It was tedious work, no doubt about it. The theoretical model had
> been set up years earlier by my Ph.D. advisor, and I was just one of
> several graduate students, each of us plugged into a specific common
> pot. It occurred to me that my particular job was a little like cutting up
> carrots to put in a soup. To the left and right of me were other
> students, equally frenzied and meticulous about cutting up their
> onions, celery, potatoes, chunks of beef, and then tossing them into
> the same huge pot. And I couldn't help thinking, All I've done is cut
> up the carrots. (p. 5)

I learned some helpful things from my brilliant and highly accomplished
PhD advisor, Pat Suppes, but never developed a passion about computerized instruction.

While working on my dissertation, I took a course from the social
psychologist Jonathan Freedman and discovered that he had an interest
in memory. He asked if I wanted to work on a project that concerned
how people reach into their long-term memory storage vaults and pro-
duce appropriate responses to questions. How can they tell you the name
of an animal that starts with the letter Z so fast, given the millions of facts
the mind holds? It was during this research on semantic memory that I
began to think of myself as a research psychologist. As a result of this
collaboration, I learned that I, almost single-handedly, could design an
experiment, collect the data from experimental subjects, analyze the data,
and write up the findings. But learning experimental skills was not the
only gift I got from the study of psychology.

I also began to appreciate what science is all about. From my professors, textbooks, and study groups with fellow students, I learned that
science is not just a huge bowl of facts to remember. Science is a way
of thinking. It's a process. Science is based on a profound insight—
namely that just because an idea seems true, that doesn't mean it is
true. The way to distinguish factual ideas from false ones is to test them
by experiment.

Well, I learned rather well how to test ideas by experiment and applied that knowledge to one particular subject matter: human memory.
Over the years I've conducted hundreds of experiments and learned some
pretty nifty things about the workings of the human mind. Discovering
fundamental facts about the malleability of memory has been very exciting. I occasionally come across an undergraduate who says, "Why should

I care about research? I want you to teach me facts." Well, one answer to this question is that there would be far fewer facts to teach if the research had not been done. When students get involved in hands-on research, they learn to be miniresearchers. This doesn't mean that they are heading to a PhD and a career in research, because only a fraction will do this. It means that they learn how to solve problems, and that skill can come in handy in all aspects of life.

The study of psychological science bestows on its students a great gift: the gift of knowing how to ask the right questions about any claim that someone might try to foist upon you. When someone tries to tell you that carbs are bad for you . . . or autism is caused by bad mothering . . . or women don't do well in math . . . or satanic ritual abuse is rampant . . . or college tuition has to increase, it should be almost automatic to ask, "What's the evidence?" Now, as psychologists we don't stop there. We can get even more specific about what we ask next: What kind of study was done? What was the dependent variable? Was there a control group? What kinds of statistical tests were used to analyze the data? Has the study been replicated?

What we're really asking here is a second question: "What *exactly* is the evidence?" Some evidence is so flimsy or fragile that it is not really evidence at all. For example, as I and others have shown, some kinds of eyewitness testimony are so fraught with the probability of error that they are not really evidence at all, and to consider them so can sometimes lead to grave miscarriages of justice.

My point is worth restating: It is important to question the evidence over and over again. Demanding to know exactly what the evidence is will come in handy in graduate school and throughout the rest of life.

A wonderful cartoon illustrates this well. Picture this: Mother and little Son are sitting at the kitchen table. Apparently Mom has just chided Son for his excessive curiosity. Son rises up and barks back, "Curiosity killed what cat? What was it curious about? What color was it? Did it have a name? How old was it?"

The son is clearly asking for the evidence, the exact evidence. I particularly like that last question. Maybe the cat was very old and died of old age, and curiosity had nothing to do with it at all.

In thinking about whether there is any evidence for the notion that curiosity killed the cat, I came to realize that in fact the saying is probably dead wrong. I contacted my former postdoctoral fellow, Maryanne Garry, now a professor at Victoria University in New Zealand, who had recently done an informal survey on the kinds of characteristics and behaviors that make for a successful student. She told me that the most common responses indicated enthusiasm or curiosity. Students should like what they're doing. They ought to be interested. Yes, they have to think, work hard, and put in the hours, but most of all they have to want to learn for the sake of learning. In graduate school, and probably the rest of life, it's the curious cats who survive and prosper.

POSTSCRIPT: A RELATED BIT OF ADVICE

Being curious is one thing, but acting on it is quite another. For as long as I have been a thinking adult, one of my mottos in life has been "nothing ventured, nothing gained." Acting on this life philosophy, I found myself spending a year at Harvard University, just 5 years after graduate school. Early in the year, I sent a note to the famous psychologist B. F. Skinner: "I'm an experimental psychologist spending a year at Harvard," I wrote, "and nothing would give me greater pleasure than to have lunch with you once this year."

A few days later the phone rang: "Hi. It's Fred Skinner. I'd be happy to have lunch."

That call began a series of lunches, during most of which I found myself saying, "I can't believe this. I'm having lunch with B. F. Skinner. He lets me call him Fred. He's telling *me* about the upcoming volume of his autobiography before it's even published!"

Write a note to someone you admire; you never know what will come of it. Skinner died some years ago. I'm glad I sent that note before it was too late.

Reference

Loftus, E., & Ketcham, K. (1991). *Witness for the defense: The accused, the eyewitness and the expert who puts memory on trial.* New York: St. Martin's Griffin.

Ian J. Wallace

Financial Considerations in Pursuing a Graduate Degree in Psychylogy 3

From: Glen Ridge, NJ

Area of study: Counseling Psychology, Virginia Commonwealth University, Richmond

Previous degree(s): BA in psychology from The College of New Jersey, Ewing; MA in clinical psychology from Pepperdine University, Los Angeles, CA

Career before graduate school: Case manager at an inpatient psychiatric facility

Number of graduate schools applied to: First time—12, second time—17

Age when started this graduate program: 25

Professional interests: Sport and exercise psychology, health psychology, group psychotherapy, and marital counseling

Career aspirations: Teaching, writing, therapy, and sport psychology consultation

The day I started driving to California to pursue graduate study in psychology was the beginning of a long lesson about managing money. My clunky Honda Accord was packed, overflowing with personal necessities and, most important, three friends who came along for the trip out West. The car was so full that its frame seemed to be expanding from the pressure inside—and the same could be said for my head, which was pressurized by conflicting thoughts about an uncertain road ahead. Yet, I was relieved because I had $2,000 in savings to get me started in Los Angeles (L.A.); little did I know that almost half of this would be spent on car repairs during the drive out. In addition to a little money, the stuff in my car, and supportive friends, I headed West with the phone number of an acquaintance in L.A. and a passion to continue studying psychology. These factors proved to be enough. I made it safely to L.A., and the trip was a successful start to my graduate school career.

Despite the financial burdens I faced driving cross-country and the many since then, I have generally been financially stable and secure, which can be difficult to achieve when pursuing advanced education in psychology. In this chapter, I discuss the many financial considerations of applying to graduate school in psychology. These include the long-term salary expectations associated with graduate degrees in psychology, finances during graduate school, and costs of the application process. The chapter proceeds in this order, from long-term considerations to more immediate concerns. But first, let me share a little more about my graduate school journey.

In spite of an early interest in and passion for psychology, my path to becoming a psychologist has been longer than I expected. I entered The College of New Jersey (TCNJ) fully committed to studying psychology. Only after returning from studying abroad in Newcastle, England, in the summer before my final year at TCNJ did I think about my future in psychology. I realized that I had spent the first 3 years of college neglecting important academic opportunities and that I had a lot of catching up to do if I wanted to make a career in psychology. Still passionate about the field, I worked very hard to improve my chances of getting into psychology graduate programs: I worked as a resident advisor in a campus dormitory, volunteered at a group home for incarcerated youth, and conducted an independent study on the mental aspects of marathon training.

I rushed to apply to master's programs because I thought it would serve as a stepping stone to doctoral study. Being ill prepared, I made mistakes, which at times made me feel incompetent and unworthy of being in graduate school. I faltered because, first, I didn't allow myself enough time to apply. I hurried to complete applications in less than one academic semester. Second, I was more concerned with the quantity of applications (i.e., 12) than with the quality. Third, I minimally consulted fellow students and professors about the process. I reviewed only one book and sought one professor's advice. In retrospect, it seemed that each step toward completing the applications required at least four steps backward.

Despite the mistakes, I was accepted to master's programs in sport psychology and clinical psychology. Although I was elated to be accepted, the programs were generally expensive and lacked student funding, both significant factors I overlooked in my haste to apply. Nonetheless, at the time I felt validated and eager to pursue a career in psychology. No matter how naive I was about the field of psychology, its subfields, common career paths, and average salaries, I believed steadfastly that as long as I was in graduate school, I would find a way to become a psychologist. My excitement and optimism overruled logic and careful planning, and I enrolled in a master's program at Pepperdine University.

I chose the clinical psychology program at Pepperdine primarily because I was always fascinated by abnormal behavior. I was also attracted to the program for its training in marriage and family therapy. Growing up with divorced parents and later learning that around 50% of marriages end that way, I was curious to know why couples don't stay together. The idea of moving to L.A. was also enticing, especially because I caught the travel bug studying abroad. Overall, I was ready for an adventure.

Living in L.A. was tough, especially because I was financially independent for the first time in my life. I had always believed that my prudent spending and modest needs would enable me to survive anywhere. However, I was overwhelmed from the start, soon doubting my ability to manage in L.A. I felt scared and homesick; I even contemplated dropping out of the program and heading back to New Jersey. Even though I knew my father could provide a financial safety net if I were ever in dire straits, I did not want to rely on him. Instead, to pay for the expenses that my part-time job did not cover, I turned to a different source: the federal government. I qualified for educational loans that allowed me to pay for tuition, books, and basic living expenses. This relative financial security actually turned my spirits around; I met new people, explored the city, and enjoyed gawking at celebrities—an entirely new experience. Even spotting a C-list celebrity was a story to share with friends back home.

For the 1st year in L.A., I lived in relative poverty. My part-time administrative assistantship job at Pepperdine paid approximately $750 per month, which basically covered the bills. For instance, rent was $300, which sounds great, but I slept in the living room of a one-bedroom apartment. Yet aside from waking up before sunrise each morning to the sound of my roommate working on his latest screenplay, I was happy with the living arrangement. Food and car expenses were my other major bills. I spent the remaining money on the bare essentials: textbooks, professional organization membership fees, and $1 beers.

After a year of penny-pinching, I wanted to make more money and also bolster my application for doctoral programs. I was able to accomplish both goals by working at an inpatient psychiatric facility as a case manager. It was my first full-time job, first managerial position, and first real-world introduction to a career in psychology. In addition, I needed research experience, and because I lived so close to a major research institution, the University of California—Los Angeles's (UCLA) psychology department seemed like the best place to start. With a little luck and focused effort, I was fortunate to reach one of the preeminent sport psychology researchers in the field. Not only was she willing to give a kid from New Jersey a place in her weekly lab meetings, but after I demon-strated aptitude and commitment, she became a mentor and gave me sound advice when I applied to doctoral programs.

After earning the master's degree and while still working at the psy-chiatric facility, I decided to take on a second full-time job, this time un-paid: applying to doctoral programs in psychology. I was determined not to repeat my earlier mistakes. I gave myself more time, bolstered my research experience, and sought advice from everyone. Although I was rejected at 14 of 17 schools, I found a fit at the counseling psychology doctoral program at Virginia Commonwealth University (VCU), where I am currently pursuing my dream of becoming a psychologist.

Before I transition into the specific financial considerations of apply-ing to graduate school in psychology, let me share a brief caveat about the information presented in this chapter. The fiscal decisions you make are influenced by your specific financial situation and personal values. Therefore, because each person is different, I do not claim to have the answers or suggest exactly what to do. Rather, I describe the financial considerations and share my decision-making process. I hope the research I have done and the experiences I share help you think about your own situation and make smart financial choices.

Money After Graduate School

Applying to graduate school in psychology does not begin with complet-ing the application form, and financial considerations do not begin with the application fee. Applying to graduate school begs important ques-tions about your financial future, specifically your expectations about annual salary, benefits, and lifestyle factors. Yet these factors are often secondary thoughts compared with personal motivations such as "to help people." From the very beginning of your career, it is also important to be aware of your financial needs and expectations. Therefore, it can help to start by asking yourself the following questions: What type of lifestyle am I accustomed to? What sort of financial situation do I want in the future? How will I achieve my financial goals? What is the cost of living at which I'd like to settle? How will others (e.g., family, partner, friends) be impacted by the financial decisions I make? In her essay at the end of this chapter, Dr. Vasquez stresses the importance of becoming comfort-able as a professional with financial issues and that achieving a successful career may require becoming desensitized to these issues. Like Dr. Vasquez mentions, when I first applied to graduate school in psychology, I neglected to ask myself these questions because they made me feel uncomfortable. Yet, I am beginning to understand that they are vital to achieving a satisfying career. If I could do it over again, I would consider each of the issues outlined in the sections that follow before applying to graduate school.

SALARY EXPECTATIONS

The salary that you can expect to earn as a professional working in the field is affected by many factors, including the type of degree, subfield of psychology, type of job, years of experience, geographic location, and managed care, each of which I review here. Generally speaking, salaries in psychology vary tremendously. Median starting salaries range from $30,000 (Singleton, Tate, & Kohout, 2003, Table 11) to upwards of $70,000 (American Psychological Association [APA], 2007a, Table 11), whereas median salaries of $75,000 (Pate, Frincke, & Kohout, 2005, Table 15b) to $250,000 (Pate et al., 2005, Table 13) are what await those with decades of experience in the field. When you are just starting out, however, salaries are somewhat lower. In Table 3.1 of this volume, you can see that starting median salaries at the master's level range from $30,000 to $48,000, whereas salaries at the doctoral level range from $49,000 to $75,000. These figures will help you gauge how much you can expect to earn during your 1st year as a professional.

The degree you hold will affect your earning power because salaries vary on the basis of the graduate degree earned by individuals. The median salary for doctoral-level psychologists across a variety of employment positions ranges from $62,000 to $110,000 per year (Pate et al., 2005). Master's recipients working in similar employment settings reported median salaries ranging between $43,000 and $80,000. These overall figures show that people with doctorates typically earn more than do those with a master's. However, it's not that simple.

Where you work will greatly determine what you are paid. As shown in Table 3.1, the highest salaries at the doctoral level belong to industrial/organizational (I/O) positions and a variety of administrative positions (except for administration of human services), which all have a median salary of around $100,000 per year. Much like their doctoral counterparts, the highest salaries for master's-level recipients are for similar positions, including school psychologists. Their median salaries range between $70,000 and $80,000 per year. In contrast, faculty members and clinical practitioners tend to earn lower salaries. Therefore, people in some master's degree positions earn approximately the same median salary as do those in doctoral positions, or even more. For instance, a master's-level educational administrator earns a median salary that is $3,500 more than a doctoral-level counseling psychologist doing clinical work. There-

TABLE 3.1

Median Overall Salaries and 1st-Year Starting Salaries for Master's- and Doctoral-Level Professionals for Selected Settings in Psychology

	Overall		Starting	
Setting	Master's[a] ($)	Doctoral[a] ($)	Master's[b] ($)	Doctoral[c] ($)
Faculty position	43,000	62,000	38,400	49,100
Educational administration	68,500	97,000	—	67,000
Research position (nonfaculty)	61,000	78,000	36,500	55,000
Research administration	57,000	95,000	—	52,000
Direct human services				
Clinical psychology	49,000	75,000	30,000	52,000
Counseling psychology	47,500	65,000	33,000	51,000
School psychology	72,500	78,000	41,300	61,200
Other	48,000	75,500	32,000	—
Administration of human services	56,500	75,000	32,000	60,000
Industrial/organizational	71,000	105,000	42,000	75,000
Other applied psychology	75,000	92,500	48,000	68,000
Administration of applied psychology	80,000	110,000	—	—
Other administration positions	58,500	100,500	34,900	66,000

Note. Dashes were inserted where data were not available. Data from American Psychological Association (2007a); Pate, Frincke, and Kohout (2005); and Singleton, Tate, and Kohout (2003).
[a]Salaries from 2003. [b]Degree recipients in 2001–2002. [c]Degree recipients in 2005.

fore, consider this information as you think about where you may enjoy working.

As an undergraduate, I knew of a student who had been accepted to a doctoral program in I/O psychology. At that time, I had no clue that she could expect to earn a six-figure salary; I wonder whether she knew. To find out more about different salaries, I suggest you talk with people in the field and your mentors, particularly those you feel comfortable asking. A quick note of caution is this: Discussing the amount of money people earn can be a sensitive topic, so you may want to initiate these conversations carefully and tentatively.

In addition to differences based on degree and areas of employment, salaries in psychology vary considerably on the basis of years of work experience and gender (Pate et al., 2005, Table 15b). Overall, the data show that the more years of experience you have, the more money you can expect to earn (see Table 3.2, this volume). Compared with starting

TABLE 3.2

Median Salaries of Master's and Doctoral Degree Recipients by Years of Work Experience and Gender

Years of experience	Master's ($)	Doctoral ($)	Median difference ($)
0–1 year			
Men	—	56,500	
Women	—	51,000	–5,500
Total	40,000	52,000	
2–4 years			
Men	—	59,000	
Women	—	59,000	—
Total	41,000	59,000	
5–9 years			
Men	—	70,000	
Women	—	65,000	–5,000
Total	50,000	66,000	
10–14 years			
Men	—	77,000	
Women	—	71,000	–6,000
Total	55,000	73,500	
20–24 years			
Men	—	90,000	
Women	—	81,000	–9,000
Total	70,000	87,000	
30+ years			
Men	—	100,000	
Women	—	93,000	–7,000
Total	75,000	98,000	

Note. Dashes were inserted where data were not available. Data from Pate, Frincke, and Kohout (2005) and Singleton, Tate, and Randall (2003).

salaries, master's degree recipients show an increase of $35,000 in median salary over 30+ years of work experience, whereas those with doctoral degrees show an increase of $46,000. Although you may not initially make big bucks with a degree in psychology, these figures indicate to me that the sacrifices made in graduate school are rewarded over the long run. According to the same data (also shown in Table 3.2, this volume), it also appears that the overall median full-time doctoral-level salaries of men are higher than those of women. This disparity is most pronounced among those with 15 years of experience or more. For example, women with 20 to 24 years of experience earn a median salary of $9,000 less than do their male counterparts with the same work experience. It is particularly upsetting to see these disparities because they represent structural inequalities in the field of psychology—an apparent violation of APA's "Ethical Principles of Psychologists and Code of Conduct" (APA,

2002; http://www.apa.org/ethics/code2002.html; see also APA, 2003). However, salary differences between men and women with less than 10 years of experience are much smaller, indicating a potential overall shift toward equal pay for equal work. The region of the country where you work will also partly determine the amount of money you can expect to earn. The salaries of doctoral degree recipients are significantly influenced by the cost of living in the metropolitan area where they work and live (Pate et al., 2005, Table 16b). For instance, faculty members and independent practitioners working in Houston earn salaries that are worth more because of the lower cost of living. They earn an adjusted salary valued at over $6,000 more than their actual median salary. Sure sounds like a great place to work! However, for their counterparts who live in costly New York City, their salaries don't go as far. Their income is valued at about half of what they actually earn. Yikes! Personally, I would like to settle in or around San Francisco. However, I must be realistic about whether my relative earning potential in that area will afford me the lifestyle I desire. I encourage you to be realistic, too, as you consider where you want to live and work.

Contrary to some data presented so far, psychology actually can be a lucrative career. In more traditional positions, work experience plays a major role in earnings. For instance, working for 20 or more years in a variety of positions can yield a median salary of six figures (Pate et al., 2005, Table 15b) and even as high as $250,000 if you work in business and industry (Pate et al., 2005, Table 13). Well-paid careers in psychology are also discovered on paths less traveled. For instance, perhaps two of the most widely recognized and wealthy mental health professionals are Dr. Laura Schlessinger (who earned a PhD in physiology and trained as a master's-level marriage and family therapist) and Dr. Phil McGraw (who trained as a doctoral-level counseling psychologist). These talking heads have hit the jackpot by pursuing unorthodox careers in psychology.

The majority of people who pursue graduate degrees in psychology are not in it to accumulate massive amounts of wealth in a short period of time so that they can retire early. Echoing many professionals, Dr. Vasquez writes in her essay that money isn't everything. She expresses appreciation for being paid to work in a career that she loves. I too am eager to earn a regular income at a job that I enjoy and look forward to each day, which is my definition of a successful career.

MANAGED CARE

If you plan to work with clients or patients in the United States, it is important to know about managed care systems, such as health maintenance organizations and preferred provider organizations, and how their growing influence may affect your earning potential. Owned and operated by private insurance companies (e.g., Aetna, BlueCross BlueShield, Kaiser, PacifiCare), these third-party payer systems provide for the delivery of health care to individuals with health insurance. In 2007, the U.S. Congress updated the Mental Health Parity Act (MHPA; 2007), requiring insurance companies to provide equal coverage of mental and physical disorders. In a review of the MHPA, APA pronounced,

> Insurers have used loopholes in the law to institute other limits to mental health treatment such as higher co-payments, separate deductibles, day and visit limits, and differing out-of-pocket caps. The Mental Health Parity Act of 2007 will improve existing law by closing these loopholes. (APA, 2007b, ¶7)

This resulted in substandard mental health coverage that has affected the incomes of clinicians in our field.

Forty-five percent of people who deliver mental health services report smaller annual salaries because of the growing influence of managed care (Singleton, Tate, & Randall, 2003). I have also heard fervent anecdotal reports from professors and supervisors criticizing insurers for providing an insufficient number of therapy sessions, requiring burdensome paperwork, reimbursing services late, and generally making it very difficult to survive as an independent practitioner. However, in her essay, Dr. Vasquez writes about some financial hurdles she overcame to build and maintain a thriving private practice. Although managed care issues may not be relevant to you right now, if you anticipate a career as a clinician you may want to store this information in your head for later.

Money During Graduate School

Whether you are certain you will apply to graduate school in psychology or just flirting with the idea, it is important to consider the financial hurdles you may encounter as a graduate student. Some common factors include paying for tuition, making money as a graduate student, and choosing to take out student loans. There are also hidden expenses in graduate school that can be costly. In the sections that follow I discuss the obvious and less obvious costs of graduate school as well as strategies and personal examples that can help you make wise financial decisions.

TUITION

Knowing the cost of tuition before applying to graduate school in psychology is important, not only because it can be expensive but also because students often incur debt by paying for tuition with borrowed money. Speaking from personal experience, I recommend that you avoid debt if you can. Paying attention to tuition costs is even more important if you are considering a graduate program that requires a lot of credits to graduate (e.g., clinical and counseling programs). To find out the cost of tuition at specific graduate programs, you can look in the latest edition of APA's (2008) *Graduate Study in Psychology*, search department or program Web sites, or phone a program. However, to start, I have a simple suggestion. Learn the following three general rules about tuition costs in graduate school (Pate, 2001, ¶37–40): (a) Private institutions are more expensive than public institutions; (b) at public institutions only, out-of-state students pay higher tuition than do in-state students; and (c) doctoral programs are more costly than are master's programs. Knowing these rules will enable you to quickly estimate the relative cost of tuition, saving you time and energy for other tasks.

In addition to knowing the three general rules, it helps to know expected costs too. The average annual cost of tuition for in-state students in master's programs is approximately $5,000; it is approximately $10,000 for doctoral students (Norcross, Kohout, & Wicherski, 2005). Out-of-state graduate students, however, generally have higher annual tuition costs, averaging about $9,100 and $14,700 for master's and doctoral programs, respectively (Norcross et al., 2005). Because of this large discrepancy, many out-of-state students apply for in-state residency as soon as possible so that they can reduce their tuition costs. States vary on the required time to establish residency and how convenient they make the process. Current graduate students or program administrators are probably your best sources for gathering information about obtaining in-state residency.

Because tuition costs were the furthest thing from my mind when I applied to master's programs, it's no surprise that I ended up with financial woes. I was an out-of-state student—at a private school—paying almost $650 per credit and taking out the maximum amount of student loans. I now carry thousands of dollars of debt, a burden that sometimes makes me wonder when I'll ever be debt-free. My example illustrates how the choices you make now, while applying to graduate school, can have long-term consequences.

ASSISTANTSHIPS AND OTHER SOURCES OF INCOME

Students enrolled in psychology graduate programs are likely to work during graduate school. They may be employed full-time or part-time, inside or outside the psychology department, and they often juggle multiple jobs. Many graduate programs provide part-time employment opportunities to graduate students during the academic year, which are generally called assistantships (discussed in chap. 2) or traineeships.

TABLE 3.3

1st-Year Students' Median Stipends and Average Hours Worked by Degree Type: 2003–2004

Assistantship	Doctoral	Master's
Teaching assistantship		
Annual stipend ($)	10,617	5,000
Hours worked per week	20	15
Research assistantship		
Annual stipend ($)	10,065	5,000
Hours worked per week	20	15
Traineeships		
Annual stipend ($)	13,648	6,000
Hours worked per week	20	16
Scholarships/fellowships		
Annual stipend ($)	11,500	2,000
Hours worked per week	0	0

Note. Adapted from "Graduate Study in Psychology: 1971 to 2004," by J. C. Norcross, J. L. Kohout, and M. Wicherski, 2005, *American Psychologist, 60,* pp. 959–975. Copyright 2005 by the American Psychological Association.

Assistantships vary in availability, payment, and required hours of work (see Table 3.3). For instance, more students in doctoral-level programs (57%) than master's-level students (25%) report receiving assistantship funding (Norcross et al., 2005). Annual median salaries for doctoral assistantships and traineeships, better known as *stipends,* range from $10,000 to $13,600 and require 20 hours of work per week. Master's stipends range from $5,000 to $6,000 and typically require 15 hours of work per week. Fellowships and scholarships, which are also shown in Table 3.3, are types of income that are discussed in more detail later in this section.

Another great perk of many assistantships is a *tuition waiver*, also known as *tuition remission*, which partially or fully covers tuition costs. As tuition credits in graduate school can be very expensive, especially for out-of-state doctoral students, tuition remission can be an essential part of a financial package. For instance, each credit at VCU costs me, as an out-of-state student, approximately $1,000, compared with about $450 for in-state students. Therefore, if not for tuition remission, I would be responsible for paying about $15,000 each semester for credits. The percentages of doctoral and master's programs that offer tuition remission for a variety of different types of assistantships, full and partial, are shown in Table 3.4 of this volume (see also Pate, 2001, Table 30). In general, doctoral programs offer full tuition remission more frequently than do master's programs. However, these data also show that master's programs are more likely to offer partial tuition remission.

TABLE 3.4

Types and Levels of Financial Support by Degree Type and Institution: 1999–2000

	Doctoral		Master's	
Assistantship	**Public ($)**	**Private ($)**	**Public ($)**	**Private ($)**
Teaching assistantship				
Depts. offering teaching assistantships	86	77	57	40
Depts. giving full tuition remission	55	33	21	17
Depts. giving partial tuition remission	33	30	42	33
Research assistantship				
Depts. offering research assistantships	85	69	52	35
Depts. giving full tuition remission	52	32	24	22
Depts. giving partial tuition remission	35	26	58	31
Traineeships				
Depts. offering traineeships	43	28	10	14
Depts. giving full tuition remission	25	16	2	3
Depts. giving partial tuition remission	9	11	25	6
Scholarships/fellowships				
Depts. offering scholarships/ fellowships	71	68	26	27
Depts. giving full tuition remission	48	41	6	11
Depts. giving partial tuition remission	26	24	17	44

Note. Adapted from *Analyses of Data From Graduate Study in Psychology: 1999–2000,* by W. E. Pate II, 2001, Table 30, retrieved July 1, 2007, from http://research.apa.org/grad00contents.html. Copyright 2001 by the American Psychological Association.

If you are contemplating clinical psychology, have you ever heard in a statistics or research methods course that within-groups differences are greater than between-groups differences? Well, that's what Norcross, Castle, Sayette, and Mayne (2004) found when looking at funding among different types of clinical psychology doctoral programs (i.e., PhD and

PsyD). Within PsyD programs, over 60% of students in university department programs received partial financial assistance, compared with 47% and 26% of students in university professional schools and freestanding programs, respectively. However, full funding (i.e., an assistantship and tuition remission) was offered to students in only 38% of university department programs, in 9% of university professional schools, and in 6% of freestanding programs. If you pursue a PhD in clinical psychology, you are more likely to be fully funded; 84% of PhD students in research-oriented programs and 57% of students in other clinical PhD programs receive full funding. You may want to consider these incredible figures if you are likely to pursue a clinical psychology doctorate.

For all graduate students, landing a fellowship or scholarship in graduate school is less likely but is a great way to be funded (see Table 3.4). Fellowships are typically grant-funded positions that may require the student to conduct research or teach. Scholarships generally are monetary awards that support scholarly activities and are given to students who demonstrate strong academic skills and achievement. Peers of mine who simply asked about these opportunities while applying landed fellowships that provided generous funding.

SUMMER FUNDING

Summers in graduate school have pluses and minuses. On the one hand, you may have a lighter schedule that allows you some flexibility; on the other hand, many assistantships do not pay graduate students during the summer. Instead, many students seek psychology-related opportunities that simultaneously provide income and experience. Having entered graduate school with a master's degree, I have taught at least one class each summer, earning both extra money (after taxes about $2,100 per class) and an addition to my curriculum vitae (CV). Some of the best opportunities, however, can be in areas unrelated to psychology. For instance, a fellow student in my program has used his specialized skills in carpentry to find work each summer. Not only does he enjoy the physical labor that provides a nice break from the mental strain of graduate school, but he makes more money than any other graduate student I know. Your experience teaching tennis, waiting tables, or decorating cakes may be an asset during summers in graduate school.

OTHER FINANCIAL OPPORTUNITIES

For clinical, counseling, and school psychology students, practicum opportunities may be funded. Practicum experiences within a university are generally unpaid. Yet, practicum experiences outside the university, known as *externships*, may be funded. For instance, I earned more while on externship at the university hospital than the average psychology stipend. Talk with students and faculty at the programs that interest you and ask about these opportunities. You might also want to ask them about funding during the official internship year, when students tend to earn a little more than they did from assistantship stipends and externships. After talking with friends of mine, I realized that, again, there is great variability in what you can expect to earn. My friends are making between $17,000 and $50,000 (which, admittedly, is much higher than average) during their internship year.

Other funding opportunities while in graduate school are available from numerous sources. Professional organizations, such as the APA, frequently offer scholarships and grants for student research, professional development, specialized training, and countless other opportunities. For more information, visit APA's Web site on student funding (http://www.apa.org/students/funding.html). Funding opportunities are also available through numerous state and national organizations (e.g., National Institutes of Health, Psi Chi, National Cancer Institute).

Psychology graduate programs also provide frequent opportunities for smaller amounts of funding, including research awards, travel grants, and money for conference presentations. In addition, because of the collegiality and close relationships inherent in many graduate school programs, faculty and administrative workers in the department occasionally present students with unique opportunities to earn extra money. These are often e-mailed around the department and may be for extra academic work (e.g., data entry, grading papers) or nonacademic work. For instance, someone in the department asked me to be the chauffeur for guests at a family member's wedding. Although some might deem this exploitative, I think differently. The job was enjoyable, it felt good to contribute to a great celebration, and I was well compensated for my hard work, which is something I can't always say happens in graduate school.

DEBT AND LOANS

More than ever before, students attending graduate school in psychology, particularly doctoral programs, are taking out loans to pay for their education, and doing it in record-setting fashion. Research on psychology doctorate recipients between 1993 and 1996 revealed that 19% graduated with more than $30,000 of debt; the next highest percentage of any other social science doctoral recipients with similar debt was 8%—a sobering discrepancy (Rapoport, Kohout, & Wicherski, 2000). In a more recent survey, 2005 graduates from practice subfields reported a median debt of $70,000 and 25% are more than $113,000 in debt; in research subfields, the median debt was $35,000 and 25% owe more than $70,000 (APA, 2007a, Table 9).

TABLE 3.5

Median Debt of Doctoral and Master's Degree Recipients by Select Subfields in Psychology

Subfields	Doctoral[a,c] ($)	Master's[b] ($)
Practice subfields (overall)	70,000	26,000
Clinical	80,000	—
Counseling	50,000	—
Forensic	97,500	—
Health	40,000	—
School	50,000	—
Research subfields (overall)	35,000	20,000
Biological	20,000	—
Cognitive	23,500	—
Developmental	30,000	—
Educational	36,000	—
Industrial/organizational	50,000	—
Social	25,000	—

Note. Dashes were inserted where data were not available. Data from American Psychological Association (2007a) and Singleton, Tate, and Kohout (2003).
[a]Degree recipients in 2005. [b]Degree recipients in 2001 and 2002. [c]Doctoral degrees include PsyD, PhD, and EdD.

As you can see, these statistics clearly show that doctoral student debt has been skyrocketing. On the basis of the trajectory set forth during the past 10 years, median debt for doctoral students seems likely to soon exceed the median salaries for doctoral students. In light of these frightening statistics, you won't be surprised to know that close to 30% of 2005 doctoral recipients reported loans as their primary source of support in graduate school (APA, 2007a, Table 7). But wait, there's more.

Because so many students pursue doctoral programs in clinical psychology, let's take a closer look at the differences within this specific group. Sixty-nine percent of PhD and 79% of PsyD graduates reported incurring debt in graduate school (Wicherski & Kohout, 2005, ¶64). Clinical PsyD graduates have experienced a dramatic increase in their debt levels: Their median debt in 1997 was $53,000, and in 2005 it reached $100,000 (APA, 2007a, Table 9). Clinical PhD graduates have also seen an increase in debt. The most recent statistics show that their median debt in 2001 was $36,000, whereas it grew to $50,000 in 2003 (Wicherski & Kohout, 2005, ¶65). To compare clinical psychology debt with that of other subfields in psychology, see Table 3.5 of this volume, and to compare debt across types of doctoral degrees (i.e., PhD, PsyD, EdD), see Table 3.6.

If you are considering a master's-level degree in psychology, there's good news: Graduates from master's programs do not appear to be incur-

TABLE 3.6

Reported and Median Debt of Doctoral and Master's Degree Recipients by Degree Type

Recipient/debt	Doctoral[a]			Master's[b]
	PhD	PsyD	EdD	
Reporting any debt (%)	64	85	40	61
Median overall debt ($)	48,000	100,000	50,000	—

Note. Dashes were inserted where data were not available. Data from American Psychological Association (2007a) and Singleton, Tate, and Kohout (2003).
[a]Degree recipients in 2005. [b]Degree recipients in 2001 and 2002.

ring significantly more debt over time. Singleton, Tate, and Kohout (2003) reported that 2002 master's graduates incurred similar debt in dollars' worth compared with 1996 graduates. Phew!

If after reading the information in this section, you are still considering taking out loans like most graduate students do, then read on, brave soul! Numerous loans are available to students, primarily from the federal government but also from banks and other private sources. If you qualify, the federal government provides Stafford Loans, which generally have lower interest rates and come in two forms: *subsidized* (i.e., does not accrue interest while student is in school) and *unsubsidized* (i.e., accrues interest while student is in school). To begin, become familiar with the Free Application for Federal Student Aid (FAFSA) form (http://www.fafsa.ed.gov) and read as much as you can on its Web site and the provided links. The information is abundant, and it is important that you read it and feel clear about what you are getting into because, well, you read the previous section, right? After you complete the FAFSA online, a determination of your financial need will be made that specifies the maximum amount you can borrow, which can be upwards of about $20,000 each year. And as long as you are enrolled in graduate school at least half-time, you can defer loans during school, meaning that you are not required to pay off the principal balance of the loan.

LIFESTYLE CHANGES

You might have guessed by now that most graduate students don't live lavishly. Therefore, a final consideration of entering graduate school is how financial changes may affect your lifestyle. Consider that 87% and 89% of doctoral and master's students, respectively, report supporting themselves during school with personal earnings and financial support from family (Singleton, Tate, & Kohout, 2003, Table 8; APA, 2007a, Table

7). If you are like these students, you are likely to spend some of your savings and income on your education. And unfortunately, this might mean less shopping at the mall, fewer Barnes & Noble sprees, and more peanut butter and jelly sandwiches! It helps to be realistic about your finances so you can find ways to make do with what you have. In her essay, Dr. Vasquez describes her relationship with money as a healthy balance between careful planning and spontaneity. As Dr. Vasquez notes, developing a healthy awareness of your financial issues will help you anticipate, manage, and effectively accommodate the changes that you experience in graduate school.

Money Before Graduate School

After you have thought about your earning potential and the financial changes that await you in graduate school, you probably also will want to consider the costs of actually applying. Although great variability exists in the amount of money people spend on the entire process, all applicants experience some similar costs. In this section, I discuss the costs associated with each step, highlight my own experience, and provide you with a running total of what it cost me to apply to doctoral programs.

INFORMATION

The first costs of applying are those incurred when finding out information about graduate school. The research and homework you do to learn about different subfields and programs will require that you invest anywhere from $20 to $100 in a few resources, many of which are listed at the back of this book (see Recommended Resources at the end of this volume). Although some of these can be borrowed from a library for no cost, I personally found it essential to own the latest edition of APA's *Graduate Study in Psychology*. For $25, I wrote all over it, marked the programs I liked, and really wore the book down, which is not something you're able to do with the library copy. Additional research into graduate programs in psychology involves Internet searches, phone calls, e-mails, and meetings with people who have been through the process. For example, I sought out a student in my master's program who had been accepted to a counseling psychology PhD program. To learn his secrets to success, I treated him to lunch and asked whether I could pick his brain about the experience; he was happy to meet, and it was a win–win situation. I also did this with an advisor of mine prior to applying. Each $20 lunch was invaluable. My total cost for researching programs was $25 for the book and $40 for lunches.

TESTS

Required examinations are the next step to consider. Most psychology graduate programs require applicants to take the Graduate Record Examinations (GRE) General Test (http://www.gre.org), which generally costs $140 per administration. Some programs require or recommend the Subject Test in psychology, which generally costs $130 (exam fees are slightly higher for international students). Another test that may be required is the Test of English as a Foreign Language (TOEFL; http://www.toefl.org). The cost of this test varies by country, but an approximate range seems to be $140 to $170. All of these tests have additional fees, such as for rescheduling, standby registration, and canceling within 1 week of the test. For those taking paper-based tests, a $12 fee is charged for calling to hear your results about 2 weeks before they arrive in the mail. Overall, the standardized exams aren't cheap, and they don't come with a refund clause if you are unsatisfied with your scores. However, the nonprofit organization that administers these tests, Educational Testing Service (ETS; http://www.ets.org), offers a fee reduction voucher program for qualified individuals to receive reduced test fees. For more information visit the ETS Web site. In my case, just a few years ago, I paid $115 for the GRE General Test and $130 for the GRE Subject Test, bringing my total application costs to $310.

TEST PREPARATION

Most students spend money preparing for the standardized tests. Workbooks or software to practice for the exams cost about $10 to $40 (don't even consider checking out a workbook from the library, unless you are going to photocopy its pages). Many applicants enroll in classes designed to improve test scores. Various courses and individual tutoring are available, ranging in cost from $300 to over $1,000. Because these options can be more pricey, I suggest that you evaluate your needs and resources and do what's best for you when it comes to preparing for these exams. I purchased a GRE verbal section workbook ($20) and study guides for both the GRE General Test ($20) and the GRE Subject Test ($20). Then I basically created my own class by developing a study schedule, making flash cards, and taking my materials everywhere I went. To this day, I still get teased by my girlfriend for taking flash cards with us on every weekend hike for 3 months straight as I prepared for the GRE—yet she always conveniently leaves out the detail that she too was preparing to take the GRE and thus benefited from my flash card mania. My total for test preparation materials was $60, bringing the running total to $370.

SCORE REPORTS

Once you have taken the standardized tests, there are fees for sending the scores to each graduate program. Immediately after completing the GRE General Test, GRE Subject Test, and the TOEFL, you can choose to send your scores to four schools, free of charge. If you know the graduate programs you plan to apply to, bring the school names and codes to the testing center and save some money. There is a $15 charge for each additional score report that you order. These can be ordered by mail or over the phone; each phone call will cost you an additional $6 and allow you to send a maximum of eight reports. If you need to report both the GRE General Test and GRE Subject Test scores, make sure, if possible, that both scores have been received by ETS before sending reports to your recipients. Otherwise, both scores may not be on each report, and then you will pay double to order them separately. I took advantage of the four initial schools, but I needed to call ETS twice to complete my order. Therefore I paid $12 in phone charges and $15 for each of the 13 additional reports, totaling $207 for these reports. This brings my total so far to $577.

TRANSCRIPTS

Graduate school applications typically require you to submit two official transcripts from each academic institution you attended. Some schools provide them for free, but others charge about $5 or $10 per transcript. I requested transcripts from my undergraduate college, my master's program, UCLA, where I took one important class, and the university where I spent a semester abroad. I ended up paying $20 in transcript fees per application because two schools were free and the other two each charged $5 per transcript. For my 17 applications, I paid $340, bringing my application costs to $917.

LETTERS OF RECOMMENDATION

Letters of recommendation may cost you a lot of time but, thankfully, not much money. The costs include purchasing envelopes, stamps, and any organizing materials, such as binders or folders, that you may use to help your letter writer. I paid about $50 for stamps, envelopes, and folders, which brings my running total to $967.

OFFICE SUPPLIES

Organization is a major aspect of applying and the folders, files, sticky notes, pens, binders, and other office supplies do add up. In addition, other minor costs of applying are writing your personal statement and enhancing your CV. While trying to perfect these parts of the application you may print multiple copies of your statement or CV, only to crunch them into balls to be tossed aside. Depending on how much of a perfectionist you are, you could waste a lot of paper and ink. Factor in organizational items, a ream of paper, some résumé paper, and a little ink for an estimated total of $30, which brings my running total to $997.

COMMUNICATION

Phone calls, especially long distance ones, made to the program you are interested in may also add up. I wanted to talk with students at each program and get their perspectives, but even 5 minutes with two people from each school still adds up to 170 minutes of long distance or cell phone minutes. Although it is uncommon, and not expected, for applicants to fly or drive long distances to visit schools before applying, you may have the desire, time, and money to spend on such an evaluation. My phone calls cost me about $25, bringing the total to $1,022.

APPLICATION FEES

The application fee itself is the next cost. You get the honor of writing a check or paying online, which is sometimes cheaper, for each school to review the application you've submitted. Prices vary: Master's programs charge an average fee of $35, whereas doctoral programs average $47 (Norcross et al., 2005). Just hope that your first-choice program isn't among the 1% of programs that charge $100! In my case, applying to 17 schools with an approximate cost of $50 per application meant I paid $850 in application fees alone. My running total jumps to $1,872.

POSTAGE

But wait, there's more. I mailed my applications in folders ($10 for a box), and I chose Priority Mail for my precious applications, for about $4 each. Therefore, sending off my applications cost me $78, bringing my total to $1,950.

   The first thing I did after sending out my applications was exhale 12 months' worth of stress. After that, I celebrated like mad for a night or two. Nights out to celebrate the mailing of applications . . . priceless, keeping the total at $1,950.

INTERVIEWS

After celebrating, I waited eagerly and anxiously before hearing that I received four interviews. Costs associated with the interviewing process will vary considerably depending on many factors. However, traveling to interview sites and paying for accommodation are often the biggest expenses. To attend three interviews, each unfortunately 2 weeks apart, I spent about $900 on three separate flights from California to New Jersey. I coordinated the trips so that I flew into my parents' place, and they let me borrow the car so I could drive to interviews in nearby states. In addition to airfare, other costs associated with each interview included gas for the car, accommodation, a suit to look professional, and a small gift to thank the student in Richmond for letting me stay the night. Overall, the interview process was very expensive for me, totaling approximately $1,500. This brings the final cost of applying to doctoral programs to $3,450.

And that $3,450 was just to apply: I wasn't guaranteed admission, I wasn't guaranteed success, and I wasn't guaranteed a degree. I have met people who applied to only one school, spent less than $200, and were accepted. I also have met people who spent twice as much as I did, applied to even more programs, and were not accepted. Throughout the process I remained hopeful that hard work, persistence, and good fortune would result in success. Today, as I write these words, I'm happy to say that my efforts were rewarded.

Conclusion

The costs of going to graduate school in psychology are numerous, vary widely, and are largely influenced by individual differences. As you apply, don't forget to think and talk about the considerations discussed in this chapter. Once you've done all the thinking, budgeting, and saving that you can do, you'll be able to focus on the important parts of graduate school and life, instead of being distracted by financial matters.

Practical Tips

1. **Take your time—if you can.** Allow yourself at least a full year from the time you are considering graduate school until the time you submit applications. This way you can ensure that you are thorough about each step of the process.

2. **Master it only if you must.** If you're ultimately seeking a doctoral degree and finances are a concern, think of other ways to bolster your application besides getting a master's degree. Although this was my path, in retrospect I realize that I could have gained the necessary research and clinical experience to improve my application without incurring massive debt in a master's program.

3. **Plan but don't scheme.** Obtaining letters of recommendation can be difficult. Therefore, it's important to make a concerted effort to get to know professors. This advice especially applies to students at large universities, where establishing relationships with professors is more difficult. Of course, don't stalk them! Be appropriate and intentional, and your efforts will likely be rewarded.

4. **Relish your naïveté.** Go head-first into psychology-related experiences to learn as much as possible. The beginning of your career is a unique chance to explore options within the field. It's also amazing how much you can learn from experiences you don't enjoy.

5. **Who do you know?** Who you know is often just as important as what you know, plain and simple.

6. **Set the precedent you desire.** Create the graduate school experience you want by being honest during interviews about your expectations for graduate school. Ask for what you want so long as you're polite and respectful.

7. **Concentrate your efforts.** In retrospect, applying to 17 programs was an inefficient use of my time and money. I thought it would increase my probability of getting in. I encourage you to be realistic about your application and focus your search. If I were to do it over again, I would apply to just 10 to 12 programs.

References

American Psychological Association. (2002). Ethical principles of psychologists and code of conduct. *American Psychologist, 57,* 1060–1073.

American Psychological Association. (2008). *Graduate study in psychology*. Washington, DC: Author.

American Psychological Association, Center for Psychology Workforce Analysis and Research. (2007a, June). *2005 Doctorate Employment Survey—List of tables*. Retrieved July 4, 2007, from http://research.apa.org/des05tables.html

American Psychological Association, Help Center. (2007b, December). *Mental health parity: Does your insurance cover mental health services?* Retrieved December 12, 2007, from http://www.apahelpcenter.org/articles/article.php?id=167

American Psychological Association, Media Information. (2003, August 24). *The wage gap favoring men doesn't just hurt women's pay, according to new research*. Retrieved July 4, 2007, from http://www.apa.org/releases/wagegap.html

Mental Health Parity Act, 42 U.S.C. § 558 (2007).

Norcross, J. C., Castle, P. H., Sayette, M. A., & Mayne, T. J. (2004). The PsyD: Heterogeneity in practitioner training. *Professional Psychology: Research and Practice, 35*, 412–419.

Norcross, J. C., Kohout, J. L., & Wicherski, M. (2005). Graduate study in psychology: 1971 to 2004. *American Psychologist, 60*, 959–975.

Pate, W. E., II. (2001, April). *Analyses of data from graduate study in psychology: 1999–2000*. Retrieved July 1, 2007, from http://research.apa.org/grad00contents.html

Pate, W. E., II, Frincke, J. L., & Kohout, J. L. (2005, May). *Salaries in psychology 2003: Report of the 2003 APA Salary Survey*. Retrieved February 12, 2007, from http://research.apa.org/03salary/homepage.html

Rapoport, A. I., Kohout, J. L., & Wicherski, M. (2000, April 28). *Psychology doctorate recipients: How much financial debt at graduation?* Retrieved July 4, 2007, from http://www.nsf.gov/statistics/issuebrf/sib00321.htm

Singleton, D., Tate, A. C., & Kohout, J. L. (2003, June). *2002 Master's, Specialist's, and Related Degrees Employment Survey*. Retrieved July 1, 2007, from http://research.apa.org/mes2002contents.html

Singleton, D., Tate, A. C., & Randall, G. (2003, January). *Salaries in psychology: 2001: Report of the 2001 APA Salary Survey*. Retrieved January 30, 2005, from http://research.apa.org/01salary/index.html#Master's

Wicherski, M., & Kohout, J. (2005, August). *2003 Doctorate Employment Survey*. Retrieved June 25, 2007, from http://research.apa.org/des03.html

Essay 3
My Financial
Considerations: The Varied
Hats I've Worn
Melba J. T. Vasquez

I am a psychologist who has been in full-time, independent practice since 1991. For 13 years before that, I served as a university counseling center psychologist at two different universities and had a part-time practice during most of that time. I entered the counseling psychology doctoral program at the University of Texas at Austin in 1974, after serving as a middle school teacher for 2 years. I'd almost completed a master's degree in school counseling by attending summer school and night classes during the school year and had just become accustomed to a nice apartment and a new car when I got accepted to the doctoral program.

To contribute to financial stresses, my partner of 2 years and I decided to get a divorce during my first semester of graduate school. At this point, I had $300 in savings and knew I had to immediately downsize and get a job. I sold my car, bought a used Volkswagen, and started tutoring undergraduates. I lived particularly frugally that 1st year (e.g., I rode the bus to save money on gas, which had become very expensive during that period).

Then, two things changed that made my 2nd year a little easier financially. I was awarded an American Psychological Association Minority Fellowship. I was lucky to be in the first cohort of 30 graduate students to benefit from what at the time was a new program. The program has been in existence for over 30 years and has funded over 1,200 fellows (Vasquez & Jones, 2006). I received funding for the last 3 of my 4 years of graduate school. In addition, I moved in with a new relationship partner who worked full-time as an educational consultant. We split expenses, which helped considerably. I continued to work when I could. As a teaching assistant, I taught adolescent psychology to future teachers in educational psychology. At other times, I served as a graduate assistant. The last 2 years of my program I obtained a paid, 2-year, half-time internship at the University of Texas Counseling and Mental Health Center. I was clear that I did not want student loans. I feel very fortunate not to have needed to obtain one, although I realize that getting through graduate school without doing so these days is rare.

As I approached graduation, I was offered a position at Colorado State University's Counseling Center as a staff psychologist as well as an appointment as an assistant professor in the university's counseling psychology doctoral program. This opportunity was ideal for me, as I was still ambivalent about whether I wanted an academic or applied position. It was also my first opportunity to leave the state, and my partner was willing to leave a job and go with me. After consulting with some mentors, I negotiated a slightly higher salary than I was offered. I was offered $14,000 in 1978 for a 9-month contract; I requested $15,000 and was given $14,500. There were also opportunities to work at the university part-time, and I started a small part-time practice by subleasing a colleague's private practice office, first, one and, then, two evenings a week. My partner, Jim Miller, took a $10,000 pay cut to be in Colorado with me; our financial status continued to be adequate, but we did not have a lot of disposable income. After 4 years, it was his "turn" to accept a better job opportunity, and we returned to Texas.

Jim took a school principal position in the Houston, Texas, area; I returned to the University of Texas Counseling and Mental Health Center in Austin. We had a 3-year commuting relationship, which increased our living costs. I negotiated a salary for a 12-month appointment and started a part-time practice. I initially rented an office on a per-hour basis and then shared an office with another part-time practitioner.

I loved almost all the work I did. I wrote papers (for presentation at conferences as well as for publication) on topics about which I had passion (i.e., ethnic minority psychology, psychology of women, supervision and training, and professional ethics) and served on local, state, regional, and national task forces, committees, and boards related to those topics. I developed expertise in these areas and began providing workshops, presentations, and keynote addresses; more times than not I was provided with an honorarium (i.e., a small payment) for my services.

I come from a working-class background and was the first college student in my family of origin. Neither of my parents graduated from high school, and both worked blue-collar jobs while I lived at home. However, my mother obtained her GED (i.e., General Educational Development) certificate and then a college degree when I was in graduate school. She was employed as a community action worker in President Lyndon Baines Johnson's War on Poverty and ended up as an executive director for central Texas, with a multimillion-dollar budget. She lifted our family from blue collar to middle class within 2 decades. My partner, Jim, had a background similar to mine. We both worked hard to obtain multiple degrees and credentials and tended to be careful with money. Jim was a school teacher, educational consultant, and school principal. He took early retirement in 1989 and obtained a second master's degree in social work, and we entered full-time practice at the same time in 1991.

Money issues have been constantly present but not a major source of stress. Jim and I fortunately shared the philosophy of living within our means. We chose not to spend money that we did not have; for the most part, we bought what we could pay for immediately. Credit cards were used only for convenience and were paid off at the end of each month. We implemented that policy early in our relationship and continue it to this day, with only rare exceptions.

Finances can be sensitive issues to address. I have found it challenging to learn how to negotiate salaries as well as become comfortable charging clients and expecting payment for workshops and talks. Early in my practice, I probably too often allowed clients to defer payments to me without clear negotiation. Learning to talk about money issues is an important developmental task that requires desensitization for most of us. Conflict in psychotherapy is an important process in which all therapists must become skilled. I can think of two clients who were very angry when I implemented my boundary about charging for missed sessions. These issues were particularly difficult for me to handle in my professional work.

As a result of working in and loving university counseling center work, I had aspirations to become the director of a counseling center. However, because of personal family events (e.g., the death of my father, wanting to stay close to my partner's daughter), I went into full-time practice in 1991. I had initially thought that the shift from a full-time university counseling center psychologist to a part-time, and then a full-time, practitioner was to be temporary. When I made the move to full-time independent practice, it was anxiety producing, as I had to pay for my own full-time office and other expenditures. However, within the 1st year I had doubled my university salary. Not only that, I found that I could continue to write and publish, could actively serve as a volunteer in various professional associations, and felt a freedom that I'd not felt before. I decided to remain in full-time independent practice. Much of what I and coauthor Ken Pope have learned about starting, growing, or improving a psychology practice is documented in our book *How to Survive and Thrive as a Therapist* (Pope & Vasquez, 2005).

After Jim and I both developed our practices, we were able to save more money to move into a neighborhood close to our office, and close to a favorite hiking and bike trail. My partner has been a bit of an entrepreneur and invested and did well in both real estate and the stock market. In the past decade or so, these investments have allowed our lifestyles to become more comfortable. It has also been very important to save for retirement, although we both wish we had started that process sooner than we did.

In retrospect, we have had, for the most part, a healthy relationship with money. Delaying gratification, balanced with enjoying life in ways that we can without overspending money, has been a very functional strategy for us. Enjoying life is not necessarily associated with money; we have both had attitudes that we could enjoy whatever we could afford. The old adage "money isn't everything" is largely true, but money does go a long way to making one feel safe! Having more money is better than having less; however, in my opinion, one's attitude and relationship to money are more significant factors in one's happiness and sense of well-being. Only once did I not have enough money put aside to make quarterly IRS payments. The stress was so uncomfortable I never allowed that to happen again.

I believe that one must become clear about how much is enough, try to obtain positions that allow one to live that lifestyle, and then make careful choices about managing money. The various career and job opportunities available to psychologists are wonderful, and the income can provide a satisfying life. For those who wish to enter full-time practice, Pope and I (2005) provided suggestions for thinking through who you are and what is important to you, as well as information about income, expenses, and how to develop a business plan (by the way, getting an occasional royalty check is a nice consequence of publishing books!).

This profession has served me well. I have thoroughly enjoyed the various hats I've worn. I love my work, and it has become financially lucrative for me over the years. It is important to assess your "fit" for the kind of work you would like to do. I believe that it is important to find work that feels natural and easy for the most part and about which you can say, "I can't believe I get paid for what I do." If you are able to do this, I believe that you are much more likely to be successful. Having a good relationship with money is an important way to engage in self-care (see Pope & Vasquez, 2005). Having a healthy relationship with money is essential if you want to achieve a long, successful, and fulfilling career.

References

Pope, K. S., & Vasquez, M. J. T. (2005). *How to survive and thrive as a therapist: Information, ideas, and resources for psychologists in practice*. Washington, DC: American Psychological Association.

Vasquez, M. J. T., & Jones, J. M. (2006). Increasing the number of psychologists of color: Public policy issues for affirmative diversity. *American Psychologist, 61*, 132–143.

Alison B. Breland

Finding a Fit | 4

From: Pennington, NJ
Area of study: Biopsychology, Virginia Commonwealth University, Richmond
Previous degree(s): BS in psychology from Mary Washington College, Fredericksburg, VA
Career before graduate school: Marketing research associate
Number of graduate schools applied to: 7
Age when started this graduate program: 24
Professional interests: Substance use and abuse research
Career aspirations: Continue researching substance use, abuse, and treatment; teach

"How do I find the best program for me?" This was the question I asked over and over again when looking for graduate programs in psychology. I had broad questions, regarding choosing a specialty, as well as more specific questions, such as finding a potential advisor. Figuring out where I belonged for graduate school was a challenging—but a very rewarding—process. Through sharing my experiences, and the experiences of my fellow students, I hope in this chapter to help you navigate the process of finding the best "fit" for you. In this chapter, finding a fit means finding a graduate program in psychology that meets your individual needs. Finding a good fit means being happy in graduate school!

In this chapter I describe many aspects of fit, such as program focus, type, structure, culture, faculty, and location. Many factors are involved in finding your fit, and the process may seem overwhelming at first. However, you will probably find that certain aspects jump out at you whereas others seem unimportant. Prioritizing certain factors can help you develop a strategy for identifying a program that will be stimulating and rewarding for you, and not all aspects need to be considered. This process may take some time, and may even surprise you. My journey to find the best fit in a graduate program definitely shocked me!

My first step to finding the best fit was choosing a particular program focus in psychology. Although I knew I enjoyed psychology, I was very unsure about an area of concentration, so I looked to my past experiences and interests for guidance. I eventually discovered that my fit was in biopsychology because of an experience in my high school chemistry class. I found chemistry extremely difficult, and I struggled to succeed in the class. Labs often ended in tears and frustration. To make matters worse, our final project was a 5-minute class presentation, and the prospect of combining my fear of chemistry with standing up in front of 30 bored, assuming, adolescent classmates was extremely intimidating.

I tried to think of a topic—any topic—in chemistry that I could discuss in front of my peers. Although I was not very interested in chemistry, I was intrigued by mental illness and psychology, probably because both of my parents are psychologists. For papers or presentations in other classes, I wrote about multiple personality disorder and how Dorothea Dix revolutionized mental health care in the 1800s. So, of course, I tried to think of a way that chemistry, something I found unpleasant, could be connected to psychology, something I found rewarding. I knew that chemicals could alter behavior and emotion and that people with mental illnesses often took medication to alleviate their symptoms, but that was where my knowledge stopped. Luckily for me, my mother was a psychology professor at a nearby college and had a colleague who taught physiological psychology who helped me understand the relationship between chemistry, emotion, and behavior. After reading some basic textbooks and a few journal articles, I learned how drugs affect the body at the synaptic level. What I learned fascinated me, and I was surprised that I could actually understand these complex discussions about chemistry. I decided to focus my chemistry project on the neurological aspects of depression, and I learned how drugs such as the selective serotonin reuptake inhibitors, monoamine oxidase inhibitors, and tricyclics function. I eventually was able to summarize the actions of antidepressant medication for my presentation. On presentation day, with my heart beating and palms sweating, I walked to the front of the room with a poster of hand-drawn synapses. At the end of 5 minutes, I did not want to stop talking and sit down. My peers even appeared interested in what I had to say. Suddenly, chemistry wasn't so bad anymore.

This high school chemistry presentation was the beginning of my interest in the biological mechanisms involved in psychology, although this interest would take many more years to solidify. I continued to struggle with chemistry and other science courses but often remembered this particular presentation. In college, I majored in psychology but focused on abnormal, counseling, and social psychology, because at that point, I thought I wanted a career in counseling or clinical psychology. However, in these classes I often wanted to know what was happening at the neurological level, which was generally not the focus of these courses. The most rewarding classes were those that focused on drugs and behavior, such as a course in psychopharmacology and another in physiological psychology. Although these courses were very challenging for me, my questions about the neurological level of behavior and mental illnesses were answered, and my interest in this field intensified.

However, even though I loved the classes in biological psychology, I did not plan to apply to graduate school in psychology because I was concerned about my chances of being admitted into doctoral programs. In college, I had learned that doctoral programs often have stringent admission requirements, and I did not feel that my grades, Graduate Record Examinations (GRE) scores, and experience were sufficient. Feeling unsure but needing to take some kind of step, I applied to a master's in social work (MSW) program and was rejected. With no backup plan, after graduation I found a job and spent the next 2 years working in marketing research. Those years were frustrating yet gave me time to consider my career goals and investigate graduate programs.

Through these experiences, I learned that choosing a path can take time and that it may not be immediately obvious. At first, finding a fit for me was overwhelming. I felt lost, unsure about my qualifications, and confused about how to find programs. By asking many, many questions, I was eventually able to find enough information to apply to several biopsychology doctoral programs, and I entered a program that fit me very well.

As I mentioned at the outset of this chapter, many different aspects to finding the best fit are helpful to consider when deciding on a program type, when applying, and when accepting an offer. To assist you in finding your fit, I frame this chapter with many of the questions I asked throughout the application process. I also include questions I didn't ask but wished I had.

Is Graduate School in Psychology the Right Fit for Me?

Although it is important to keep in mind the big picture of graduate school in psychology (see chap. 1), thinking about graduate school in psychology as an overall career choice is also a part of finding a program that will suit you well. This overarching question was a huge part of finding the best fit for me. You may wonder whether you need an advanced degree to reach your goals. Many people with undergraduate degrees find that a graduate degree is required to reach their career goals, but some do not. If you are unsure about your ultimate career goals, considering your current job opportunities can help you decide. For example, with only an undergraduate degree, can you get a job that will make you happy professionally? If not, continuing your education may be a wise option. Second, consider the sacrifices involved in getting an advanced degree, such as the time, money, and motivation required. Are you willing to make these commitments?

For me, I needed some time in the workforce to realize that I required an advanced or different degree to reach my career goals. During this time, I wasn't entirely sure what my career goals were, but I knew I was not happy with my career path. For example, with only an undergraduate degree in psychology, I found that appealing jobs and attractive salaries were unavailable. During the 2 years I spent doing marketing research after college, I was briefly content with my own little cubicle, my business cards, and my new business wardrobe. However, the actual work was not challenging and was generally unrelated to my psychology degree. In addition, I discovered that my salary and prospects for advancement were limited.

On slow days at the job, I kept busy by contemplating different possible degrees, such as library science programs, massage school, social or personality psychology PhD programs, and a master's degree in public health, among others. Fortunately, my boss didn't notice what I was working on! I also kept returning to my interest in biological psychology and began talking with other graduate students in psychology about this avenue. While gathering information, I asked many of the questions that head the sections that follow, and as I obtained more information, I became more confident in my decision to apply.

Will a Master's or Doctoral Program Fit Me Better?

While I was doing some initial research into biopsychology programs, one of my first goals was to figure out what type of program would fit me best. I spent a long time trying to determine whether I should get a terminal master's degree, a doctoral degree, or both. For most areas of psychology, both terminal master's-level and doctoral-level degree programs exist, and each has advantages and disadvantages. The degree that will fit you better depends on your career goals, the time you can commit, and financial considerations. For example, a terminal master's program can often be completed in 1 to 3 years and may give you all of the training you need for your career of choice. As an example, if you are interested in counseling, but not research, a master's in counseling or social work may be a great option. In addition, some (yet certainly not all) master's programs tend to have less competitive or different admission requirements than do doctoral programs. For example, the MSW program to which I initially applied did not require GRE scores. Unfortunately, most master's programs require you to pay for tuition and living expenses, and opportunities for professional advancement may be more limited than with a doctoral degree.

The benefits of a doctoral program can include greater career opportunities, and many programs offer tuition remission and a stipend. However, doctoral programs take longer to complete (4–6 years or longer), and most have very competitive admission requirements. Most doctoral programs require GRE scores, and many require prospective applicants to have high GRE scores along with stellar grade point averages (GPAs). Also, many doctoral programs provide education in multiple domains: research, teaching, writing, consulting, and providing therapy (however, not all doctoral programs provide education in every domain). Gaining expertise in all of these areas can be very rewarding and can increase your career opportunities.

Another option is to get both a master's degree and a doctorate, and many students choose to follow this path. Some students find that getting a master's degree first can strengthen their applications to doctoral programs and help them focus on a particular area of interest, thus increasing their chances of being admitted to competitive doctoral programs. In addition, some master's-level programs in psychology are general programs, so students graduate with a well-rounded knowledge of psychology. Others focus on particular areas, such as clinical or social psychology. You also can choose a master's-level program in a particular area, and then decide to switch to another area for a doctoral degree (e.g., PhD, PsyD, EdD). For example, I know one student who obtained a master's in clinical psychology and then changed tracks by entering an experimental psychology PhD program. Of course, getting both a master's and a doctoral degree might mean more years in school (i.e., if you attend two separate programs), but many students find success with this strategy.

Overall, there isn't necessarily a "right" choice for program type; your choice will depend on your interests and what is feasible for you. After being out of college for several years, I decided I was primarily interested in research, which requires a PhD because few research-related jobs are available for people with just a master's degree in psychology. Because I was unsure whether I would be admitted to PhD programs, I applied to both general master's and biopsychology doctoral programs. If I was rejected from the PhD programs, my plan was to get a master's first and try again for PhD programs on completion of the master's degree. I had used a similar strategy when applying to undergraduate colleges; that is, I chose a range of schools with different admission requirements. For graduate school, applying to a range of programs provided me with a greater sense of security by increasing my chances of being admitted somewhere and, therefore, decreasing the likelihood that I would be stuck in my boring corporate job.

Can I Find a Program With a Focus on a Very Specific Area?

In addition to choosing between master's- and doctoral-level programs, another hurdle I encountered was finding a program in which I could do research in my area of interest. By this point, I had narrowed my interest to programs in biopsychology with research in psychopharmacology, specifically research related to substance abuse. Also, I was interested in working with humans, not animals. This distinction was important because many researchers in the substance abuse field work with animals. I learned that faculty doing substance abuse research with humans were often part of medical schools, and I wasn't interested in applying to medical school; however, after talking with various people, I found that some psychology programs did have opportunities for biological or physiological research with humans—I just had to find them.

So, even if you have very specific research interests or have a particular clinical population you want to work with (e.g., a population with a particular mental disorder or specific characteristics), you may find programs that fit your interests and psychology faculty members with similar interests. In addition, there are entire programs with specific concentrations. For example, programs exist in sports psychology, health psychology, psychology and religion, marriage and family therapy, child therapy, and psychopathology, among many others. Sometimes finding these programs can require some extra investigation, so be prepared to do your research thoroughly.

What Programs Match My Qualifications? (or, Will Any Programs Accept Me?)

Finding the best fit for you involves taking an honest look at your overall qualifications and comparing them with the characteristics that are valued by programs. You can run into trouble by thinking too highly of your credentials or by thinking that you are underqualified. Finding the best fit in this context means matching your qualifications with the requirements of various programs. For example, consider your clinical and research experiences, course work, undergraduate GPA, and GRE scores.

Several resources can help you match your qualifications (at least roughly) with the qualifications for particular graduate programs in psychology. First, I found that the American Psychological Association's (APA) book *Graduate Study in Psychology* (see Recommended Resources at the end of this volume), which provides the requirements for many available programs, categorized by state and type, was an excellent source of information. This resource provides information about current students' mean GRE scores and GPAs, the number of applicants and the number accepted, and various programs' areas of specialty. Although this guide can be helpful, all program "requirements" listed are not necessarily definite and may be slightly out of date, so make sure to consult program Web sites for the most updated information. For example, I applied to several programs that listed minimum GRE scores that I did not quite meet and was admitted anyway. However, even with these limitations, this book gave me some idea of how my qualifications matched the requirements of various programs.

Second, I spent a considerable amount of time researching program Web sites. The information provided online usually includes admission requirements. Web sites also frequently provide detailed information about faculty members, course work, and other learning opportunities. Sometimes, I was able to make online requests for information about specific programs to be mailed to me, which was very helpful.

Third, I found that current or recent graduates of psychology doctoral programs were an invaluable resource. While trying to find my fit, I spoke with current and former graduate students wherever I could find them. Through contacts with friends and relatives, I found graduate students in various psychology programs. I also contacted psychology professors at a local college, as well as my alma mater, to find recent college graduates who went on to graduate school in psychology. I also talked with newly hired psychology professors about their graduate school experiences. I obtained extensive, valuable advice from each person I spoke with and learned from each person's unique experience. Plus, everyone I spoke with was eager to help and glad to tell me his or her strategies and experiences.

A major stumbling block for me was figuring out just how good my qualifications needed to be and exactly what kinds of courses, training, GRE scores, and experience I needed to be a competitive applicant. Although I wanted to pursue a degree in biopsychology, I thought I required extensive science-related course work in addition to psychology course work. I was also unsure about my GRE scores, which were not the best. It took me a while to realize that my GRE scores needed improvement, and I initially balked at the idea of retaking these tests to improve my scores. Fortunately, after dragging my feet for some time, I finally admitted that to increase my chances of being accepted to graduate school in psychology, I would need to improve my GRE scores. I enrolled in a GRE preparatory class, studied intensely, and dramatically boosted my scores.

Some of my early beliefs about qualifications for graduate school in biopsychology were incorrect; for example, many programs did not require extensive undergraduate work in basic science. I had a great GPA, and most important, I had a strong history of undergraduate research experience, in addition to my work in marketing research. Even though most of my research experience was not specifically biopsychology-related, research experience in general helped make me a strong applicant.

It is also critical to assess the requirements of a graduate program during your search for a good fit. Various components of the graduate training experience differ by institution and program type (e.g., biopsychology vs. counseling psychology). Possible components include courses, teaching, practicum, and research. You may find that the experiences you gain as you acquire your degree may be the most valuable aspect of your education, which has certainly been true for me.

What Program Requirements Will Fit Me Best?

Course work is a core aspect of program structure. Depending on your interests, you may want to consider the amount of time you will need to commit to course work versus the time you will need to spend getting hands-on experience. It may be useful to determine how many credits are required for the degree and how many credits students typically take each semester. I suggest finding out whether the required courses reflect what you want to learn. Investigate credit requirements and course listings by consulting program Web sites and handbooks. While in graduate school, I was surprised to learn that some programs (e.g., counseling and clinical PhDs and PsyDs) tend to have heavy course requirements, whereas other programs (i.e., experimental PhDs) tend to require fewer courses. Although we may all be psychology graduate students, we spend our days engaged in very different activities.

In addition to course work, teaching experience can be another valuable aspect of your graduate education in psychology. In many programs, students earn their stipends by serving as teaching assistants or by teaching an entire course. In other programs, teaching is not required or is optional. If you are interested in gaining teaching experience, you may want to find out what courses graduate students teach and the level of responsibility expected. For example, some teaching assistantships require students to assist a professor with teaching responsibilities, whereas other assistantships require students to teach courses independently. For programs in which teaching is not the focus, you may want to ask about teaching opportunities if this is something you want to do. For me, teaching was not required in the biopsychology program I chose, but because I was interested in teaching, I asked about potential teaching opportunities before I applied. I have found that the teaching experience I gained in graduate school has been rewarding, and it can increase job opportunities after graduation, particularly if you are looking to work in academia.

Integrated into clinical, counseling, and school psychology graduate programs, practicum experiences provide training for developing therapists. Aspects that may vary by graduate program include the theoretical orientations of faculty, the setting (e.g., clinic, counseling center, hospital, school), the populations with whom you may work (e.g., individuals, couples, families, children, adults), and the particular disorders you may treat (e.g., phobia, borderline personality disorder, obesity). In addition, you may also want to inquire about APA accreditation status, the number of clinical hours required for graduation, opportunities to attend workshops, and other training opportunities.

Another important requirement of many programs is research. For students in PhD programs, research experience is particularly important, although it may be less emphasized in master's programs, depending on the type of master's program. When I considered program requirements, my focus was almost solely on research. I looked for programs with several faculty members researching a somewhat broad area (for me, substance abuse research) because I wanted a program with a strong emphasis on that type of research. I asked faculty members how involved students were in research and what kind of research responsibilities I might expect as a graduate student. In addition, I asked about potential opportunities for publications and how many publications I could expect to submit to journals while in the program, because I had been advised that publications would be an important part of my curriculum vitae. I also asked about opportunities to attend national and international conferences where I would be able to present research and network with colleagues in the field.

The emphasis on each of these requirements will differ depending on the type and focus of the program you choose. For example, students in clinical and counseling doctoral programs often are expected to balance course work, teaching responsibilities, clinical work, and research. If you are considering these fields, researching all aspects of each program is important. For these doctoral degrees, you may want to determine whether the program has ample clinical and teaching opportunities, interesting courses, and faculty with strong track records of research and clinical skills. In contrast, students in graduate programs with a primary research focus usually conduct research and take classes and may also teach. Students in clinically focused programs (such as PsyD or school psychology programs) may concentrate on clinical work, courses, and teaching, with less emphasis on research. Again, requirements differ by institution and program. Thus, determining the program requirements will help you meet your goals, which is a very important aspect of finding the best fit in a graduate program.

What Kind of Program Culture Will Fit Me Best?

As a student, your experience of graduate school will be colored by the culture of the program. Programs have very different cultures; they vary by work expectations, flexibility, balance, and diversity. For example, some programs have a "weed out" mentality, and not all students who are admitted actually complete the degree. Other programs are less demanding (which is subjective, of course) and may not be challenging enough for you. Many programs are in the middle. Likewise, some programs are more flexible than others and allow students to finish quickly or take more time, depending on the individual. Other programs have stricter schedules to which students are expected to adhere. Also, some programs offer evening classes, which may be preferable for working students or students with families. Depending on your personal needs, you may want to consider these and other factors related to program work expectations and flexibility.

Related to work expectations and flexibility is program balance. For example, you may want to find out whether the faculty members themselves strike a balance between work and family. Do faculty demonstrate interests and hobbies not related to their professional endeavors? If they work day and night, they might expect the same from you. As Dr. Sternberg explains in his essay at the end of this chapter, balance is a key consideration as you seek a good mentor.

Finally, some programs are more culturally diverse than others. Finding a program with faculty and students of different backgrounds and abilities may be important to you. Some students find it helpful to assess the ratio of ethnic minority students in a program or talk to students of diverse backgrounds to assess their experiences. Also, some programs are more diverse than others in terms of the types of research conducted and the populations studied.

Overall, finding a program with the level of work, flexibility, balance, and diversity you want will strongly influence your overall satisfaction with graduate school. Learning about program culture can be more difficult than finding out requirements, but I found that talking with current graduate students was an excellent way to get a feel for the graduate program's culture. Other graduate students have mentioned that visiting schools helped them get a sense for the program. During visits they observed the lives of current graduate students, thus getting a glimpse of how students in the program socialize together and how students and faculty interact.

How Do I Find a Fit With a Particular Faculty Member?

Individual faculty members can have a huge impact on your graduate experience, particularly in programs with a mentor model in which you will work primarily with one faculty member (this is more often the case in programs that emphasize research). The program I attend uses this model, and I work closely with my advisor. Because you may be spending a lot of time working with a particular faculty member, it's best to find out what he or she is like before you apply. You may want to consider the faculty member's research, funding, position, availability, and personality.

Start by looking for programs with faculty doing work that particularly interests you. See whether the faculty have recent publications in your area of interest and whether students are listed on recent publications. PubMed (http://www.ncbi.nlm.nih.gov/entrez) and PsycNET (http://psycinfo.apa.org) are excellent search engines to consult for publication references and articles, and many college and university libraries have a subscription to both. If current students in a program have publications, the likelihood is greater that you will also have the opportunity to publish.

If research is important to you, you may want to investigate whether the faculty member is grant-funded. If you are looking at psychology programs that are biomedically oriented, you can review a particular faculty member's grants online using the Computer Retrieval of Information on Scientific Projects database (http://crisp.cit.nih.gov). Another resource to find faculty grant funding is located on the National Science Foundation's Web site (http://www.nsf.gov). Also, university Web sites often list faculty grants. Grant money is very important for research-oriented programs because more grant money often means better equipment and more opportunities. In addition, your stipend may be grant-funded, although this depends on the program. You can also ask faculty members about their previous or past funding as well as whether they intend to apply for grants in the near future.

When considering individual faculty members, you may also want to learn the person's position in the university and whether they are tenured. Working with tenured faculty can be safer, because untenured faculty could leave the university if they do not receive tenure. If you choose an untenured faculty member, it's best to identify other faculty members at the same university with whom you could work with, just in case your mentor leaves the university (and, thus, the program).

A factor related to position is availability: Some mentors are readily available for students, whereas others are not. In some cases (certainly not all), as professors become more senior, their availability decreases. I think that availability is a critically important quality of a good mentor; a good mentor will have time to give you expert guidance, and he or she will likely be key to helping you obtain publications and awards, as well as helping you advance your career. Students who are extremely self-motivated may succeed with a mentor who is rarely available, but I recommend finding a mentor who has the time to advise you. In his essay, Dr. Sternberg also emphasizes the importance of having an attentive and available mentor, and I have found that these qualities in a mentor are absolutely critical.

Last, consider the personality of the faculty you'd like to work with; working with someone you can develop a rapport with will make your experience more enjoyable. In considering an advisor, it is best to seek out someone you can work with, as opposed to seeking out a new best friend. Although you need not always agree with your mentor, it is important to have an advocate who wants you to succeed and who will fit your mentoring needs, as Dr. Sternberg also mentions in his essay. A good backup plan is to find a program with several professors who are doing work you find interesting. Therefore, if your personality clashes with one mentor, you may be able to switch to another. Again, current students can be a resource regarding information about faculty members whom you may not otherwise be able to access. Yet although soliciting this information may be helpful, keep in mind that everyone's experience with a particular faculty member is different.

Because I was interested in research programs with a mentor model, my strategy was to first look for programs with faculty who were doing research in my field of interest. Then I found some of the faculty members' published articles and familiarized myself with their work. Next, I

FIGURE 4.1

Dear Dr. Brown:

My name is Alison Breland, and I am interested in applying to the Biopsychology PhD program at Science University. In particular, I have read some of your work on nicotine self-administration and have found it very interesting. I am wondering what research you are currently working on and whether you are accepting students for the upcoming school year.

Thank you,

Alison B. Breland

Sample e-mail for contacting prospective advisors.

contacted faculty members via e-mail, mentioned my interest in their work, and asked whether they were planning on accepting any new students for the coming year. Figure 4.1 shows example of an e-mail similar to ones I have actually sent.

I found that most professors were eager to discuss their work, and if I was unable to reach a particular professor, I figured that he or she was likely too busy to be a good mentor. As I mentioned earlier, having a mentor who was attentive (e.g., who responded to e-mail) and available was very important to me. If I was able to develop a rapport with a particular faculty member over the phone or via e-mail, I then asked more questions about the program and also asked to speak with current graduate students.

I obtained very helpful information from other graduate students regarding each professor's availability and personality. Although each student's relationship with a mentor may be different, I used these graduate students' opinions to help with my program selection. If I heard that a particular mentor was great to work with, I would move that program higher on my list. Hearing that a mentor did not treat all students fairly moved a program down on my list.

In many programs, you may not work with one particular professor; instead you may work with several. It is still useful to contact professors and discuss their specific work and the program in general. Depending on your interests, you may also want to contact the clinicians with whom you might work. Once again, current graduate students are an excellent source of answers and insight regarding your future working relationships in graduate school.

What Else Should I Consider When Looking for a Good Fit?

Several other considerations regarding a good fit include the location of the school and your financial circumstances. For some, the location of a program is critical, whereas other people may be willing to move to wherever the best school happens to be. You may need to consider the importance of location, especially if you have a partner or family to relocate. You may also want to consider whether you have a preference for an urban or a rural campus, and what type of climate you prefer. You may also want to consider whether your work requires access to unique resources (e.g., special equipment) or populations (e.g., medical patients) that may be available only at some universities. The answers to these questions should be factored into your decision-making process when finding a fit.

The relevance of funding and the type of stipend you can expect to receive is another factor to consider (see chap. 3). Financial packages at colleges and universities vary greatly. I found that each program I was accepted to offered different stipend amounts, although many were comparable. I did not make my decision on the basis of a stipend; rather, I focused more on choosing a mentor and location. Of course, the importance of a program's funding depends on your financial situation.

What If I Can't Find the Answers to All of These Questions, or What If No Program Meets All of My Requirements?

The goal of this chapter is to help you think about what program aspects will make a program the best fit for you. As you prioritize your preferences, you will find that particular factors are most important to you and thus consider them when deciding which program is the best match for you. Of course, finding the answers to all of the questions posed in this chapter may be difficult, and some questions may go unanswered. Also, probably no program will be perfect, so you may have to compromise in some areas. The goal is to get as much information as possible to make the most informed decision.

In my case, although I applied to many different programs, I compromised and took risks in several areas. First, I decided to attend a program that was geographically close to where my husband could find work. Second, I chose to work with a new, untenured faculty member, which was a bit risky. Third, the program I chose did not have multiple professors with whom I wanted to work; this choice nearly turned my life upside down when my mentor seriously considered taking a job at another university. Fortunately, my mentor stayed and received tenure, and my program has turned out to be an excellent match for me.

And don't forget, mistakes happen. If you enter a program and find that it does not fit you, this problem can be remedied. There are many options, such as switching to a different program at the same university, changing your mentor, or leaving the program. Depending on the circumstances, you might choose to tough it out, even if you had hoped for a better overall graduate school experience.

Conclusion

I found that the process of finding suitable graduate programs and applying was more difficult than finding an undergraduate institution. Unfortunately, there are few resources for finding graduate programs, which places the responsibility of researching programs on applicants' shoulders. In addition, finding the best fit often involves asking many soul-searching questions, which are often difficult to answer. However, investing the time and energy to find the best program will increase your chances that your graduate experience will be valuable and satisfying.

Fortunately, the graduate program I chose ended up being an excellent fit for me. Although not every aspect of my program is perfect, I am grateful that I found a dedicated mentor doing research in my area of interest. During graduate school, I have had many opportunities, such as working on a variety of research studies, teaching, publishing several peer-reviewed articles, obtaining my own federal funding, and traveling to both national and international conferences. I have also strengthened my public speaking and writing skills and will graduate having learned exciting and valuable knowledge.

I encourage you to find the program that fits you best, and I hope it leads you to a thrilling and rewarding graduate school experience. Simply thinking about the various topics addressed in this chapter will help you develop a strategy for finding a good fit.

Practical Tips

1. **Talk with other graduate students.** Find other graduate students in your field and talk with them. Ask for honest evaluations of their programs. Most likely, they will be happy to tell you their experiences. However, remember to not fixate on particular students' individual paths. Everyone's path to finding his or her fit is unique.

2. **Get a second opinion.** Keep in mind that even if you talk with a student who is dissatisfied with a particular program, *you* may not end up being dissatisfied. If you experience this situation, consider talking to multiple graduate students for several opinions and look for clues in other places as well.

3. **Make contact.** If considering applying to programs with a mentor model, contact individual faculty members and introduce yourself (having already read their recent publications). Ask whether they will be accepting students for the following academic year, because even if you are the "perfect" applicant, if they are not accepting students that year, you won't be accepted.

4. **Keep your options open.** Apply to programs with varying admittance requirements, thus increasing your chances of being admitted somewhere.

5. **Make a good impression.** In most programs, individual faculty members are key in determining who is admitted, so making a good impression is important. Therefore, make sure you thank faculty for providing information and assistance (e.g., if you talk on the phone, consider sending a thank you e-mail or a card).

6. **Graduate school doesn't decide your future.** It's helpful to know that your future is not completely determined by where you attend graduate school. The focus of your work and your geographical location may change as you advance in your career.

Essay 4
What to Look for in a
Graduate Mentor: Ten
Qualities to Find a Fit
Robert J. Sternberg

One of the most important decisions you can make is the choice of a graduate mentor. Mentors play a crucial role in graduate education. The exact role they play varies by degree and program. I was extremely fortunate with my own mentors: Endel Tulving was my undergraduate mentor at Yale, Gordon Bower was my graduate mentor at Stanford, and Wendell Garner was my mentor when I was a junior faculty member at Yale. I would like to talk about what made them so great so you can learn about the qualities you will want to look for in a graduate mentor (see also Sternberg, 2004).

1. Caring for and about you. The single most important attribute of a mentor is that he or she cares for and about you. You want to choose someone who will look out for your interests, certainly in graduate school and, if possible, throughout your whole career. My mentors have become lifelong friends. I am frequently in touch with them, and they *still* advise me on important matters—and I'm 57! That is care. What you don't want is a mentor who is exploitative, who works with graduate students primarily or even solely to advance his or her own career. Good mentors know that on average they will get back from a student in proportion to what they give. They are therefore giving of themselves because it helps the student and at the same time helps them. Bad mentors want to get but not give. You can find out how caring a mentor is by talking to past mentees and getting their perspectives. You can also talk with a potential mentor before working with him or her to assess whether the mentor exhibits genuine interest in you.

2. Willingness to devote time and effort to mentorship. Graduate mentorship is time-consuming. There is no quick fix for it. You need someone who wants to invest time and effort in you. In the end, I am convinced that you will learn more from a good mentor than you will from all the courses you take in graduate school. However, you can learn only if the mentor is willing to invest in you. Again, you can find out about investment by talking to other students and by observing the mentor in action with current mentees. In reality, there is oftentimes something of a trade-off between seniority and time. Many more senior mentors simply do not have as much time as more junior ones. However, if the person is not going to be there for you, it does not matter how senior he or she is: You won't get anything from the mentor. When I was in graduate school, Gordon Bower was at the peak of his career. He still found time for his students. He has continued to find time to help me even in the 30 years since I left Stanford.

3. Willingness to go to bat for you. One of the reasons you go to graduate school is to get a good job after graduation. Mentors have very different views on how much they should do to get their students jobs. Almost all mentors will write you a letter, but some will invest a lot of work in the letter; others will not. Moreover, some mentors will pass your name on to colleagues who might be looking to hire, help you network, make phone calls for you, and give you specific tips about how to succeed in job interviews. In the end, you want someone who will support you when the time comes to get a job. Look at what the mentor has done for others in the job market. That is the best predictor of what he or she will do for you. Also, be sure to find a mentor who will go to bat for you while you are still in graduate school. You will need an advocate during your graduate years, and it should be your mentor.

4. Fit to your mentoring needs. Graduate mentors have different styles of mentoring. At one extreme, they may expect all their students to get heavily involved in the mentor's own projects and only later in their careers to become involved in independent work. These mentors tend to provide a very structured experience to graduate students. Other mentors may expect you to find your own project to do. These mentors tend to provide less structure during the graduate experience. If you are quite uncertain as to what you want to do, then having a mentor who provides a lot of structure can be a blessing. However, if you want things your own way, having a mentor who imposes a lot of structure can be a curse. It is important, therefore, to find a mentor whose style fits your own. It is good for a mentor to be flexible, but not all of them are. So you need to work with someone whose style works for you. When I was in graduate school, I needed to be left alone. Gordon Bower left me alone, letting me do what I wanted. Other students of his worked directly on his projects. He adjusted his mentoring style to fit the student, which is probably why he has had so many successful students over the years.

5. Excellence in your chosen field. Much of what you learn, you will learn from your mentor. For example, from Endel Tulving I learned the importance of not assuming that because a lot of people believe something it necessarily must be true. From Gordon Bower I learned the importance of asking questions that will interest people and thereby having an audience. From Wendell Garner I learned the importance of making a positive contribution to the field, rather than contributing negatively by knocking down other people and their work. They were, all three, outstanding role models. And their excellence as role models was because of their excellence in the field. A mentor can be willing to invest in you, but if he or she is not a great role model, what you learn may not be the lessons you most want to learn. Excellence must be found in those things that matter to you, which usually will be teaching, research, and, possibly, practice.

6. Balance in life. A mentor is more than an academic role model. Academia is very demanding of one's time and energy. Many people in academia live personal lives that are much less than ideal. Part of what you want to learn from a mentor is how to achieve some balance in life, not just how to be a researcher, teacher, or practitioner. All three of my mentors have led full lives. They did many things besides just teach and do research. You want to learn how to achieve balance, lest you get older and wonder where your life went. Very few psychologists on their death-bed regret that extra paper they did not write; however, they may well regret the extra time they did not spend with their family. In my own case, I feel that the best use of my time has not been writing papers but rather spending time with my family. My children are doing very well today, and I would like to think it is due at least in small part—perhaps very small part!—to the role I played when they were growing up. Had I not had those two kids, I think I would have missed a great deal in my life.

7. Resources and willingness to share them. Having a mentor with resources and a willingness to share them can greatly facilitate your graduate career. It is important to note that resources are not just financial. One of the trickiest things to look for is a pool of resources that may come with a mentor. Some mentors have a lot of resources. They may have grants or contracts or great lab space or an active lab with lots of people with whom to speak. Other mentors may have fewer resources or may not be willing to share what resources they have. In my experience, it is better to choose a mentor who has more resources rather than fewer. Neither the other graduate students nor I fully appreciated his generosity. The money he spent on us was money not spent on other things to which he might have allocated the funds.

8. Kindliness. One of the things that I greatly appreciated in my mentors was that they were, when all was said and done, kind. Every graduate student makes mistakes, usually many times. There is nothing wrong with making mistakes. That is how you learn. However, mentors vary greatly in their tolerance of and willingness to help students learn from mistakes. Some faculty have many graduate students; others, very few. A major factor in how many students they have is simply whether they are kind to their students. However, those who are not kind often do not even realize it and wonder why students either do not come to work with them or do not stay with them. No matter what the mentor's other qualifications, do not select a mentor who is mean: You will regret it.

9. Helping you find your niche. My interests were almost totally different from Gordon Bower's. I was interested in human intelligence; he, in memory. Yet he supported my interests in a topic very different from that of his research. It is always good to have overlap in interests between you and your advisor; however, most important is that your mentor helps you find who you are and what you have to contribute to the world.

10. Being there for you. There likely will be some point in graduate school when you feel like things are falling apart. It may be in your professional life, it may be in your personal life, or it may be in both. You want someone who is there for you when you need him or her.

In sum, choosing a good mentor is one of the most important decisions you ever will make. I hope this essay has provided some guidance as to what you should look for when you meet potential mentors.

Reference

Sternberg, R. J. (2004). *Psychology 101½: The unspoken rules for success in academia.* Washington, DC: American Psychological Association.

Kristine M. Molina

The Application Process | 5

From: Miami, FL

Area of study: Joint Psychology (Personality and Social Contexts) and Women's Studies, University of Michigan, Ann Arbor

Previous degree(s): BA in psychology from Smith College, Northampton, MA

Career before graduate school: Research assistant

Number of graduate schools applied to: First time—16, second time—13

Age when started this graduate program: 23

Professional interests: Intersectionality, immigration, social marginality, education, mental health, and Latina/os

Career aspirations: Become a university professor and conduct research

The application process for graduate programs in psychology demands much consideration and many resources before you even submit a completed application. In this chapter, I provide information about the details worth knowing when applying: mentoring and organization throughout the process, components of the application, and the logistics involved in finalizing the application package. To highlight these topics, I also share my personal journey through the application process and admittance to graduate school.

I am grateful to my family, friends, and mentors, who all provided much needed support and encouragement when I needed it most throughout the application process. I couldn't have done it without them.

As a first-generation college student who is a low-income Latina with multiple learning disabilities, I have experienced challenges at every step of the educational pipeline. Even today, as a graduate student, I continue to face challenges because of my ethnicity, class, and ability status. However, I have also had (and continue to have) support from family, friends, and mentors to help me succeed and become the influential figure I hope to be in academia and within my community. Because of my membership in stigmatized and marginalized groups, I have developed a heightened awareness of the specific needs that people within these groups face on a daily basis. In fact, this awareness fuels my passion for pursuing an academic career so I can conduct research and ultimately influence public policy.

At the start of my undergraduate career, I wanted to attend medical school and become a pediatrician, but that soon changed after I took an introductory psychology course. The class exposed me to various areas within psychology and left me wondering whether psychology was a field that I might pursue. My interest deepened the following year, when I took a clinical research course. This course opened up an activity I had never experienced before: research. Until then, I had always thought psychology meant becoming a therapist. In this class, I, along with other students, was asked to develop an empirical study on behavioral inhibition. Although my peers wanted to focus on behavioral inhibition in college women, I wanted to understand the relationship between ethnicity and behavioral inhibition during a public speaking task. Being the only woman of color in many of my classes provided me a lens from which to study this question, because I sometimes felt marginalized and silenced. We developed an empirical study that incorporated both concepts and collected data, and I later presented the findings at a national conference. The conference experience made me realize that pursuing a doctoral degree was something I wanted to do so I could ask the types of questions I did not see addressed within my psychology textbooks or course material—specifically, questions about how women of color experience, cope with, and resist systems of oppression (e.g., racism, sexism, classism). I knew that if I wanted to see these questions addressed, I would have to obtain a doctoral degree so that I could research them myself.

Although I knew I wanted to pursue a doctoral degree, I had not decided whether social–personality psychology or clinical psychology programs would best fit my interests. Thus, in the summer after my college graduation, I was still researching both types of programs because they equally intrigued me and spoke to my personal experiences. As I describe later, I ended up applying to both types, which gave me an in-depth awareness of the application process from two angles.

Knowing that research experience was necessary to apply to the graduate programs that interested me, I became involved in various projects in college and sought out research experience during summers. I interned at the Child Development Unit at Harvard Medical School and Children's Hospital and the Pediatric Psychology Department at the University of Miami's School of Medicine. I also took a year off after graduation to work as a research assistant at Florida International University's Community-Based Intervention Research Group, which gave me further research experience, especially with Latina/o and African American youth. In these research positions, I learned how social identities are studied differently in various subfields of psychology. Doing social–personality psychology research and taking classes in clinical psychology guided my decision to apply to both social–personality psychology and clinical psychology graduate programs.

I went through the process of applying to doctoral programs twice. The first time I applied to 16 programs in clinical psychology; however, with only some research and little clinical experience, I was not accepted to a graduate program. The second time around, I applied to 13 doctoral programs that included both clinical, and social–personality programs. I broadened my search because I thought that I might have a better chance of getting into social–personality programs. These programs tend to be research-oriented and seemed like a good fit because of my extensive research experience, especially within the area of ethnic minority research. Actually, applying to social–personality programs made me feel more confident about my chances of getting into a doctoral program the second time around, especially after a year of figuring out the specific research areas that I wanted to delve into as a graduate student. I was also more excited to apply to the social–personality graduate programs because they would allow me to research the social issues that interest me.

After the application process, I was happy to be accepted at the joint PhD program in personality and social contexts and women's studies at the University of Michigan. Two mentors from my undergraduate school, who were graduates of the program, encouraged me to accept the position. They believed that I would fit well because of my research interests, the resources available, and the diverse faculty in the department. I also noticed that many of the authors from journal articles I read were from the University of Michigan, which suggested that it was a place where I could become an influential scholar and leader. Furthermore, finding a fit with this particular program was easy for me. I learned from my visit to the University of Michigan that I could do the research that I wanted to, and I could see myself working with at least three faculty members. This definitely gave me a sense I had found my perfect fit.

The program's recognition of the importance of diverse faculty, students, and research was a vital feature for me when I applied, because diversity is central to my research and personal well-being. In particular, when I was selecting a doctoral program, it was important for me to choose one that valued and supported my work on ethnic minorities and other disempowered groups. Although I would love to see more Latina/o psychology faculty at Michigan, I do appreciate the diverse faculty we have in the department. Learning from professors who share similar research interests and with whom I can collaborate is critical to my productivity as a young scholar of color. I also enjoy taking part in the Latina/o Student Psychological Association to build relationships with other up-and-coming Latina/o scholars.

Applying to Graduate School

In all honesty, applying to graduate school was an exhaustive and difficult but also very rewarding process for me. It was a struggle to stay optimistic through the process. As a first-generation college student coming from a financially disadvantaged home, my parents were not able to assist me with the costs of applying, nor were they able to help me with the actual applications. Although they did give me moral support, it was hard not being able to share the experience with them. It was important to me to explain the application process to them; otherwise, they might not have understood why I spent so much time on my computer completing applications. This experience kept me humble as I sought to apply to doctoral programs, because I realized that although this process was difficult for me, I was privileged to have the opportunity to seek higher education—something my family members were never able to attain.

So, if I knew that the application process would be difficult, why did I apply? And why did I apply to so many programs? I definitely wanted a career in academia and to work as a professor, and therefore I needed to obtain a PhD. I also knew that I was interested in two different subfields of psychology and had not made up my mind as to which I preferred. Looking back, I see the importance of making sure that you know exactly why you want to attend graduate school and why you are applying to particular programs. It is essential because exploring degree options and personal motivations, as well as researching programs and contacting faculty and current students, can help you identify programs that might suit you.

In fact, identifying the most suitable graduate programs is difficult because there may be many more programs that fit your interests than to which you have the time and money to apply. However, identifying and applying to only a few programs can be problematic because graduate programs tend to be very competitive, although there is some variance by subfield. Therefore, it is important to consider the number of programs to which you will apply. Of course, this decision will be based on many factors that are unique to you, which might include geography, willingness of your family or significant other to move, cost of the program, and funding available. In my experience, I was told to apply to a minimum of 10 graduate programs because they are extremely competitive and sometimes accept only a handful of students. Friends I know received similar advice—that they should consider applying to at least 7 to 10 programs. Even so, when I applied to 16 clinical psychology programs, my mentors told me that if I did not get in, it wasn't necessarily because I was not good enough, but that many applicants apply two or three times. Of course, this does not mean that *you* won't be accepted, but this information helps all applicants to recognize the competitiveness of the field.

Acceptance rates to graduate programs vary greatly by type of program, rank of school, and available funding for students. I would suggest consulting the American Psychological Association's *Graduate Study in Psychology* (see Recommended Resources at the end of this volume) to find out the average number of applicants to each program annually as well as acceptance rates. This useful book also contains statistical information about each graduate program, including the typical applicant's credentials (e.g., average test scores, grade point average [GPA]), average age of applicants, percentage of ethnic minorities. Use this information to identify programs that accept applicants with credentials similar to yours. In addition, apply only to programs you would actually attend. I would also take into consideration the selectivity of each program, such as those that seem to be "reach" schools versus "safety" schools, and apply to a range of programs.

Mentoring Through the Process

Applying to graduate school can be a lengthy and even scary task. Therefore, finding support while you go through this process is very useful. I fortunately had mentors who served different purposes while I was applying to programs. Some helped me cope emotionally with the process, because at times I felt down because of my test scores, felt hopeless that I would never get accepted to a graduate program, and felt pressured to do something that no one else in my family had done. Other mentors invested time in providing feedback on my personal statements and curriculum vitae (CV). Still others just gave me advice about what they felt would be essential when choosing a graduate program. Therefore, I encourage you to talk to current and previous professors and mentors about the application process. If you ask for it, they may provide valuable support and advice that can help you be more calm, informed, and successful.

Graduate students are also a rich resource for knowledge and support. Talking with graduate students helped me figure out what programs are looking for in applicants and how to best present myself as an applicant. They also helped me think more clearly about how to articulate my research interests. Having the support of current graduate students who had recently survived the application process motivated me to keep going and also gave me hope—like them, I too could actually complete it and possibly be accepted to a program. As such, I highly recommend that you contact successful graduate students and ask what the process was like for them as well as request their feedback on your applications.

Staying Organized and Focused During the Application Process

Many steps are involved in the process of applying to graduate school, and it is easy to get confused about deadlines, requirements, and submissions. Because I had a busy schedule at work and at home, I realized quickly that organizing my application materials was necessary to ensure I met the deadlines. To avoid unnecessary pressure, mistakes, and missed deadlines, consider an organizational system that works for you. For example, you might want to keep an actual file cabinet system with hard files in separate manila folders, a binder separating the various programs to which you are applying with different sections for different types of information for each program, or an Excel spreadsheet that you can access from your computer. In fact, when I applied, I developed an Excel spreadsheet—categorized as shown in Figure 5.1—that listed the programs and helped me keep track of program details, such as deadlines, addresses, Graduate Record Examinations (GRE) test requirements, faculty of interest, and pass codes for online applications.

Another strategy that definitely helped me stay on top of everything was keeping track of what I had completed for each program. I created another Excel file, this time a program-specific to-do list of each task that

FIGURE 5.1

University name	Science University	First Choice University
Type of program	Clinical psychology	Social psychology
Contact at program	Dr. B. Jones	Sarah Smith (graduate student)
Program phone number	(379) 555-2368	(973) 555-8632
Address	ATTN: Dr. A. Kamdar Department of Psychology Science University University Lane City, State 10001	Ms. Sarah Smith Department of Psychology First Choice University College Road City, State 20002
Pass codes for online applications	1234	N/A
Faculty of interest	Dr. B. Gimon Dr. R. Deller Dr. L. Samples	Dr. P. Premkumar Dr. I. Ufferman Dr. S. Anderson
Fee	$50	$60 for paper application. $50 for online application
Deadline	Dec 15	Dec 31
GRE tests required	GRE + Psychology GRE	GRE
GRE/program codes	1212	5532
Separate department application?	No	Yes
Number of recommendation letters required	3	3
Extra material required?	Writing sample	No
Awards/fellowships offered?	No	Yes, application due in January
Miscellaneous notes	Fee waiver available	Requires recommendations to be sent separately

GRE = Graduate Record Examinations; N/A = not applicable.

Sample Excel spreadsheet of program details.

needed to be done (e.g., complete personal statement, fill out application, contact faculty). This file was especially useful as some programs have unique application requirements. Once I had marked off all items for each application, I could move on to the next program on the list. Checking off each item and moving on felt good and helped me stay motivated. No matter what system you design or adopt, I encourage you to become organized; it will help you meet your deadlines and minimize the feeling of being overwhelmed.

In addition, making sure that you give yourself ample time to complete the application process is very important. I took a total of 6 months (i.e., June–November) to complete all my application materials, because I had to take the GRE twice, wait to hear about my testing accommodations, and make many revisions to my personal statements. Sometimes people procrastinate and wait until the last minute to submit applications and write personal statements; however, I would not recommend this, because major, unforeseen problems can arise, even some that might be out of your control. For instance, applicants occasionally miss test dates or experience online computer glitches that prevent the submission of application materials. Had I procrastinated and waited until the last minute to get everything completed, I don't think I would have submitted such strong applications.

One of the most important things I realized during the application process was the necessity of giving myself time to rest and reflect. Researching programs, revising personal statements, and filling out countless forms sometimes felt exhausting. In fact, I believe that getting away from my computer gave me the energy I needed to continue being focused, thoughtful, creative, and productive. When away from my computer, I enjoyed activities that were not related to applications—such as watching music videos, talking with my sisters, or taking our dog to the park. These everyday activities helped me feel partially sane even though most of my time was spent writing and revising my essays. In addition, stepping away from my personal statement for at least 3 days helped me gain perspective that enabled me to see ways to improve it. Ample time and self-care not only enhance your personal well-being but also help ensure you submit strong applications.

Parts of an Application

The graduate application has many components, each important and requiring specific attention. Admissions committees evaluate each document to determine whether you might fit into and succeed in their program. Therefore, it is essential that you submit all relevant documents.

With such stiff competition for coveted slots in graduate school, an incomplete file can be reason enough to discard an application.

A typical graduate application to psychology programs includes the application form, application fee, academic transcript(s), GRE score(s), personal statement, and letters of recommendation. On occasion, programs request a CV and other supporting documents such as a writing sample (e.g., a research paper or proposal), departmental application, or other test scores. In the sections that follow, I discuss each component of a typical application.

APPLICATION FORM

The application form usually requests that you provide personal information such as name, contact information, and demographic information, as well as the department and program area to which you are applying. You are also asked to list your references and school information, such as GPA, test scores, and sometimes the psychology courses you have taken. Usually, the application form is no longer than two or three pages.

Although all programs require an application form, programs differ regarding the type of application they use; some require applicants to complete an online application, whereas others request paper applications. Sometimes, you are given the option of using either, although as I understand, most programs prefer the online application. Make sure to read the application instructions or check the program Web site to see whether the program instructions state a preference. I found that one advantage of the electronic application is that you can usually save a draft online and work on it as you go.

When you are ready to begin either the online or the paper application, make sure you have all required materials with you so that you won't be distracted trying to find information that is required on the application form, such as Social Security number, courses taken, or contact details for your references. Having my binder with all my materials in hand proved to be extremely helpful and saved me time. You can spend the extra time reviewing the information on your application form right before submitting it (either by sending it off by mail or by clicking "submit" in the online version), because it is important that all your information is accurate. If you are planning on submitting an online application, you should also know that programs cannot view your application until you have clicked the "submit" button.

APPLICATION FEE

Schools often have different fees for the paper and online applications. Application fees typically range between $35 and $50, depending on the institution and type of application. Online applications can be less expensive than paper applications. If you do submit online applications, make sure you know what form of payment is required (e.g., check, credit card) and be sure to remember to pay the fee in a timely manner. For instance, if you pay by check, mail the check well before the application deadline, because some programs will not process your application until the payment is received.

Also, if finances are a concern, it is useful to know that some programs will provide fee waivers. I encourage you to be proactive in seeking out financial assistance and support. For instance, I contacted programs such as the Committee on Institutional Cooperation (http://www.cic.uiuc.edu) and Project 1000 (http://mati.eas.asu.edu:8421/p1000) and explained to them that I desired to attend graduate school and needed financial assistance. I also suggest, if you are a student, going to the financial aid office at your campus and requesting help seeking funding support. If you qualify for financial assistance, you might also qualify for graduate school application fee waivers, as well as one GRE General Test and GRE Subject Test fee waiver. I was able to use 10 application fee waivers and GRE fee waivers, which significantly reduced the burden of application costs.

TRANSCRIPTS

A *transcript* is a document, specific to each school, that lists all courses you have taken and are currently enrolled in, as well as important information such as your GPA, credit hours, and honors received (e.g., dean's list, honor societies). Different types of transcripts (e.g., unofficial student copy, official sealed copy) can be submitted with your application, but most programs require an official transcript that bears the school seal and is enclosed in an envelope with an official school stamp or signature across the envelope flap. Most programs request transcripts from all institutions you have attended, including community colleges and study abroad programs. Therefore, make sure to give yourself time to request transcripts from former schools attended in case there are any delays. Transcripts are typically issued by a school's registrar's office.

Some graduate programs require that the school mail your transcripts to them directly, whereas others allow you to mail them with the rest of your application or even prefer that you do so. If you have the option, I think it is most helpful to request the transcripts be sent to you, so you can include them with the rest of your materials and decrease the chances of their getting lost. Some schools offer rush processing for transcripts, but remember that they cannot guarantee that the post office will get them to your programs on time, so order them early! Many schools charge a small fee for transcripts, so budget accordingly if money is a concern.

Fortunately, my undergraduate institution did not require that I pay for transcripts, but did suggest that I submit my transcript requests early in the fall because many students order transcripts during October and November (i.e., the busy season, when applications for many graduate school disciplines are due). If your budget permits, I also suggest ordering a few extra transcripts because sometimes materials get misplaced or lost in the mail, or you might decide at the last minute to apply to one more school. For a few more dollars, it is better to be safe than sorry. Also, I would order at least one extra transcript for your own records and so that you can check the document for accuracy.

EXAMS: THE GRE, GRE SUBJECT TEST IN PSYCHOLOGY, AND THE TOEFL EXAM

Another important component of an application are the standardized exams. Nearly every program requires the GRE General Test, which assesses an applicant's aptitude by measuring three domains: verbal reasoning, quantitative reasoning, and analytical writing. Admissions committees tend to focus on the verbal and quantitative reasoning scores, which are sometimes used to screen applicants because graduate programs receive a large number of applications. The GRE is a computerized test in the United States, Canada, and other countries and can be taken at nearly any time during the year. Test-takers in other countries may take a paper-based test.

Another test that some psychology graduate programs require is the GRE Subject Test in psychology, typically a 205-item multiple-choice exam. This exam measures your knowledge of psychology within three areas: (a) experimental, usually consisting of questions about learning, language, memory, physiology, sensation and perception, and comparative psychology; (b) social science, consisting of items on clinical, abnormal, personality, social, and developmental psychology; and (c) the general category, which includes questions on the history of psychology, research design, measurement, applied psychology, and statistics (Educational Testing Service [ETS], 2007a). The GRE Subject Test in psychology is administered on paper and offered only three times a year: November, December, and April (ETS, 2007a). Because not all programs require the Subject Test, I would recommend browsing the Web sites of the programs you are interested in to see whether they request this test. Although none of the social–personality psychology programs required me to take the Subject Test, most of the clinical psychology programs did, so I ended up taking it.

For international students, many graduate programs require the Test of English as a Foreign Language (TOEFL), a 140-item test that evaluates English language skills through listening comprehension, structure and written expression, and reading (ETS, 2007b). Some programs have strict minimum TOEFL score requirements for international graduate students, which can often be found on a school's Web site. Meeting a score cutoff is important because it indicates to the admissions committee whether a nonnative speaker of English possesses the language skills necessary to succeed in graduate-level education. The TOEFL is administered in computer- and paper-based formats, depending on the location, and can be taken in many countries around the world. The TOEFL has limited dates and locations for when and where the exam can be taken, so it is important to find out whether your country or city has a testing site and the dates when the test is offered.

Because I cannot claim to be a standardized test expert, I encourage you to check out the ETS Web site (http://www.ets.org), which can provide you with relevant information about when and where the tests can be taken, costs involved, and much greater detail about how the tests are evaluated. In addition, practice tests are available on the ETS Web site. In the next few paragraphs, I highlight useful information on the basis of my experiences.

In general, my advice regarding the standardized tests is to take sufficient time to prepare for them (see chap. 6, for suggestions). Taking the GRE caused me a great deal of anxiety and fear because I do not perform well on standardized tests. In fact, even after taking a summer prep course, studying weekly with friends, and taking practice tests on my own, I still did not score within the range of scores that many programs required. I knew that, regardless of what my scores were, I would continue with the application process; however, I struggled with feeling like a failure and thinking I would never be accepted into a program. Although very influential, GRE scores are not the sole indicator of your potential to succeed in graduate school; many other components are assessed as part of the application. Many programs have minimum score requirements, but admissions committees may look beyond numbers depending on an applicant's situation. As Dr. Hill suggests in her essay at the end of this chapter, her program may admit a student with mitigating circumstances, such as a learning disability, minority status, or English as a second language, among others. If you test poorly on the GRE, I suggest retaking it only once or twice because scores generally do not improve much with subsequent administrations (ETS, 2007a). In fact, once I knew what my scores were, I put them aside and devoted my energy to completing the rest of my materials, making sure that the people who were going to read my application would see my GRE score as the outlier of my complete application.

Once you have taken the required tests, you need to have your scores reported to each program to which you are applying. You must submit requests to ETS to send a score report to each program. Each graduate program has a specific program code as assigned by ETS (these can be found at http://www.ets.org) to ensure accurate reporting. As mentioned in chapter 3, on the GRE testing day, you have the option to report your scores to four institutions free of charge. Therefore you should give some thought to four schools to which you plan to apply, and make sure to bring the specific program codes with you on the test day. If you are applying to additional schools, you need to order scores by mail, fax, or phone.

If you are required to take the GRE General Test *and* the GRE Subject Test in psychology, you will need to be more mindful of when and how you report your scores. These tests require different times for the scores to be reported: The General Test score is reported immediately after administration, whereas the Subject Test scores take 4 to 6 weeks to be calculated. Therefore, if possible, try to wait until both scores are available before sending your official score reports to graduate programs that request both exams. This will save you money and hassle. However, if you have already reported your general GRE scores, you will need to request that ETS send separate GRE Subject Test score reports.

THE PERSONAL STATEMENT

It is key to convince the admissions committee that you are a good fit and can be successful in their program. The *personal statement* (also called a *statement of purpose*), which is required by nearly every program, is an ideal place to communicate your fit. This document is taken very seriously by admissions committees. In fact, I have always considered the personal statement to be the core of an application package; it is here that you can showcase who you are, how your professional interests developed, what talents and strengths you possess, how you fit with the program, what faculty member(s) you'd like to work with, how the program can help you become a scholar or clinician, and what you hope to do with your degree in the future. In addition, as Dr. Hill suggests, the essay can be used to highlight your uniqueness. Thus, I encourage you to use the personal statement as an opportunity to distinguish yourself from other applicants.

For me, writing the personal statement was the most challenging yet rewarding experience of the application process. It was tough because I had to be concise when communicating my varied research experiences and, most important, showcase how and why I fit with each program. The rewarding part of the statement was being able to write about what brought me to psychology and my passion for the field. For example, I wrote about the inequities that marginalized communities face, and how my personal and research experiences, such as growing up in the inner city and conducting studies on social issues, spoke to these inequities. I also discussed the skills I acquired while doing research and how using them could help me better understand structural systems of oppression. I believe the combined description of personal and research experiences created a strong statement that helped readers understand how both experiences shaped each other and ultimately enriched my life.

Because the personal statement is an opportunity to communicate directly with faculty members, it is important that your statement be authentic and represent you in an honest manner. I believe that admissions committees have an uncanny knack at deducing when students might be lying, stretching the truth, or not using their own words to describe themselves. Presenting yourself in a way that speaks to your numerous strengths, but not in an aggrandizing manner, is preferable to boasting about honors, awards, or the number of As you have received. Readers want to get to know who you are when they read your statement. In mine, I shared how coming from an educationally and financially disadvantaged family and having daily experiences with discrimination motivated me to pursue a PhD; I wanted readers to know that I planned to bring about change through scholarly work. Having them sense my passion for research was also important; I believe this helped compensate for my lower-than-desired test scores. I wanted them to understand that I could be a successful graduate student despite what the numbers seemed to indicate about me. For example, mentioning the various qualifications I had (e.g., practice with manuscript preparation, conference presentations) helped highlight my capabilities and enthusiasm for research and my potential as a graduate student.

Choosing the topic of your personal statement is critical, and I encourage you to talk with your mentors, family, and friends about your thoughts. In the statement, you need to strike a balance to ensure that it is not too personal, lacking in credibility, or too professional, prohibiting readers from getting to know the real you. You want it to stand out for the authentic story you tell. I strongly suggest you avoid revealing too much personal information, especially aspects that could be damaging. For instance, you probably don't want to write about a time when you had to seek mental health services because you couldn't handle the stress of college life, or that you have had financial problems that led to bankruptcy. As Dr. Hill writes, she does not look favorably on applicants who disclose information inappropriately.

A good idea when drafting your personal statement is to develop a template of your statement. You can tailor the template, or "standard" statement, to each program. I developed a standard personal statement that I used for the clinical programs and another for the social–personality programs. To personalize each statement, I changed the paragraph where I mentioned the program to which I was applying, the unique reasons why the program appealed to me, and the names of the faculty members with whom I would like to work. However, if you are applying to different types of programs or want to highlight different aspects of yourself and personal experience, you probably will need to further tweak your standard statement.

LETTERS OF RECOMMENDATION

Admissions committees like to hear from others that you would be a successful graduate student, and the letters of recommendation allow them to learn about your potential. A letter of recommendation is an opportunity for professionals (i.e., professors, supervisors, mentors, and other well-positioned people) to write about you as a complete person, not just a student who gets good grades. Just as the personal statement communicates that you are capable of doing graduate-level work and have much to contribute, positive letters of recommendation do so as well. Each letter is an evaluation of you that carries a lot of weight for the admissions committee. Dr. Hill mentions in her essay how the admissions committee pays particular attention to letters to see whether an applicant is distinctive when compared with peers.

You will be asked to provide two to four recommendation letters for most psychology graduate programs; three letters is quite common. As such, you will need to decide who to contact for letters. Although there are always exceptions, an ideal letter writer is usually an academic who is in the field you are applying to and who knows you well enough to speak to your strengths and possible weaknesses. Graduate programs often want at least two of your letters to be from academics because they are well positioned to assess your abilities as a future graduate student. When possible, ask a professor instead of a graduate student; a student will have less clout. However, if you really, really want a letter from a graduate student—because she knows you very well and can attest to your skills—you could ask her to have the letter reviewed and cosigned by one of her professors.

In addition, you may want to ask for a letter from someone who has known you in a different capacity other than through your college or university. You would want them to write about your other strengths. For instance, a work supervisor or volunteer coordinator may be able to articulately describe your clinical skills if you intend to apply to a clinically oriented graduate program. However, always keep in mind that letters typically carry more weight if they are written by a professional in the field of psychology who holds a reputable graduate degree.

Strong letters inform a committee about the type of person you are inside and outside of the classroom. Thus, when I selected recommenders, I chose people who could write about my academic strengths, community service, scholarly work, classroom performance, and personal qualities. Each letter writer held a PhD in psychology and had supervised me on research projects, and they knew me as a person beyond academic work as well. I also chose people who could mention how I have struggled with learning disabilities but have triumphed despite the adversity. It would have been difficult for me to completely explain this to a committee myself, but my recommenders were able to do so in an appropriate, professional manner.

You want to select people who will write a glowing letter that comments on your strengths and suggests that you will be a successful graduate student. However, if you do have a weakness in your application (e.g., low GRE scores, low GPA), you might consider asking one or more of your letter writers to address it in the recommendation letter. They may able to explain, for example, that your grades were lower in the year following your father's death or that although you may have lower than expected GRE scores, you demonstrate exceptionally strong academic writing skills. If they address a weakness, you definitely want to encourage them to provide examples of how you managed the issue and coped with it.

After identifying who you would like to provide letters of recommendation, you have to contact them to see whether they are willing and able to write a complimentary letter, because you don't want just any old letter! So how can you be sure that a particular person will write you a good letter? Although you may want to defer to Dr. Hill's advice, I suggest being direct and politely asking the prospective recommender whether he or she feels comfortable writing you an honest, yet strong, positive letter, rather than just asking whether he or she would write you a letter.

Meeting in person with your letter writers (if possible) and being prepared in the meeting is quite important because it shows them how committed you are about going to graduate school as well as how valuable you think their letter is to your application. Knowing how to ask and what to ask for when talking with them shows that you have done your homework about what you need from them as recommenders. However, if you have already graduated or cannot meet with potential letter writers, I recommend e-mailing or phoning them. If you don't think they remember you very well, attach a current CV to the e-mail to remind them of who you are and to inform them of your activities after graduation. Also, it is a good idea to provide them with information regarding the courses you took with them (e.g., name, term, and year of the course taken; grade earned in the course) as well as any projects you worked on with them. If you've been out of school for a year or more, it helps to update your letter writers about what you have done since graduating, so that they can address relevant activities in their letters.

In my case, while still a college senior, I approached two faculty members in person before applying. I arranged to meet with them in their offices, asked whether they were willing to write strong letters, and provided suggestions with regard to what I would like them to address in their writing. I contacted my third letter writer by e-mail. The second time applying to graduate programs I contacted my former college professors through e-mail. After they agreed to write recommendation letters, I provided them with all of the necessary materials (i.e., recommendation forms, address labels, CV, and all other application materials) as early as possible. I did promise to give them at least a month to complete the letters before the application deadlines. I wanted to be considerate of their time, knowing they also were writing letters for other students. If possible, make sure the materials you give your letter writers are well organized and supplied in a timely manner. I cannot tell you how much my recommenders appreciated being given a neatly organized folder that contained all relevant materials and deadlines.

In addition to letters of recommendation, some programs require you to submit recommendation forms completed by your references. Although the forms vary among programs, most serve the same purpose: They require a recommender to evaluate you on various characteristics such as independence, creativity, intellect, and potential as a graduate student. One important point to note is that the forms usually have an option to waive your rights to see the evaluation that is being submitted on your behalf. Although there is no official penalty for not waiving your right to view the materials, not signing may undermine the credibility of your recommendation because the letter writer may not feel comfortable being candid if he or she knows you will be reviewing the evaluation. Therefore, it is highly encouraged that you waive your right to see the recommendation before giving the materials to your letter writer. Doing so assures the admissions committee that your recommenders are providing them with an objective evaluation of you.

CURRICULUM VITAE

Some programs request that you include a CV as part of your application. In short, a CV is an academic résumé. If a CV is not requested, you may want to include one as an additional document. Many students, including myself, submitted a CV in their applications regardless of whether it was requested. Including a CV in your application allows you to highlight many experiences and skills that you might not be able to fully discuss in a personal statement. For example, on a CV, you list your scholarly accomplishments, such as research, clinical, and teaching experiences as well as conference presentations and publications. Most people also include relevant jobs (e.g., being a resident assistant), volunteer activities, honors and awards, and service in organizations (e.g., serving on a diversity committee). I included a CV so that each admissions committee would get more detailed information about my research experience, the specific role I had on each project, and where and with whom I worked. My CV also reflected my leadership roles as well as the mentoring and volunteering activities with marginalized communities that were extremely relevant to my research interests. If you want information about how to structure an academic CV, you can consult books or online resources, visit the career counseling center, or talk with current graduate students, an academic advisor, or your mentor.

EXTRA DOCUMENTS

Including additional documents in your application can be a little risky because some programs and individuals can get annoyed if applicants send in more materials than those requested. Their irritation is understandable because they are dealing with many applications and they don't have time to go through extra documents. If a program specifies that applicants are to submit a sample paper or some other academic work, then of course it is advisable to submit it with your application. However, if a program does not request supplemental materials, I would think carefully about sending extra documents. Consult with a mentor about whether an extra document serves a purpose and its inclusion strengthens your application.

Although many programs do not like to receive additional documents beyond those required for the application package, sometimes it is helpful or necessary to include them. For instance, you might want to submit an extra document that emphasizes a significant academic achievement, such as a published journal article for which you were the lead author or a conference presentation or poster for which you received an award. You might also consider attaching something that can explain any discrepancies in your application (e.g., low grades or test scores). In my case, I attached a brief letter as an addendum, in which I explained why I could be a successful graduate student regardless of my test scores and GPA. Having the admissions committee take a closer look at my application was very important to me because of my learning disabilities and the functional limitations that were imposed at times as a result. However, I worked hard to word the letter so that it did not sound defensive. Again, it helped to have my mentors review drafts before I submitted the final version.

Finalizing the Application Package

Submitting a strong application takes time, money, patience, and dedication. You want to make sure that the amount of work you've invested pays off. Be sure to see this process through to the last step, which is finalizing each application package. I encourage you to proofread and double-check all parts of the application several times to catch typos or mistakes. To avoid anything getting misplaced by the institution, I suggest making sure your full name is on each document in the application package (some programs also request that you include an ID number, which they give you, on each page). You may want to put your finished application aside for a 1 or 2 days before submitting it (whether online or through the mail) so that you can revisit it and possibly catch mistakes that went unnoticed. Doing this final review is extremely important, especially because it increases the likelihood that you will submit a clear and well-prepared package, which indicates that you will be a responsible graduate student.

Putting your application package together (if sending by mail) requires you to be attentive to small details such as writing the correct postal addresses and making sure that all relevant materials are included in the package and sent to the proper school. As such, I recommend putting each application package together one by one, so that you can fully concentrate. You might also want to have another person double-check each package before mailing it—someone who isn't as stressed as you might have become by the end of the application process!

It is important to realize that postal delivery involves many details that can make or break your chances of getting admitted into a graduate program, and after having done so much painstaking work, you don't want these details to jeopardize your future. Therefore, if you are mailing your applications, it is essential that you allow sufficient time for them to arrive at their respective destinations. To be on the safe side, try to send off your materials at least 2 weeks before the deadline. If sending it a week or less before the deadline, I would consider paying for priority mail. However, planning ahead really benefits your finances as the priority mail fees are more expensive than first-class postage. Also, make sure you have the proper postage on your applications. You don't want such a simple issue to delay all your applications. When sending them off, consider paying a nominal fee for delivery confirmation, so that you have proof that they've been received. That said, you should check each program's application instructions to see whether it has specific requirements about how to send mail; some programs will not accept packages that require delivery confirmation.

Once you have mailed an application, you naturally will wonder whether it has been received. As programs do not like to be bothered with hundreds of phone calls regarding applications, you might consider enclosing a self-addressed stamped postcard with your application that can be sent back to you to confirm the receipt of your application. If you have not received the postcard or there are other extenuating circumstances, you may need to follow up with a program to learn whether your application was received. If you do this, be mindful that the application season is a very busy time for graduate programs. Be polite if you call or send a brief e-mail. Your understanding will be appreciated.

Conclusion

The application process to graduate school can be complicated, but your energy and hard work can pay off, especially if you give yourself ample time to prepare and you are tenacious. The process can be further complicated by weaknesses in your application, which can invoke much anxiety because most of us don't have perfect transcripts or test scores. As I mentioned, I worried whether I would be accepted to graduate school because of my lower-than-desired GRE scores. I couldn't predict what exactly would get me into graduate school, but I could make my application as strong as possible. Focusing my energy on the factors that were under my control helped me stay focused on the application process. My mentors were instrumental in helping me remain optimistic; they continuously complimented me on my strengths and helped me see that I had what it took to get into a graduate program. Fortunately, I was accepted into a top program in psychology and was able to share this success with both my family and my mentors. I hope the advice and suggestions in this chapter help you get through the application process. I also sincerely hope you enjoy a positive outcome as well.

Practical Tips

1. **Get Started!** Although you might initially think that applying to graduate school requires only a few documents, much more goes into this process. I suggest talking with mentors, professors, and graduate students as soon as you start considering graduate school as an option.
2. **Mind your manners.** Once you have finished the application process, say "thank you" to everyone involved: mentors, parents, friends, and so on. It probably took a village to get you into graduate school.
3. **Celebrate!** As a mentor suggested to me, I encourage you to celebrate your efforts at every step of the application process, not just if and when you get accepted to a program. And of course, submitting graduate applications deserves extra-special celebrations because it is a process that

requires much hard work. Mark the milestone by celebrating with family and friends.

4. **What to do after applications are completed and the celebrations are over?** I encourage you, if possible, to take time off and rest. Forget about graduate school for a while. Then, you might consider alternative plans in case you are not admitted, because it is always great to have a backup plan if things don't turn out well. I applied for jobs right after I learned that I had been wait-listed to my programs, and it felt good to have options.

References

Educational Testing Service. (2007a). *GRE—Graduate Record Examinations*. Retrieved June 13, 2007, from http://www.gre.org

Educational Testing Service. (2007b). *The TOEFL Test—Test of English as a Foreign Language*. Retrieved June 13, 2007, from http://www.toefl.org

Essay 5
The Application Process
From a Faculty Member's
Perspective: How I Evaluate
Applications
Clara E. Hill

Each year when we do admissions to our counseling psychology graduate program, I think back to when I applied to graduate school. I knew that I wanted to become a counseling psychologist because of my experiences working in the psychology department at Southern Illinois University (SIU), my work on an undergraduate honors thesis examining why students do not go to counseling when they could benefit from it, and my summer working in a mental hospital (after that, I knew I wanted to work with "normal" people). I applied to three schools and was delighted that I was accepted at SIU with funding. I remember the agony of waiting to hear and knowing that my life would differ depending on where I went. I wish I had known more then about what goes on in the admissions process.

So here is the other side. In our program at the University of Maryland, we are faced with the daunting task of choosing eight students from approximately 200 applications each year. There are usually about 50 students who would fit well in our program, 50 who are clearly inappropriate, and 100 who are marginal. So how do we go about deciding to whom we will extend offers?

The easy answer is "It depends." It depends on the pool of students any particular year and who looks best given the competition. However, a number of things help certain applications rise to the top.[1]

FIRST CUT

The first thing we do in our program is look at basic credentials. Students applying to our program must have a 3.5 GPA in their last 60 hours of undergraduate course work and a minimum of 550 on each of the Verbal and Quantitative subtests of the GRE to make it to the next stage. We

---

[1] I need to add a caveat here that our counseling psychology program has the luxury of being highly selective because we receive many applications from highly qualified applicants. Other programs might have fewer applicants, apply less stringent selection criteria, or have different values for selecting students.

sometimes, however, make exceptions for applicants with mitigating circumstances (e.g., several years since obtaining the undergraduate degree, a very stringent undergraduate major, a learning disability, English as a second language, minority status). Also, applicants need to have completed a minimum of 15 hours of psychology course work so that they have a foundation of knowledge in the field of psychology. Students who switch from other majors often go back to an undergraduate or graduate program to obtain these hours before they apply to our program.

Using these criteria, we cut many applicants from the pool. I should mention, however, that the number of applications cut for these reasons has declined over the years as students have become more aware of the criteria and do not apply unless they have a relatively good chance of making it past this first cut. If you are an applicant who does not meet these basic criteria, should you despair of attaining your goal of graduate study in psychology? Well, the answer is mixed; it is always a good idea to realistically appraise your abilities. If your GPA is less than 2.5, you are probably not going to be accepted into a graduate program; it may be time to reconsider. If your GPA is between a 2.5 and 3.5, consider retaking courses and trying to raise it, and consider applying to a less competitive graduate program. If your GRE scores are low, you might consider studying hard and retaking the test; we look at the best scores no matter how often the test is taken. If after studying and retaking the GRE several times you still get low scores, though, it may be time to reconsider options. (Sorry, but it is better for me to be honest than to paint a rosy but false picture.)

SECOND CUT

From among the applicants left at this stage, we choose a final pool of about 30 to consider further. At this point, a number of factors weigh equally in our decisions. We want to select students who

- know about and have experience in our field. For counseling psychology, that means we want students who have experience in both research and counseling practice. Students need to know what they are getting into and have some idea that they like it and are good at it.
- are a good fit with at least one faculty member in the program. In our doctoral program, we usually take one student per faculty member each year because we work closely with students. Each of us wants to take students who share our interest areas because we have more to offer them than we do if we do not share interests. For example, I study therapy process and outcome, therapist train-

    ing, and dream work, so I want a student who shares these interests and really wants to learn from working with me.

- bring something special to the program. The majority of our applicants are 22-year-old White women who say they want to do teaching, research, and practice when they graduate from the program. These applicants all look alike, and their applications are boring because there is nothing to distinguish them from the others.
- can handle the graduate course work, particularly in core psychology and statistics.
- show evidence of persistence and hard work.
- are passionate about both research and clinical practice.

To determine whether students fit these criteria, we look closely at the following:

- The personal statement. This is how we get to know the applicants and get a feeling for who they are, what their passions are, why they want to go into counseling psychology, and how well they can write. We look for what they offer that is special, but we are wary if they disclose excessively or inappropriately.
- Letters of recommendation. We read the letters to see if the applicant truly stands out from other students and whether there are any red flags.
- Grades in psychology, statistics, and math courses.

FINAL CUT

The final cut is the most difficult because everyone who makes it into the final pool could most likely succeed. In our program, we try to strike a balance between choosing applicants who are top on all criteria (i.e., grades, GRE, experiences, writing ability, and evidence of persistence) and who fit the interests of specific faculty members. We talk extensively about each applicant in our admission meeting because we often see different things in applications.

    In making our final decisions, we interview the final applicants by phone. We ask a standard set of questions of everyone, and also ask individualized questions based on our review of the application. We do not interview in person, although many programs do. We make our final decisions by picking the best overall candidates given the pool of applicants.

    The ideal student is a bright, motivated, interesting person who shows evidence that he or she can write, can think of original research ideas, is passionate about psychology, understands what counseling psychology is, and is persistent. Please note that brilliance is not the sole criterion. I have seen students who were brilliant but did not have to work to get ahead. I have also seen students who were bright but not brilliant but worked really hard. I think the latter are more likely to succeed because they are hungry and willing to go the extra mile. So we look for people who are both bright and motivated—who really want to succeed and are willing to work hard.

RECOMMENDATIONS

I have several recommendations for prospective students:

1. Think carefully about what you want out of life. Make sure that psychology is what you want and that you are ready, eager, and mature enough for a rigorous graduate school experience.
2. Do your homework (e.g., read books like this one). Really think about the different programs and what they are like (e.g., check the Web sites). Read about the faculty in the various programs, and know with whom you would like to work.
3. Do *not* ask to set up appointments to talk with faculty members. I get many, many calls from prospective students; I cannot meet with all these students. If you have a specific question, yes, please e-mail the relevant faculty member, but do not ask to meet just so you can try to make a good impression.
4. Apply to a range of programs: places you would love to go, acceptable places, and backups.
5. Put time into your applications and think through the answers.
6. Spend a lot of time on your personal statement. Make sure it reflects who you are. Be honest; don't try to be someone you are not. Have others read it and give you brutally honest feedback. Then rewrite it until you are pleased with it and feel that it represents who you are.
7. Get all your materials in on time.
8. Choose your letter writers carefully. Make sure they know you well enough to write about you. Sometimes students I taught 3 or 4 years ago ask me to write letters, but I don't remember them in enough depth to write a compelling letter. Do *not* ask people whether they can write you a positive letter; ask for an honest evaluation of your ability. Give your letter writers plenty of time to get the materials in before the deadline.
9. Check to make sure all the materials are in before the deadline.

CONCLUSION

One of the best parts of my job is working with students. I feel blessed that I have a job in which I can sit around talking about ideas with students, read great books, and design and conduct research. I also love to mentor students, to help them grow in their development as both therapists and researchers; it is very gratifying to see students change and learn more about themselves. It is also extremely distressing for me when we select a student who does not fit well in our program. So I, and most faculty members I know, are very committed to making good choices in terms of student selection. It is certainly not an exact science; I know of situations in which we selected people who were not right for the program and others in which we failed to select people who have been stellar students elsewhere.

In closing, my best advice is "know yourself." Make sure you want to be a psychologist and that you are willing to work really hard to become one. And then, find the right program that can help you get where you want to go. Finally, be ready to think of alternatives if you don't immediately get what you want.

Best of luck in your journey!

Sangeet S. Khemlani

Bolstering an Application | 6

From: Alexandria, VA
Area of study: Cognitive Psychology, Princeton University, Princeton, NJ
Previous degree(s): BS in psychology and electronic arts from Rensselaer
Polytechnic Institute, Troy, NY
Career before graduate school: Student
Number of graduate schools applied to: 10
Age when started this graduate program: 22
Professional interests: Higher level cognition, representation, reasoning,
semantics, and categorization
Career aspirations: Become a professor of cognitive science

I n an ideal world, this chapter would present five quick-and-dirty secrets that an applicant can use to race to the top of an admissions committee's short list. The secrets would be effortless, would require no planning or foresight, and could be exploited by everyone. Oh, if only it were that simple! The bad news is that an admissions application cannot be bolstered without planning and foresight. It takes time and thoroughness to strengthen an applicant's qualifications. The good news is that students

My sincere gratitude goes to my advisor, Philip Johnson-Laird, and my colleagues, Geoffrey Goodwin and Louis Lee, for their many helpful comments and suggestions on this chapter. I also thank Bram van Heuveln, Selmer Bringsjord, Konstantine Arkoudas, Hansjoerg Neth, and Wayne Gray for their invaluable guidance and support throughout my undergraduate career.

who make the effort to develop strong applications are more likely to be rewarded with admission to graduate school in psychology.

If a secret tip to bolstering your application exists, it is this: Throughout your application process, it helps to think like an admissions committee. In particular, it helps to think like the professor or professors who will be looking at your application most critically. Appreciate the difficult decisions graduate committees are faced with: They are searching for bright and capable students among hundreds of talented applicants each year. What elements will impress them? What will they be concerned with? You can make your application stand out by considering the various questions these committees ask themselves. For instance, they might ask themselves the following questions: Can this student think and conduct projects independently? Can this student work with diverse individuals and organizations as an effective therapist? Does this student demonstrate initiative in the work he or she is involved with?

To help answer these questions, in this chapter I examine ways you can bolster your application by demonstrating that you can handle the rigors of graduate school. I start by recommending the course work and test grades that will demonstrate your preparation to admissions committees. I then explain how to find opportunities for experience in research and clinical work before you apply. This experience can provide a strong foundation for your application. I then move on to reviewing ways to strengthen your personal statement, recommendations, and other application materials. But, I will start by telling you a bit about my path to academia.

In my first semester at college, I programmed a smart robot. It was not the most serious research project—it was a simple Lego robot that could solve spatial reasoning puzzles—but building it was exhilarating. My robot's name was Walter, and Walter could metareason, solve puzzles of arbitrary sizes, and even learn from its mistakes. As my team spent tireless nights programming Walter, I pondered the fact that we were imbuing a mechanical object with the ability to reason—simple reasoning, yes, but reasoning nonetheless. The very notion that thought processes could be broken down, analyzed, and pieced back together was intensely intriguing to me.

Walter became my first successful project as an undergraduate; more important, the robot ignited in me a fascination with the power of the human mind and the way it functions. I began to engage in similar projects that challenged my understanding of both technology and psychology. My interests in research became more serious when I was exposed to psychological experimentation at National Public Radio Labs during a summer internship. I realized then that psychology and cognitive science were the fields that intrigued me the most. I spent my subsequent years of college working at two separate research labs: the CogWorks Laboratory and the Artificial Intelligence and Reasoning Lab. My work focused on artificial intelligence (AI), reasoning, task analysis, and cognitive engineering, and the years I spent working at those labs were the beginning of my intellectual growth as a researcher.

I had not considered graduate study until the summer after my sophomore year in college. I spent the summer doing research at the AI lab where I had been working, when the pace of the research picked up considerably. During the year I had conducted research as a part-time job and worked on one project, one task at a time, but over the summer I spent 40 hours a week working on several projects. I began to engage in the research in a much more intimate way. The work was both challenging and rewarding, and I realized that the intellectual rush I felt over that summer was something I wanted to continue.

Once I had decided to pursue further study, my parents were supportive of my decision to attend graduate school in psychology, but skeptical as well. They had witnessed my academic promiscuity since high school: I was initially interested in technology and computer science, then moved on to hone my artistic skills by pursuing studies in art and graphic design, later took several courses in math and logic, and finally decided to major in psychology. It came as no surprise that I would want to continue my studies, although they worried about whether I would be able to focus on one subject for an extended period. (To tell you the truth, I am still worried about that myself!) But, they encouraged me to apply nevertheless. My mom quipped once that she wanted a doctor in the family and always needed a therapist to deal with her kids, so a son with a PhD in psychology might be the best of both worlds.

After receiving my bachelor's degree at Rensselaer, I decided to pursue graduate school immediately. I applied to nearly a dozen graduate schools and chose Princeton University's Department of Psychology as the setting for my doctoral studies because of the school's strong emphasis on higher level cognition, reasoning, and representation in the labs where I hoped to work. In retrospect, I am grateful for having been patient when developing my application to graduate school. The whole process can be intimidating, and it is often difficult to know where to begin. In this chapter, I offer some insights from my peers, my advisors, and my own experiences to help you put together a strong, successful application package.

Get Ready: Self-Awareness, Classes, and Tests

An application to graduate school begins long before you consider to which schools and programs to apply. Self-awareness and academic preparation mark the beginning of a successful application. This section will examine the ways to get yourself ready for the application process.

SELF-AWARENESS

As I learned when applying, much of what it takes to put together an effective application happens before you even fill in your name on the application form. Strong classroom performance, good scores on standardized tests, and independent or thesis work in psychology all help establish your interests and capacity for additional scholarly work. However, first it helps to become more self-aware, specifically to better understand your motivations for applying to graduate school. You have already decided on, or at the very least considered, enhancing yourself with a more rigorous and concentrated education. Because you will need to articulate this decision in each and every application you send out, it pays to spend some time to think about your reasons for applying. In my case, I knew that I wanted a career that included exchanging ideas, running empirical studies, designing models, and developing theories of human cognition. Likewise, your motivations for applying to graduate school and your interests in higher education will guide and shape your application package, graduate school interviews, and final decisions.

It can feel intimidating to make the initial decision to apply to graduate school in psychology. After all, the most brilliant individuals I had ever met were my professors, and the thought of rising to their intellectual stature was (and still is) daunting. I recognized that the disparity between my potential and my abilities at the time was quite large, so I spent some time thinking about my strengths and, more important, where my education and experiences were weak. As an applicant, it pays to reflect on your areas of weakness and to know that you may need to address them before or after you embark on graduate study. Most admissions committees do not demand perfection; instead, they demand potential. I recommend that you bolster your application by thinking about what your interests are, why you are applying, what your strengths and weaknesses are, and what it will take to become successful as a professional in your field. Then, as Dr. Myers suggests in his essay at the end of this chapter, stay focused and pursue your vision.

CLASSES

Graduate study begins with solid preparation at the undergraduate level. Classes and good grades are important because they not only demonstrate your discipline and intellectual diversity but also suggest that you take a general interest in education and learning. What courses are appropriate for a person interested in psychology? What grades suffice?

TABLE 6.1

Most Frequently Required or Preferred Classes for Graduate Psychology Programs

Class	Programs that require or prefer the class (%)
Statistics	85
Research methods/experimental design	66
Childhood/developmental	36
Abnormal/psychopathology	33
Learning	28
Personality	28
Physiological/biopsychology	24
Social	23

Note. Adapted from "Graduate Study in Psychology: 1992–1993," by J. C. Norcross, J. M. Hanych, and R. D. Terranova, 1996, *American Psychologist, 51,* pp. 631–643. Copyright 1996 by the American Psychological Association.

Were all psychology graduate students 4.0 psych majors in undergrad? (Answer: No.) Before going further, let me address an important question: Do I *need* to major in psychology to become a graduate student in the field? Absolutely not. As you will read in the following essay, Dr. Myers didn't major or even minor in psychology. Of course, an undergraduate degree, or at least some course work in psychology, is a strong asset; it suggests that the material is of general interest to you and that you are comfortable with psychological theories and methodologies. However, competitive applications can come from a wide range of disciplines. For instance, the graduate students in psychology at my school have backgrounds in psychology, computer science, art, philosophy, English, neuroscience, biology, and chemistry. Of course, there is a caveat: The further your discipline is from mainstream psychology, the more you will have to demonstrate how your interests and abilities fall within the purview of the field. This can be accomplished through related clinical, research, or work experience. In addition, some programs require a certain number of prerequisite hours of psychology course work or call for applicants to have passed certain courses, such as statistics or research methods. This information can be found on the program's Web site or by contacting the admissions coordinator.

If you plan to take psychology classes, I suggest that you be strategic about the classes you take, study hard, and earn good grades. When you select courses, it helps to know which ones are most frequently required or preferred by graduate programs, as seen in Table 6.1 (Norcross, Hanych, & Terranova, 1996). Doing well in undergraduate classes is the first step, and its importance cannot be stressed enough. Also, if you can take more than the standard psychology curriculum, enroll in advanced or graduate courses in psychology (even if you are not a psychology major). Because current psychology graduate students often take these courses, attending them will also introduce you to a more advanced dialectic; that is, you will become part of a discussion at a level higher than what occurs in most undergraduate classes. If you do well in the advanced courses and highlight that in your application, you can communicate to graduate schools that you are motivated to pursue in-depth study and can excel at it.

I also strongly suggest that you take courses in research methods and statistics. I know, I know—if you cringed after reading that sentence, I feel your pain. Statistics courses can be dry and unappealing for some people. Nevertheless, it will help to take them and make every effort to excel at them. These courses are important because they are often required by graduate programs (Norcross et al., 1996). Even if they are not, I recommend that you take them, as you will need to read and understand papers that use many powerful statistical techniques. Experience with these methods cannot hurt an applicant and can demonstrate that you have skills in multiple domains. Not only do admissions committees pay close attention to classes in statistics and research methodology, but doing well in them will help prepare you for the more rigorous versions of the courses that will likely be required in graduate school.

Finally, I encourage you to do a senior thesis if your school offers such an option. Many students have no experience working on one project for an extended period when coming straight out of undergraduate school, and regardless of whether or not your project is a significant contribution to psychology (although they often can be), the mere fact that you were able to conduct the research and write about it is demonstrative of your preparation.

TESTS

The Graduate Record Examinations (GRE) test is often seen as an enormous obstacle, a test crucial to your acceptance into a competitive graduate program. Although doing well will increase your chances of acceptance, a phenomenal score rarely secures an applicant a spot in a graduate program, and an average score on a single test rarely prevents anyone from opportunities for further study. Often a GRE score is seen as one of many components that are evaluated as part of your application portfolio.

That said, the GRE is not inconsequential. Psychology is challenging in that it demands expertise in both verbal and quantitative skills. Because of this, some graduate schools have absolute score cutoffs, whereas others are more sensitive to extenuating circumstances (e.g., disabilities, cultural hurdles, medical issues) when they evaluate GRE scores. Your scores will indicate where you stand and what you may need to overcome to achieve your career goals. Use your scores as rough measurements of your ability to write, compute, and reason relative to your peers, but don't *ever* equate them to general intelligence; they do not predict what you or anyone is capable of doing in psychology or life. The following are a few suggestions to help you improve your scores on the test, although they are not comprehensive for GRE preparation; for more help, consider purchasing a self-paced GRE prep book.

Try To Be "Good Enough"

Your goal should be to spend as much time studying for and taking the test as is necessary to get a decent score. Often schools post median scores of their successful applicants in admissions brochures and on their Web sites; I suggest you compare your scores with the typical scores at the programs where you hope to apply. When this information is not available, evaluate yourself carefully. Ask yourself whether your work will require deep mathematical or computational prowess, or whether it will demand rigorous training in communication and analysis, or perhaps both. Set goals for the scores you want to achieve, but do not be too ambitious. If you are working diligently toward an off-the-charts score, you may be wasting time and money that could be much better spent doing research or getting clinical experience. Be aware of the point of diminishing returns: A minor boost in one's GRE scores might not be worth the monetary and temporal cost of attending specialized courses. In fact, the admissions committee may glance at your score, see that it is "good enough," place a little check mark on your application evaluation sheet, and move on.

Consider Studying in the Summer

If you are currently a student, the summer before you apply to graduate schools is often a great time to study for the GRE. With a reduced workload, you will be able to soak up a lot more vocabulary and practice many more math problems than when you have 15 credits to manage, a weekly shift at a crisis hotline, a couple experiments to conduct, and dozens of parties to attend.

Take Practice Tests

If you are short on time, lose the vocabulary cards and quit trying to memorize the equation for the volume of a cone. Instead, take practice tests on the computer and by hand. Take as many tests as you can, and when you have run out of those, take the old ones over again. Be sure to time yourself on the practice tests as well; often students get less-than-desirable scores on the GRE because they have spent months memorizing vocabulary while not realizing that the format and pace of the test itself influence performance. Because the GRE is typically conducted on a computer, the dynamics of the test are different than those of a paper-based test. For instance, the GRE does not allow you to leave a question and come back to it later. If you practice the GRE in the same format in which it will be given, you will be more prepared than if you study only the content of the test.

Some schools require you to take the GRE Subject Test in psychology in addition to the GRE General Test. Be aware that the format of the Subject Test is different from that of the General Test; it stresses memorization and general knowledge of psychology over analytical reasoning. A good way to study for this test is to review an introductory psychology textbook and to take a few sample tests. It may not be a waste of time to take the same sample tests over and over again, because doing so will hammer in some of the salient details that are asked about on the real exam.

Get Set: Immerse Yourself in Professional Activities

Admissions committees must sift through piles of applications and choose individuals who demonstrate both achievement and aptitude. They often try to tease out applicants who are naively applying straight out of college because they once took an interesting course in psychology from those applicants who have a more disciplined rationale for applying to graduate school. Students who are the most likely to excel in graduate school are those who have already pursued scholarly or professional activities. Those with research or clinical experiences have a significant edge in the admissions process because they have already begun living the life of a graduate student. Experience in domains outside your schoolwork demonstrates to admissions committees that you are motivated to be independent, seek out opportunities, cooperate with others, learn, and excel in the field. There are plenty of ways to engage in professional activities: You could work in a laboratory or a clinic that is managed by a professor or graduate student, get an internship in your field, or volunteer in a related organization (e.g., nonprofit organization, hospital, school).

Be judicious about where you choose to work. It is not necessary to work on the same problems you want to study in graduate school. That is, if you want to study prejudice and stereotyping in the long run, do not be apprehensive if you are presented with the opportunity to work on research that examines personality or human sexuality. In fact, use your preliminary professional activities to gain insight on different lines of research in psychology. On a similar note, if you one day hope to do neuropsychological testing, do not shy away from volunteering at an assisted living residential home. Working with the elderly could be a good chance to develop your clinical skills in general and will help you develop familiarity with a population that often requires neuropsychological assessments. The people who will evaluate your application are not likely to criticize the fact that your background experiences do not line up perfectly with your future plans; rather, they are more likely to be impressed that you have taken the initiative to pursue extracurricular work in your field of interest.

That being said, it always helps when your previous experiences and your future plans are congruent with one another. In my case, I had worked at a laboratory that focused on AI and reasoning before I started applying to graduate programs. In particular, I worked with systems of logic and deduction. My developing interest in human reasoning influenced the schools and programs to which I applied. I never ran experiments or conducted any empirical research at the AI lab where I worked, but that did not hurt my application portfolio because my work was relevant to my research interests. Professors and clinicians are not looking for students with comprehensive preparation in their line of work. They are looking for students who will be productive members of their laboratory and future collaborators, so initial interest in the research is often sufficient to impress the admissions committee. As an added benefit, the more work experiences you have, the greater your perspective will be when you begin your work in graduate school. I currently tend to compare problems in human reasoning with problems in machine reasoning, and my work is guided by understanding and accounting for the discrepancies between the two. But this type of perspective could not have come without prior work in a lateral field. Likewise, a colleague of mine had spent several years working in the magnetic resonance imaging (MRI) unit of a hospital while he was an undergraduate before he came to graduate school to pursue research on working memory. His background experiences now play a big role in his doctoral work because he uses functional MRI data to investigate cognitive control and working memory.

RESEARCH EXPERIENCE

Research experience is always an asset, and if you intend to pursue a research-oriented psychology degree, experience in conducting research projects is a key component of your application. When I was applying to graduate school, I talked to a professor about what criteria his research-oriented department used when evaluating applications. He said, "Well, first we divide the applications into two piles: students with research experience and students without research experience. We don't look at the latter." The professor may have been exaggerating, but I doubt he was exaggerating much. Students with a background in research in psychology are better prepared to be productive and successful graduate students. Not a single 1st-year graduate student in my department arrived without significant experience in conducting research. Some students had even presented at conferences and coauthored publications as well. In particular, research experience for anyone interested in experimental psychology is of the utmost importance.

Before you embark on research, remember to—well, do some research. If possible, seek out opportunities for research as part of a lab; that is, consider the benefits of a small community of researchers working on similar projects. You will learn from your collaborators and develop skills in teamwork and cooperation. My experience as a research assistant in a lab convinced me of the value of, and prepared me for, the pursuit of further education. If a laboratory environment is not available to you, don't fret; there are often opportunities for internships and independent studies, and I encourage you to pursue them. Some of these will be volunteer opportunities and others will offer compensation, but your experiences in research will be far more valuable than whatever monetary gains you may make.

Good research opportunities are sometimes difficult to come by. Many colleges and universities do not have an active undergraduate research community, and private labs and research centers often have stringent background requirements (e.g., prior training with animals, children, or specific types of software). Many students who have not obtained a background in research decide to postpone their application to graduate school for 1 or 2 years to gain more research experience after college. This recommendation is also applicable to those students who have conducted research in a different field (e.g., marketing, pharmacology, sociology). Students are often apprehensive about taking this route, believing that it delays their career. However, adequate preparation in research is a critical factor in graduate admission, especially in experimental psychology and other research-oriented graduate programs. Thus, spending a few months or years as a research assistant can be very useful. I have found that the students who have taken time off before graduate school to conduct research often develop new perspectives to guide their work. Because you will be conducting research as a job instead of as a sporadic contributor (as is often the case with undergraduate researchers), you will gain better insight into the graduate student life you will soon experience. Time spent as a research assistant does not limit your chances of gaining admission to your preferred programs in psychology; older students are quite common in psychology graduate programs. Again, if you decide to bolster your research background, try to be productive by publishing, attending conferences, networking, and developing technical skills.

CLINICAL EXPERIENCE

In experimental psychology, with which I am most familiar, research experience is a crucial and often necessary element of a successful application. It is not surprising that clinically oriented programs put much more weight on clinical experience. Although it is not essential to have completed extensive clinical work before applying to a clinical, counseling, or school psychology program, some experience strengthens your application and demonstrates to your potential advisors that you are familiar with the professional activities of a clinician.

To get clinical experience, you may want to pursue activities that interest you and look into both volunteer and paid positions. For instance, opportunities available at my college included suicide- and abuse-prevention hotlines and placements in a local hospital. You might also want to look into related positions at community mental health clinics, college counseling centers, psychiatric centers, prisons, schools, group homes, addiction treatment centers, and universities with clinical research labs. Of course, you will not be qualified to be a therapist, but even working or volunteering in a mental health setting will allow you to get a feel for the professional environment and relevant issues, which you can discuss in your personal statement and interviews. For instance, a friend of mine had a part-time job at her college counseling center. Although she did not treat clients but did administrative work, the on-the-job learning helped her understand issues such as confidentiality, theoretical orientations, and developmental issues of college students. She was able to articulately discuss her experiences with professors during her interviews, which she credits with landing her a place in graduate school.

If you are starting your senior year of college without much clinical experience or even have worked in an unrelated field for the past 20 years, it is never too late to begin clinical training. More experience is always beneficial, but even a few months of working for a crisis hotline or as a psychology technician demonstrates your interest in clinical work. The point, again, is to get involved. Clinical experience will begin to prepare you both emotionally and intellectually for the challenges you will face in graduate school, and will suggest to the admissions committee that you are both committed to your field and dedicated to making a difference.

PRESENTATIONS AND PUBLICATIONS

Psychology is a field in which professionals share ideas by presenting and publishing their work. These professionals are researchers, clinicians, teachers, consultants, and other types of psychologists. Graduate students are also encouraged, and sometimes expected, to present and publish.

Although attending a local Toastmaster's club and joining the debate team are good ways of getting accustomed to public speaking, inevitably the best way to become a good communicator is to present your work. Thus, actively look for opportunities to present your projects and ideas. Whether you are presenting at your school's psychology club, in class, or at a conference, any presentation experience whatsoever will help you for the future. In particular, presentations at academic conferences are highly regarded by admissions committees and indicate that an applicant is actively involved in the scientific process and professional activities.

A crucial part of life as a professional is writing and communicating, and I encourage you to practice writing up your work or research results. If the opportunity to publish arises, seize it. Some admissions committees rank applicants higher if they have at least one publication. Although any publication is an asset, articles in academic journals tend to be the most highly regarded within academia. I am most familiar with publishing research articles, which shows admissions committees that an applicant's research experience touches on all the facets of the scientific process, from theorizing to operationalizing to analyzing to documenting. It also suggests that an applicant is capable of scientific discourse and can summarize and synthesize background research effectively. Writing is a crucial component of graduate study, and publishing as a graduate student is usually encouraged, particularly for research-oriented programs. Therefore, honing your skills in writing and familiarizing yourself with the publication process will give you a great advantage and will prepare you for the discussions you will have with your mentors and peers. If you have further questions, I recommend asking professors and colleagues for advice; some of the most insightful and helpful comments I have received have come from my friends who had learned much from their own experiences. If you are interested in getting experience with publishing, I also encourage you to let your professor and other mentors know that you are interested and willing. I have often seen professors involve students in their publications when they know the students are willing to help and learn.

NETWORKING

In his essay, Dr. Myers discusses an important facet of his career: networking. Networking is a powerful way to get exposed to your field without burying yourself in journal articles and textbooks. One way to network is to attend conferences and, if possible, present your work. During the conferences, you will most likely have the opportunity to socialize with others who have similar interests. In fact, as subcommunities in psychology tend to be close-knit, you may have the opportunity to chat informally with well-known figures in your field of interest. The idea is to develop a reputation as someone who is capable and eager to learn and may even have good ideas.

Even if you don't have the opportunity to attend conferences, you can still network effectively. When I became interested in applying to graduate school, I sat down with some of my professors and chatted about my interests. They were able to provide names of researchers I might be interested in, and inevitably they recommended researchers with whom they had worked in the past. I e-mailed the researchers my professors had recommended, and I received many positive responses because the researchers were aware of who I was working with. For instance, one researcher remarked, "So you've been working with Professor Gray then? That's good training. I have a great deal of respect for him." I ended up chatting with that researcher over the phone, applying to the school, visiting, and gaining admission, and none of it would have been possible had I not taken the initiative to network and contact him in the first place.

It is often unclear how to best prepare for effective networking. I have always found it helpful to practice what I call the *30–30 sell*, wherein you learn to sell yourself and your professional interests in two different formats: a 30-second format and a 30-minute format. Each format presents different challenges. For the 30-second format, imagine that you have met someone in an elevator and she inquires about your work. Your goal is to give her a snapshot of your work but to avoid complicated information that will confuse newcomers to your field. Effective sells are those in which you are able to explain a few interesting things about your field, as well as what your work entails and why it is important. Remember, the 30-second sell is but a sample of a rich tapestry of work. People who converse with you should walk away with both more knowledge and more questions.

The 30-minute sell is crucial for many forms of networking, when psychologists and colleagues are interested to hear about the pertinent details of your work. Often it does not take place in an office but rather at a conference, party, restaurant, or bar, where scholarly socialization can be informal and relaxed. The 30-minute sell is an extended sales pitch for what you are working on within your field of interest. You should be able to frame your work in the form of a story and, in particular, a dialectical story, in which your work advances or critiques other work. It helps to include interesting details of the theoretical orientation, methodology, or approach, but be sure to concentrate on the main idea of your work. When critiquing others' approaches, do so respectfully and intelligently. A good 30-minute sell will take you far, so invest some time in thinking about it.

GETTING INVOLVED

Other ways to gain experience include getting involved in various organizations on campus or in your community. These organizations can be psychological or academic in nature, but need not be. Even experiences in disparate domains such as marketing, journalism, and computer science can add perspective and often inspiration to your application portfolio. For instance, a friend of mine who is interested in the social psychology of poverty worked at soup kitchens before she applied to graduate school. Her experiences undoubtedly shaped her motivations for applying. Inspiration does not always come from textbooks or lectures; do not hesitate to highlight your nonacademic influences in your application portfolio. You could use your years in the military, or your ability to communicate in sign language, or your experience as an entrepreneur to show admissions committees that you are engaged, motivated, and ready to pursue future study.

Go! Bolstering the Application Materials

Okay, so you have hit the books, taken the tests, and worked in the field—it is now time to put together your application. This is arguably the most difficult activity of the entire process, because you may not know what is expected of you. Chapter 5 illuminated many of the components of the application itself. Here, I address a major concern: What distinguishes a great application from the rest of the pile? The answer is recommendations and personal statements.

RECOMMENDATIONS

Recommendations can make or break your application, so choose your recommenders carefully. You do not need just positive recommendations; you need excellent ones, or at least the best you can get. What characterizes an excellent recommendation from merely a good one is often the amount of detail the recommender goes into. Recommendations ideally should come from individuals who can comment on your abilities, performance and successes, potential, work ethic, personality and amiability, respect for others, and interest in the field. Further, recommendations that compare you positively with other students (e.g., "Student X is among the top three finest students I've ever worked with") are especially powerful. Of course, only individuals with whom you have worked closely will be able to provide such information. Although not necessary, recommendations from well-established psychologists add clout to your application as well. That is because they have worked with lots of students and are able to recognize potential for future success in the field. Also consider getting recommendations from those who have taught you. Your professors can comment on your intellectual voracity, ability to communicate and express your ideas, and involvement in classroom discussions. The key point is to develop close relationships with individuals in your field so that they will be able to talk about you in as much detail as possible, and to explicitly ask them to provide a detailed recommendation for you. If they are open to it, you may even want to provide the people writing your letters with your curriculum vitae and a page of highlights about your strengths.

PERSONAL STATEMENT

Your personal statement is your one chance to demonstrate to the admissions committee your interest in furthering your education. A common mistake in personal statements is making them too general and vague. Avoid this mistake by distinguishing yourself from others and highlighting specifics about you. It helps to be unique; consider opening the statement in an engaging, lively manner and demonstrate that you are a creative thinker (without being too eccentric!). In addition, share the academic interests that inspire you. It is clear you have been involved in your work for a reason, but what experiences in particular have prompted your intentions for future graduate study? If you focus on your innovative ideas and enthusiasm for learning, it shows that you are excited to work in your field and communicates your passion for psychology in general. Finally, be bold. Although arrogance should be eschewed (because graduate school is nothing if not a humbling experience), feel free to emphasize your skills and your competencies. Talk about successes you have had in the past and how they relate to your current work. Address specific events that highlight your work ethic and demonstrate your capacity for rigorous training. Communicate the strengths and qualities that make you cut out for graduate school. Sell yourself; it is your job to convince admissions committees that you can handle the course work, learn the appropriate skills, and be innovative in your research and clinical duties.

Conclusion

The night of December 27 found me staring at the mailbox with 10 graduate school applications in my hands. I had spent months preparing the application materials themselves, and I had spent years preparing myself intellectually to even get as far as standing at my mailbox with the silly, deer-in-the-headlights expression I wore at that moment. In that situation, I found it difficult to stop doubting my abilities and criticizing my experiences; I was praying for a clerical error in my favor. That is why I found it rather surprising when, instead of hesitating even more, I simply shoved the applications into the mailbox with self-confidence. Although I was not at all confident that the applications would be successful (I was rather pessimistic on that front), I realized that I had done my best. Whatever the outcome, I could rest easy knowing that I had constructed the strongest application I was capable of. I hope you can say the same when you submit your applications, and that my advice and personal experiences in this chapter help you submit strong applications.

Practical Tips

1. **Start early.** I encourage you to start your applications early and keep track of deadlines. I started the summer before I applied to graduate school, 6 months in advance. I filled in all the boring details first and then updated each application periodically, whether on paper or online.

2. **Put a premium on advisors when applying to graduate programs.** Study their work, contact their advisees with questions, and look into where their students get jobs after graduation. Because you will be spending the next few years working with an advisor, make sure he or she is worth working with.

3. **Talk with professors about the application process.** When I was applying, I sat down with six professors with whom I had either conducted research or taken a class. They not only suggested programs and researchers I would be interested in but also gave me honest advice about some of the strengths and weaknesses in my application package.

4. **Apply to multiple schools.** No school is perfect for you, but some may come close. If you apply to several schools that offer you a good fit, you will appreciate the choices you have if you are accepted.

5. Use undergraduate research experiences as a stepping-stone. If your only option is a lab or research group that is just vaguely related to your field of interest, consider working there anyway. Research experiences help most applicants, and they will afford you a perspective that many of your peers might not have.

Reference

Norcross, J. C., Hanych, J. M., & Terranova, R. D. (1996). Graduate study in psychology: 1992–1993. *American Psychologist, 51,* 631–643.

Essay 6
Bolstering a Career: The
Supports and Satisfactions
of Networking
David G. Myers

As a teenager in Seattle, I worked in my family's insurance agency and became a licensed insurance salesperson, but the family business became the first road not taken. In college I instead pursued a premed program—majoring in chemistry, minoring in biology, and working three summers on wards and in the emergency room of Seattle's county hospital. After taking the Medical College Admissions Test and half-completing my medical school applications, I never mailed them in, having wearied of peering at slides and watching doctors pore over X-rays.

What, then, could be my vocation? Perhaps a college professor? But what could I profess? Looking back on my first 3 years of college, I recalled enjoying my only psychology course. So I took several more, applied to graduate schools without even a psychology minor, and, partly on the strength of my science background, was welcomed by the University of Iowa.

When I arrived to begin Iowa's graduate program in 1964, having declared my interest in personality, my advisor explained that their one faculty member in personality had just left: "So we've put you in social psychology." And that is how I became a social psychologist.

During my 2nd year, I assisted my advisor, Sidney Arenson (here begins my networking), by engaging 40 small groups in discussing story problems that assessed risk taking. We replicated the phenomenon of increased risk taking by groups, dubbed the "risky shift," and before long the college teacher wannabe had, to his surprise, also become a research psychologist. Moreover, the research mutated unpredictably—from risky shift, to a broader group polarization phenomenon, to studies of the subtle influence on one's own opinions of mere exposure to others' opinions.

Such is the adventure of life. You can't know your future, I tell students. Your interests on entering college will likely change during college and will change again during your working life. And that is why a broad education for an unpredictable future—a liberal education—serves most students better than does a focused vocational education.

As I began my teaching at Hope College, I also continued doing experiments and was able to make some modest contributions to the understanding of group influence, which led to an invitation to join 7 other Americans and 16 Europeans at a 1978 group research symposium in a

German castle. As we entered the seminar room the 1st day, I found myself seated near two heroes of my field, Irving Janis, of "groupthink" fame, and Ivan Steiner, author of many books and articles. During the breaks and on some outings, I enjoyed getting to know them, and when we all returned to the United States both showed me great kindness. Irving Janis brought me to speak at Yale (a scary experience for a person from a then little-known Midwestern college) and hosted me at a dinner in his home.

Several months later, Ivan Steiner received a phone call from McGraw-Hill's psychology editor, wondering whether he could recommend someone to work on developing a new social psychology text. When my phone rang a short while later, on that January day in 1979, I couldn't have been more surprised by the invitation to consider textbook writing. I thought it an outlandish idea, especially for a relative unknown such as myself. However, the editor persisted, over many calls, and I eventually decided that by writing the textbook I would, at least, learn more about my discipline.

From that networking came a book (now, over 25 years later, in its eighth edition) and a whole new career (note again the unpredictability of life, thanks to what Albert Bandura has noted is the life-shaping power of chance encounters). Developing that text led to an invitation to write an introductory psychology text (another shocking idea when first proposed). And all the reading and reporting for those texts then led to opportunities to contribute to the public understanding of psychological science through magazine articles, general audience trade books—on happiness, social change, hearing loss, intuition, and sexual orientation—and nearly 600 media contacts and interviews related to these topics. None of this would have transpired without networking.

I began the work with little confidence in my writing ability (I recall English composition being my lowest college grade). So I sought the help of others by reading helpful writing manuals and by seeking out an even more helpful Hope College colleague, poet–essayist Jack Ridl. Jack closely edited some 5,000 of my manuscript pages while patiently teaching me what it means to develop a voice, to order words to maximize punch, to write with rhythm. The lesson this experience taught me is that it pays to have enough self-confidence to risk undertaking a project and enough self-doubt (i.e., "defensive pessimism") to think you'll fail if you don't focus your efforts and network with others.

Indeed, two heads are often better than one, as famed creative teams such as Watson and Crick and psychology's own Kahneman and Tversky illustrate. Many of us working together are often smarter than any of us working alone. I suspect I speak for all my text author colleagues in at times feeling slightly embarrassed by people who are too impressed with what we seem to have written, as if we just sat down and wrote it. In fact, what's delivered is the end product of a collaborative effort involving countless expert consultants, reviewers, and multiple editors. If it is true that "whoever walks with the wise becomes wise," then text authors are wiser for all the wisdom and advice we receive from our expert colleagues.

Networking enabled my becoming an author and improved my skill and content, but it also has become a result of authoring. My work connects me with all sorts of interesting people and occasionally enables me to connect them with one another. Within the past day, as I write, I have helped link one colleague to a foundation that has also connected me with lots of people, pointed an inquiring ABC *Primetime Live* producer to five other professional colleagues, and reciprocated the help of a fellow author by assisting her with her new trade book manuscript. Writing *The Pursuit of Happiness* led to my connecting with the growing positive psychology movement, which Marty Seligman has effectively facilitated by aggressively bringing together early-career and senior scholars through networking opportunities.

Networking may sound best-suited to outgoing, self-confident, assertive people. Perhaps it is. However, as one who is a tad shy about hobnobbing with our distinguished colleagues at conventions and still not confident enough to call and interview them, I am especially grateful for e-mail. With time, my comfort in reaching out to them has grown. My colleagues, I've learned, are nearly always happy to answer questions, send papers, and read and critique drafts of what I've said about their work.

In my experience, people in psychology are overwhelmingly kind, positive, and supportive—and so are many people outside of psychology. I recently e-mailed kudos to a well-known writer (whom I recalled having briefly met) in response to one of his *New York Times* op-ed essays. I also dared to share with him a kindred-spirited draft essay of my own. In reply, he suggested how I might better focus it. When I did, he then, with my blessing, shared the revision with the new editor of the *Los Angeles Times* op-ed page. Voila! The essay appeared shortly thereafter. Such are the benefits of electronic networking.

Another way to reach out to people is with reprint request cards. I send a few hundred each year, mostly requesting published articles that I've spotted in *Current Contents in the Behavioral Sciences,* a wonderful but expensive little periodical that provides the contents pages of all English-language psychology and psychiatry periodicals. When this comes to me on our department routing, I just initial any article I'd like a copy of and, using the author addresses provided with each issue, a department assistant makes out the request card. Often, respondents include their other pertinent work as well.

Finally, for those of us who need to vacuum up information from all corners of psychology, numerous resources can assist us in sifting and identifying interesting and important new information. The British Psychological Society, the American Psychological Association, the American Psychological Society, and the American Association for the Advancement of Science all offer publications, conferences, press releases, research digests, or e-mail networks that inform us of developments outside our specialty area, as, occasionally, do quality public news sources, such as the *New York Times* and *Scientific American*, and news sources that feed these and other periodicals.

The lesson I have learned from all the supportive networking, and even from critiques and rejection, is this: Be open to others' ideas and advice. Listen to criticism. But if you have a vision, hold to it. Keep your eye on the goal. You and your life's work will be the better for it.

Darby E. Saxbe

Campus Visits and Interviewing 7

From: Oberlin, OH

Area of study: Clinical Psychology, University of California—Los Angeles

Previous degree(s): BA in English and psychology from Yale University, New Haven, CT

Career before graduate school: Marketing director for several Internet start-up companies; freelance writer

Number of graduate schools applied to: 11

Age when started this graduate program: 26

Professional interests: Close relationships, stress physiology, and the family environment

Career aspirations: Combine research, teaching, and possibly clinical work in an academic position

Y ou've slaved over your essays. You sweated through the Graduate Record Examinations (GRE). You may have made contact with faculty at your target schools. However, the visiting and interviewing process is likely your first chance to kick the proverbial tires of your prospective graduate institution. Despite all the thinking and preparation that went into your application, you may not have set foot on the campuses of some of the schools you've been considering—until now. In this chapter, I explain how the campus visit is your best, and maybe your only, opportunity to figure out which of the schools on your list are actually right for you. You can also bet that the programs are wondering the same thing about you. After having seen you only on paper, as a disembodied set of credentials, the faculty and students on the admissions committee will be excited to put a face to your name and get a sense of you as a real person, someone they might enjoy seeing in class or chatting with at a lab meeting. Having been on both sides of the process, as an applicant and an interviewer and admissions committee representative, I've come to see interviewing and visiting as crucial pieces of the application game. In fact, ideally, the interviewing process should be at least as valuable for you, the candidate, as for the programs that are interviewing you.

For me, the road to graduate school was long and winding because it took me a while to settle on psychology as a career. I always loved to read and, as a child, I dreamed of writing children's books or mystery novels. I started at Yale University as an English major, thinking I'd go into journalism or maybe academia. But then I discovered Freud's case histories one summer and realized they were as gripping as any mystery novel I'd ever read. I loved the idea of helping people get to the bottom of their problems, and as a bossy older sister, I thought I'd enjoy life as a therapist or professor. I added a bunch of psychology classes to my schedule in my junior and senior years, and even did research with a psychiatry professor, but I definitely didn't feel ready for graduate school right after college. When I graduated in 1999, dot-com mania was at its height and everyone I knew was starting an Internet company. So I followed the trend. I ended up working with a few friends who were developing a career-oriented Web site for college students, which led me to another dot-com job for journalists. It was definitely not research psychology, but I did learn a lot about working with people, especially those who are slightly "unhinged"!

After more than 3 years in the work world, I wanted to change course and decided it was finally time to apply to graduate programs in psychology. Given my unconventional background, I did a lot of catching up to become a credible applicant. I contacted a professor at a local university and started working with her on a research project that interested me. I also bought every GRE test preparation book I could find and spent hours checking out graduate programs online, e-mailing faculty, and writing and rewriting my essays. I eventually sent off 11 applications, was invited to interview at nine schools, and made the trek to seven of them.

As soon as I started getting interview invitations from schools, I started to feel anxious. Writing essays and sending e-mails was one thing, but how was I going to "sell" myself in person, especially after years away from school? What if I slipped up and said the wrong thing? What if I spilled coffee all over my interview suit? As it happens, one of my graduate school interviews did turn out a little disastrous: My student host came down with an eye infection the day I flew in, so the department had to scramble to find another host. It ended up being an older student who lived far from campus, and we got stuck in traffic en route to my morning interviews. Worse, the airline lost my luggage, and I didn't get it back until halfway through the interview weekend. Not having had the foresight to bring my suit as a carry-on, I ended up conducting my first few interviews (scheduled the day I arrived, so no time to shop) in the clothes I'd worn on the plane: a T-shirt and a pair of red sweatpants.

In an ironic twist, that disastrous interview weekend was at the University of California—Los Angeles (UCLA), where I was accepted and eventually chose to go. As I discovered, having almost everything go wrong turned out to be a good thing. The department secretary felt sorry for me and took me under her wing and, joking about my very unprofessional attire, helped break the ice with my interviewers. Best of all, I had a chance to show the admissions committee—and myself—that I could survive bad luck and keep my sense of humor. So my first piece of advice to you as you gear up for interviews is to relax and be yourself. Sure, you can practice and prepare until you've got the so-called perfect answers to every possible interview question memorized, but, as Dr. Hector Myers explains in his essay at the end of this chapter, admissions committees aren't looking for canned perfection. They want to know whether you will be happy and successful in their program, and to figure that out, they need to get to know *you*. (By the way, if you don't think you will be happy and successful at any of the programs you're applying to, put down this book and go into another career instead. Psychology graduate school is tough, so don't bother to apply if you're not passionate about it.)

Getting the Word . . . and Deciding Whether to Go

After you send off your applications and cross your fingers, it might be anywhere from a few weeks to a few months before you are invited to interviews, depending on the admissions timetable of your program. In fact, not every program requires or even offers interviews, so you may not hear from some places at all. I sent off applications at the end of December and heard in mid-January about interviews that were to take place in February or early March. If you're applying to a lot of faraway schools, try to keep your winter and spring calendar pretty clear to accommodate weekend trips. You will probably hear about the interview via phone or e-mail, and you will sometimes receive a follow-up letter as well. Most contacts are made by a program administrator—in my case, the departmental secretary—but sometimes you will get that first call from a graduate student or a faculty member on the admissions committee. In any case, remember to be polite and pleasant; you are making an impression, even before you arrive on campus. To that end, it's worth double-checking that your outgoing voicemail message includes your full name, clearly enunciated, and no one is in the background making funny sound effects. Also be sure to use a professional-sounding e-mail address. Crazyfan35@hotmail.com, for example, might give your committee pause. You might consider opening an application-only e-mail account. This will help ensure that you don't miss any important application-related e-mails because they got mixed up with one of those online-pharmacy ads or because your school or work address has expired.

If you're traveling to numerous campuses, the interviewing process may quickly get expensive. As addressed in chapter 3, you'll need to anticipate and budget for these costs as you start to apply. Some programs—such as the one at UCLA—offer travel allowances to help applicants defray the costs; if a program offers such assistance, you'll probably hear about it in the initial phone call or e-mail. It's okay to politely ask whether a program helps cover travel costs. If it doesn't, and money is tight, you might have to think about interviewing by phone instead. In my opinion, it's always best to bite the bullet and go on as many visits as you can; you have an opportunity to convey your enthusiasm for the program and to make an impression on faculty, and you also get a chance to learn more about each program on your list. You'll spend 2, 4, 6, or even 8 years of your life in graduate school, so it might be worth an extra few hundred bucks to find the best place for you. Also, the more interviews you attend, the more comfortable you'll get, so it also doesn't hurt to interview at not-quite-right programs just as practice—and who knows, you might fall in love with that last-choice school. That said, I was broke during the year I applied and ended up saying no to two faraway interviews—one because the school was last on my list; the other because I had just been accepted to my first-choice school and didn't feel the need to look anywhere else.

Many schools try to coordinate their interviewing schedules so as to prevent double-booking, but it still happens every year. Interviews at different schools are scheduled during the same weekend or even the same day. If this happens to you, don't panic. It's not uncommon that interviews get double-booked. Let the admissions coordinator know about the situation and see whether he has any suggestions. When there's a conflict, some programs are willing to host you on a different day, although you may miss out on the social aspects of the interview weekend. If the campuses are relatively close together, you could also try splitting up your weekend; spend Thursday and Friday at School A and Saturday and Sunday at School B. If all else fails, travel to the school that appeals to you the most and ask to do your other interviews by phone, if the program allows it. I know a few people who interviewed only by phone and still got into their target schools. Admissions committee members know that applicants are busy and that scheduling conflicts are inevitable. If you can't make it to the interview but you can convey your skills and enthusiasm via phone and e-mail, your nonvisit often will not ruin your chances. In my opinion, the main argument in favor of going to interviews isn't to better your chances of acceptance—although it helps—but to get your own firsthand sense of what different programs are like.

I Forgot My Toothbrush! Preparing for Your Visit

You've bought your plane ticket or fueled up your car—what now? Depending on how your program conducts interviews, your campus visit could last for a few hours or an entire weekend. My seven interview experiences ran the gamut. For an interview at one program in New York City, where I was living at the time, I didn't even make it onto campus; I just took the subway a few stops uptown and spent an hour meeting with a faculty member in his private therapy office. I took an early-morning train trip to check out another program in Philadelphia, where I spent most of the day—interview, lunch, interview, afternoon reception—before heading home that night. For visits to North Carolina and California, I devoted a full weekend, staying with graduate student hosts and attending every organized social event. How much time to put into each visit depends on the program itself, travel and distance considerations, and your interest in the school. I certainly got more out of my longer visits—and it is no coincidence that I ended up at UCLA, where I spent the whole weekend.

The length of your visit will dictate most of your packing, but you'll certainly need at least one thing: an interview suit. As a graduate student, you'll probably live in jeans, but it is important to wear business attire for interviews: a suit or decent jacket–tie–pants combination if you're male, a suit or dress and jacket if you're female. It's better to err on the side of dressed up rather than dressed down. Also, steer clear of anything too flashy, distracting, or revealing. This may seem obvious, but I am always surprised, during UCLA's interview weekend, to see a few applicants in casual wear or worse, skimpy skirts and tops. If your attire looks unprofessional, the admissions committee might wonder how you will present yourself to clients and research participants. That said, this is from the girl who interviewed in red sweatpants! Remember that admissions committees do not expect—or even desire—total perfection, so don't get hung up on every detail of your wardrobe.

In addition to at least 1 day's worth of interview wear, you may need to bring more informal clothes for social events. If social events are scheduled directly before or after interviews, you may want to stash a few "convertible" items: a sweater that you can substitute for a suit jacket, for example, or a comfortable pair of shoes to slip on if you're going right from an interview to a walking tour.

If your campus visit includes an overnight stay, the department may make arrangements for you to stay with a current graduate student. In some cases, you'll have a choice between bunking with a student and booking a room at a local motel or hotel. You may even have friends in town who are willing to host you. I strongly recommend staying with a graduate student host, if one is available; you will learn much more about the program. You'll see what kinds of housing you'll be able to afford on a student stipend and get insight into the nuts and bolts of student life, from commuting and parking to how much time students really spend in the lab. There's just no substitute for the kind of firsthand perspective on a program you can get by tagging along with someone already enrolled. If you've got friends in town, you might want to meet up with them, but remember to keep your focus on the program you're visiting. I was torn when I made arrangements to visit UCLA, because my sister lived in Los Angeles at the time and wanted me to stay with her. I ended up extending my trip by a few days so that I could stay with a student host and still spend time with my sister.

If you are staying with a graduate student, your sleeping accommodations might vary; it's a good idea to contact your host before your visit to find out whether you should bring anything (e.g., extra pillow, sleeping bag, alarm clock). I am completely addicted to my morning coffee, and on one visit, I stayed with a graduate student host who kept no caffeine in the house. Needless to say, I was a little slow the following morning. On my next school visit, I brought individual packets of instant coffee, just in case. You get the point: If there's anything that you want or need, bring it along, whether it's toothpaste, a cell phone charger, an extra laptop battery, warm socks, contact lens solution, something to read, and so on.

As you pack and prep for your campus visits, consider making an interview folder that you can customize for each visit. Include copies of your application essays as well as a printout of your senior thesis or any other academic work you discussed in your application; your interviewers will ask you about this material, so make sure it's fresh in your mind. If you're visiting a research-oriented program, include research statements and recent abstracts for each of the faculty you are expecting to meet with, so that you can be "up" on their current work. Don't go overboard with this folder—you don't need to memorize the contents—but it helps to keep everything in the same place.

"So, Tell Me About Yourself . . .": What to Expect During Interviews

As someone who'd been out of college for a few years, I wasn't as savvy about the application and interviewing process as some students, and my first interview was pretty rocky. I erroneously assumed that graduate school interviews would be like undergraduate interviews: You'd meet some nice friendly alumnus who would ask about your hobbies and favorite novels and try to get to know you on a personal level. Nope. I discovered that graduate school interviews are closer to job interviews: You're meeting with professors and they want to see how you'll perform.

I knew that most research-oriented programs had an mentor model, but I thought that meant that you showed up, worked in different labs, and then chose someone who would advise your dissertation. Nope again. As Dr. Myers explains, many schools pair students with a specific mentor right from the get-go. As I was surprised to discover, a big focus of their interviews is to assess the "fit" between applicants and potential faculty advisors. I found this out the hard way at that first interview, when I couldn't figure out why my fellow applicants kept asking me, "Who do you want to work with?" I replied, "I don't know; all the faculty seem really good, and maybe I'll figure it out if I go here." When I gave the same response to the first professor who interviewed me, she looked at me blankly and explained that I was supposed to identify a particular faculty member's lab. Not having done much homework on the different professors and what they focused on, I ended up asking her for suggestions. Needless to say, I didn't get into that school. By the time I made it to the next campus, I had printed out each faculty member's research statements (which are usually available on the school's Web site) and read the most recent publications from the two or three professors whose interests seemed closest to mine. These all went into my interview folder. When I was asked, "Who do you want to work with, and why?" I was able to cite specific aspects of each faculty member's work and explain how it fit with my interests. That said, don't zero in on only one advisor. You may discover that she's not taking students that year, or that there's stiff competition for the spots in her lab, or just that you and she don't have great chemistry. Be able to make a strong case for how well you match with two or even three of the faculty members in each program and you'll improve your odds of getting accepted. If you've read chapter 5 of this volume, you may have already identified particular faculty members in your essays, but the interviews are a chance to actually make face-to-face connections with professors. And, as Dr. Myers writes, your interviewers will be trying to figure out whether your interest in specific faculty members is genuine, so be sincere.

In addition to referencing specific faculty, at a research-oriented program you should also be able to articulate, clearly and concisely, what kind of research you're interested in doing and where you might expect your interests to take you during the course of graduate school. Although the following advice may not be as helpful to those applying to other kinds of graduate programs, the general principle still stands: It's good to think about what really motivates you and to be able to present it in adaptable, easily digestible sound-bite form. By the time I'd finished the interview process, I had winnowed my sound bite into something like this:

> I'm interested in the family environment and how it is related to mental and physical health. More specifically, I want to study how adverse experiences in early childhood influence later coping with stress, and what kinds of qualities make some children more resilient than others. In this program, I could pursue this interest by getting involved in (*insert potential mentor's project*). For example, you just told me about the data you've been collecting on X. I would be interested in exploring how X is related to children's ability to handle stress by looking at Y and Z aspects of that data.

Formulating this sound bite helped me define myself better in interviews and stand out more from other students who had not clarified their interests. It also helped me with my decision-making process: By working to identify what really interested me, I was better able to decide what programs and faculty members really were a good fit.

If you're applying to a clinically focused program that does not emphasize research, you will not need to work as much on articulating your research interests and finding a specific faculty fit. However, it's still good to give interviewers a clear sense of who you are, what you want to do, and why their program suits your specific interests. For example, you might say something like, "Ever since I spent a semester in Madrid, I've been interested in cultural issues. One of the reasons I'm attracted to First Choice University (FCU) is that you're located in a diverse city where I could work with Spanish-speaking clients" or "I enjoy working with children on their social skills, and I'm impressed that you have several placement opportunities at local preschools." You get the point: If you can be

EXHIBIT 7.1

Sample Questions You May Be Asked in an Interview

- How did you get interested in the field of psychology?
- What appeals to you about this program?
- What kinds of clinical (or research) experiences have you had? What were the most challenging aspects of those experiences? What did you enjoy most?
- What have been your most challenging or enjoyable academic experiences?
- What was your undergraduate senior thesis (or biggest undergraduate academic project) about? What did you learn from this project?
- What would you like to be doing in 10 years? Twenty years?
- Why are you interested in working with Dr. Johnson?
- Are you primarily interested in research, in clinical work, or both? Why?
- What type of research do you hope to conduct in graduate school?
- Do you subscribe to a particular theoretical orientation? If so, what and why?
- What are your major strengths and weaknesses?
- What do you like to do for fun?

specific in explaining why you will thrive at FCU, admissions committee members will have an easier time picturing you there. So consider what settings (e.g., hospital, clinic, private practice), populations (e.g., gender, age, ethnicity), and pathologies (e.g., level, diagnosis, symptoms) interest you and why, and try to find out what resources are available at FCU. You may also want to mention your interest in a particular clinical orientation, such as psychodynamic, family systems, or cognitive–behavioral. Just do your homework and be sure that it matches the approach of the program or professor.

Depending on what kinds of programs you're visiting, interview questions will vary (see Exhibit 7.1). However, be savvier than I was at my first interview and expect to be asked for specifics on your clinical and research goals and your interest in particular faculty members. Interviews will also cover your previous experiences, whether in research or clinical domains. Be prepared to talk about what you learned from these experiences and what was both difficult and rewarding about them. You'll get questions about your academic work as an undergraduate, particularly your senior thesis, if you wrote one. If you've been out of college for a few years, as I had, it pays to dust off that thesis and read through it before your interviews. I was glad I'd done this when, at UCLA, a professor asked me what statistical approaches I'd used for my analyses. Interviewers will also likely ask about any experiences you've detailed in your application essays, so skim through these as well; you may have forgotten what you wrote a few months ago!

If you're applying to a program that requires clinical work, you should also be prepared for questions about your experiences in clinical settings. You may not have many such experiences (and many applicants don't), so mention other opportunities you've had to develop your interpersonal skills and get to know people from other walks of life, whether volunteering at a retirement home, tutoring, or even interacting with people from other cultures. I had worked at a day care center, so I talked about how teaching young children challenged some of my assumptions about developmental psychology. If you're applying to research-oriented clinical programs, as I was, you may want to be careful about expressing too much enthusiasm for clinical work. Keep in mind that faculty at research institutions will be investing a lot of their time, energy, and even grant money into your training. They do not want to take on a mentee who will spend his or her time in graduate school seeing clients rather than logging hours in the lab or writing up results for publication. So expect questions about whether you prioritize research or clinical work and what kind of career trajectory you envision. As Dr. Myers notes, faculty may doubt that you are truly research-oriented if you seem vague about your research goals or plan to maintain a busy clinical practice on top of an academic appointment. Interviewers will also be curious if your curriculum vitae is chock full of volunteering, tutoring, counseling, and other clinical-type experiences but light on research. Be prepared to respond as honestly and diplomatically as possible to questions about balancing research and clinical work. After all, if clinical work is truly your passion and research leaves you cold, you may want to pursue more clinically oriented programs.

Remember that interviewers are interested in not only what you have to say but how you say it. Smile, make eye contact, sit up straight, and try not to ramble. This is especially important if you're interviewing at a program that involves clinical work. If you are friendly, relaxed, and professional, faculty members will be more apt to trust you with clients in the future. As Dr. Myers writes, nearly every applicant is anxious; it's how you cope with your anxiety that matters. Graduate school can be stressful, and faculty want to know that you can hold up under pressure. If you're an anxious interviewee, devote extra time to practicing and polishing your interviewing skills and experiment with diaphragmatic breathing techniques, stretching, meditation, or any other relaxation exercises that will help you. Remember your goal is not perfection—just a slightly more articulate, calmer version of yourself. Pretty much everyone on the admissions committee was once in your shoes, and they're really not out to make you feel bad or uncomfortable (even if it seems that way). They genuinely want to get to know you and find out what interests you. So if you get a tough question that catches you off guard, it's okay to admit that you're not sure how to respond and that you need some time to think. You can also say "My best guess is X, but before I could really answer that question, I would want to review the literature on the topic more carefully." That's better than getting annoyed or defensive, or visibly rattled. If you're asked a really impossible question—say, a specific statistics question—it's better to admit that you don't know but that, for example, "I'm really eager to learn more about statistical approaches, and I know Professor Baird teaches a course on that topic," than to make something up on the spot. After all, psychologists are often required to make educated guesses, so how you handle the holes in your knowledge is just as important as what you do know.

Finally, remember that your interviews are not a chance for you just to talk, but to ask questions. Take advantage! This is often your only chance—until you start graduate school, that is—to spend one-on-one time with the faculty members who will ultimately mentor you and shape your career. If you think you might go blank when you're asked for questions, jot down a few in advance (see Exhibit 7.2). If you're meeting with a professor who might become your advisor, ask about her mentoring style and current research program. Don't ask her to repeat information that's already available online (e.g., "What kind of research do you do?"); instead, give her a chance to fill you in about current programs and future directions: Say, for example, "I see that you're developing a new study about genetic influences on schizophrenia. How soon are you expecting to start collecting data, and how long will data collection take? What will graduate student involvement be like?" Ask about research early in the interview so that the answers can inform your later responses (e.g., "I was really intrigued to hear that you're looking into the developmental trajectory of schizophrenia; that ties into my interest in stress and childhood"). If your interviewer is a graduate student representative on the admissions committee or another faculty member, ask about course work, housing, or other aspects of the program. Don't fly home with a bunch of unanswered questions still on your mind.

All of my interviews were one-on-one with faculty members or graduate students (I met with two or three faculty members and one or two graduate students at each program). However, some programs may also include group interviews, either to increase efficiency or to get a sense of how candidates interact in a group setting. If you end up in a group interview, the same general rules apply: Stay calm and friendly, ask well-informed questions, and try to stay on message about who you are and what you want to do. Speak up and be vocal, but be careful not to dominate the group or interrupt others.

EXHIBIT 7.2

Sample Questions to Ask During an Interview

If you're interviewing at a clinically oriented program	▌ How much clinical experience do students typically get in the 1st year? ▌ How much supervision time do students get for each client? Do supervisors usually observe sessions live, or on video- or audiotape? ▌ What kinds of clinical populations can students work with? ▌ Is it possible to work with both children and adults, or are students encouraged to specialize?
If you're interviewing with a potential research mentor	▌ How closely do you typically work with graduate students? ▌ Do you have regular lab meetings? ▌ Do you consider yourself more of a hands-on or hands-off mentor? ▌ What do you hope to see from students over the course of their time in graduate school in terms of publications or presentations? ▌ Do you typically encourage students to collect their own data, or do your students tend to work with preexisting datasets?
If you're interviewing with another faculty member or graduate student	▌ What is the 1st-year course work like? ▌ Where do most students live, and how do they commute to campus? ▌ Are there opportunities for students and faculty to socialize outside of class? ▌ How challenging is it to live in this town/city on a graduate student stipend? ▌ What do students do on the weekends?

So Now I'm Supposed to Socialize? Handling the Rest of the Weekend

Sit-down interviews might be the official reason for your visit, but they do not mark the end of the interview process—especially if you're on campus for the whole weekend. You will probably have plenty of opportunities to socialize with current graduate students, faculty, and even your fellow applicants. Most schools organize at least one lunch or dinner event for interviewees, and graduate students sometimes arrange additional get-togethers, ranging from sightseeing tours to late-night parties. This social whirlwind can feel exhausting, especially if you've been sleeping on a graduate student's lumpy couch all weekend. However, it can also be a lot of fun and one of your best chances to meet people and get candid responses to your questions. So go to as many events as you can! Smile, and don't be shy about striking up conversations with current graduate students and other applicants. You should have plenty of common ground. If you feel especially tongue-tied, remember what you probably learned in Psychology 101: People love to talk about themselves, so give them the opportunity by asking questions. Also, if you're going on many interviews, you may start to see many of the same applicants on the "circuit." These folks might become a great source of information and insight, so don't let your competitive urges keep you from being friendly. In fact, if you don't get into any first-choice programs this time around and end up reapplying, your fellow applicants might become your best contacts during your next round!

As with the formal interviews, you might feel unsure about what to ask or what to look for when checking out a program. It pays to think this over before your interviews because you'll be swept up in a maelstrom of activity during your visit. What makes you happy? How do you envision spending your time as a graduate student? If you aspire to a prestigious research career, make sure you're joining a lab where you can be productive and can take the lead on research projects or publications. If you want to do clinical work with a particular population—say, cancer patients—look for programs with ties to hospitals. For me, quality-of-life considerations were important. I wanted to live in a diverse city with a nice climate and a good music scene. I also wanted to join a program that was fairly social. At a couple of campuses, I noticed that the majority of graduate students seemed to be older and married, whereas at other schools, the students tended to be younger, single, and more socially active. Because I knew I wouldn't be settling down anytime soon, I gravitated to the schools that seemed to have more single folks. It's up to you to figure out what's important, but the big question is this: "Would I feel comfortable spending several years here?"

Many applicants get nervous about the social aspects of the interview weekend, worrying that they're being watched and evaluated by some mysterious hidden critic. However, I can attest that applicants' off-hours conduct is rarely a major focus of the admissions committee at the meetings I've attended at UCLA. Social behavior usually enters into discussion of an applicant only if there's a concern—that is, if the candidate did something inappropriate that raises questions about his judgment. For example, a few years before I applied, an applicant made an offensive remark about homosexuals. The comment didn't sit well with his host, who happened to be gay. The host told another student, who was on the admissions committee, and the incident was then discussed during the admissions meeting and the candidate was rejected. Such instances are pretty rare, so don't worry that your every word will be dissected by the admissions committee. That said, whether or not it affects your eventual acceptance, be courteous and respectful to your graduate student hosts, who are sacrificing a weekend of their time to show you around. Don't expect them to drive you places at the drop of a hat or cater to your every dietary need. Also, every year at the interview weekend party at UCLA, some nervous applicant drinks way too much alcohol and ends up having to be hauled home by irritated hosts. Don't be that person. It's fine to have a beer at an after-hours event—you've certainly earned the right to unwind—but ultimately, you're visiting to check out a program, not to party.

It's Over! Or Is It? Following Up After the Interview

You've made it home in one piece, and you're convinced that FCU is the school for you. Now's the time to say so! Many applicants neglect to do any follow-up after their interviews, but contacting your hosts and interviewers is a great way to express your interest in a program. Most admissions committees meet fairly soon after their interview weekends—sometimes even the next day or week—so don't hesitate to send out thank you notes promptly. Some applicants mail cards, but an e-mail thank you is quicker and easier. If you can't decide whether to send a printed card or an e-mail, send both. Either way, make sure that your note conveys enthusiasm for the program, and try to be as specific as possible. See Figure 7.1 for a sample note.

If you are convinced that you would attend FCU if accepted, you could include the following statement in your note: "FCU is my number one school, and if accepted, I would be certain to attend." Admissions committees don't want to offer their spots to candidates who are uncertain and might ultimately turn them down—that's a waste of their time—so your strong interest will be a selling point (as long as it's genuine; if not, you'll find yourself in a bind after you get accepted to more than one "number one" school). Also, bringing your student host a card or small thank you gift is certainly not mandatory, but it's a thoughtful gesture that can only improve your standing at FCU. Consider a simple bouquet, a bottle of wine, a set of soaps or lotions, or a yummy snack. Dash off an e-mail thank you to your host, as well, as soon as you return.

Now it's time to cross your fingers again and wait. As mentioned, many programs make admissions decisions fairly soon after the interviews. At UCLA, the committee meets the Tuesday after the interview

FIGURE 7.1

Dear Professor Hernandez:

Thank you for taking the time to sit down with me on Friday and tell me about your current research program. I enjoyed hearing about your work on childhood shyness and your ongoing therapy study. As someone who is fascinated by children's social behavior and temperament, I am really excited about the data you are collecting. I had a great time at First Choice University, and I appreciated the opportunity to see such an excellent program in action.

Yours truly,

Darby E. Saxbe

Sample thank you note.

weekend, when the candidates are fresh in everyone's mind. So you may hear about your fate within a few weeks of your visit. However, other schools take much longer, and there could be a lag of a month or more between your visit and your official accept or decline notice. You might also end up on an official or unofficial wait-list if the program is waiting to hear from students who might go elsewhere. If decision deadlines are approaching, other schools have gotten back to you, and you still haven't heard anything, you may be in this kind of limbo. If so, continue to convey your interest in a polite, nonpushy way: "I continue to feel that FCU is the best school for me, and I hope that I am fortunate enough to be offered a place." Don't deluge the admissions committee with phone calls or e-mails; a simple reconfirmation of interest is enough. If all goes well, you'll be packing your bags a second time—to move and attend FCU next fall.

Conclusion

Campus visits can be a critical part of the application and admissions process, a chance to check out the place that may form the backdrop for the next chapter of your life. Take these visits seriously, and give yourself the time and energy you need to prepare for them. At the same time, remember that, at the end of the day, you're looking for the program that will help you to flourish and develop the most. Keep that "selfish" agenda in the back of your mind and perhaps the visiting process will seem a little less onerous and a little more fun. Those weekends of schlepping around the country and sleeping on graduate students' lumpy couches may seem like a hassle, but at the end of the process, you will have made valuable connections (both at your eventual "home" and at other institutions) with professors and future colleagues and possibly even a few new friends.

Practical Tips

1. **Explore what makes you happy.** I really benefited from taking time off after college to explore other (i.e., nonpsychology) career options. Even though those years didn't enhance my academic curriculum vitae, they've helped me feel more secure about my choice of a career in psychology, and as a result I'm a happier and more focused graduate student. Give yourself time to explore what makes you happy; your sense of self will come through in your interviews.

2. **Make the most of your connections.** When getting information about programs, contact graduate students or alumni, even if they're distant acquaintances; most people will be flattered to be asked for their opinions. If you don't know anyone who went to First Choice University, ask around! Chances are you know someone who knows someone who knows someone, and they might give you a very candid insight into your potential advisor.

3. **Proofread!** Get a second, third, and fourth pair of eyes to look over your application essays. Enlist professors, friends, and current graduate students to give you feedback on drafts. I sent my essays to everyone who would agree to look at them, from a former professor to my mom, and I got a lot of useful suggestions.

4. **Prevent grumbling and hunger pangs.** Pack a couple of energy bars or other favorite snack foods when you head off on campus visits; no one should have to interview on an empty stomach.

5. **Relax and enjoy the process.** The application process can be stressful, but it should also be fun; it's a chance to really think about what you want to do with your life, and why. It's also a chance to meet people who are pursuing interests that are similar to yours. If you're finding the process more overwhelming than enjoyable, maybe it's time to revert to the first tip and give yourself some time off.

Essay 7
Admissions Interviews From
a Faculty Member's
Perspective: The Challenge of
Honest Self-Presentation
Hector F. Myers

For many applicants to graduate school, one of the most stressful aspects of the process is the admissions interview. In this essay I try to demystify this aspect of the review process by placing it in proper perspective and offering suggestions about how to make an interview less distressing and more effective. First, I discuss the purpose of the interview from the perspective of the interviewer and the program. Then, I describe how the interview is an important opportunity for interviewees. Finally, I draw on more than 25 years of conducting graduate admissions interviews to identify some *dos* and *don'ts* that might be helpful for prospective applicants.

Before I discuss interviews in detail, it is useful to first discuss some procedural issues that can influence how many interviews applicants are likely to have and with whom they are likely to interview. Graduate programs differ in their model of training: Some programs follow an apprentice model in which students are assigned to work primarily with one faculty member, whereas other programs have students work with several faculty members. In the former model, the primary mentor typically selects the applicants he or she wants, and therefore, applicants are likely to be interviewed by only one or two faculty members who will ultimately make the admissions decision. In the latter model, however, the program admits applicants, and therefore, applicants are likely to be interviewed by many faculty members. Also, in many graduate programs only faculty conduct the interviews, whereas in others graduate students are also included as interviewers, and their input carries weight in the admissions process. Therefore, it is important for applicants to find out as much as possible about the programs' training model and how interviews are conducted before visiting the program so that they know what to expect.

WHY DO GRADUATE PROGRAMS CONDUCT INTERVIEWS?

The major reason graduate programs include interviews of applicants as part of their admissions process is to get to know applicants beyond what is in their application folder. Interviews give programs the opportunity to obtain additional information and clarify questions they might have about the applicants' preparation for graduate training, beyond grades, GRE scores, self-statement, and letters of recommendations. For example, many applicants believe that to be admitted they need to describe their interests and goals to match those of the program and the interest and expertise of the faculty. However, it is not always clear whether these "stated interests and goals" are real or simply packaged to make the applicants more attractive to the program. Therefore, the interview gives faculty the opportunity to carefully evaluate how real these stated interests are and whether the candidate actually understands what will be required to achieve his or her stated goals or has the background training to accomplish them. Thus, for example, a candidate may claim to be interested in an academic or research career but have only vague ideas about specific areas of research interest or only limited research experience. Some candidates may also indicate that they want to have an active clinical or counseling practice along with their academic teaching and research, which suggests that they are unaware of the focus and commitment necessary to have a successful academic or research career and may be unrealistic about all of the professional roles they hope to fulfill.

The interview also affords faculty the opportunity to identify candidates' areas of strength and deficits and to reconcile these with what may not be as evident in their admissions folder. For example, some applicants may exaggerate the extent of their research experience and suggest that they played a more significant role in the studies than they actually did. With careful questioning, however, faculty can determine very quickly the applicant's depth of understanding and ability to discuss the relevant research issues. This process can either reinforce their initial positive impression of the applicant or allow them to reevaluate their impression.

The interview also allows faculty to assess applicants' interpersonal style. This initial impression is very subjective, but these first impressions can carry substantial weight either positively or negatively. Of course, interpersonal style and personality are likely to be given more weight for clinical and counseling programs because of the requirement for service training. A strong academic record predicts success in the classroom and in research; however, an interpersonal style that conveys an applicant as being awkward, excessively anxious, overly chatty, pushy, overly controlled or guarded, or inappropriate predicts problems with clients. Therefore, graduate clinical or counseling programs are likely to be reluctant to admit these applicants. In fact, such applicants might be advised to pursue other career paths in psychology.

The interview also allows faculty to assess the relative "fit" of applicants with the program and, in a sense, to market the program and to recruit their top applicants. Graduate programs, especially the more competitive programs, have a limited number of slots to fill each year, so their ultimate goal is to select those applicants who have the best fit with the program. Thus, in the final analysis, the ultimate goal of the faculty is to select the best candidates for their program, so the key question they are interested in answering with the interview is whether this is the type of applicant they want in the program.

WHAT VALUE DO ADMISSIONS INTERVIEWS HAVE FOR APPLICANTS?

One of the things I tell undergraduates with whom I discuss graduate admissions is that admissions interviews should be considered opportunities for mutual assessment. Therefore, applicants should take this opportunity to find out as much as possible about the program, the university, and the community at large. Remember that you will be spending anywhere from 2 years for a master's degree to 5 years or more for a doctorate, so you want to make sure that you select the program that is likely to best meet your needs. You will need to consider not only the specifics about courses and other academic requirements but also the social climate of the academic program, department, university, and surrounding community. For many students, having a community that they identify with because of religion, race/ethnicity, sexual orientation, and so on is very important, so you should also consider these issues when evaluating graduate programs.

Therefore, graduate admissions interviews provide candidates with the opportunity to obtain a more in-depth understanding of the program. As a faculty member, I am very impressed with applicants who ask a lot of questions, including questions about our model of training; about what expectations we have of students with respect to research, clinical training, and teaching; about whether students work with only one professor or can work with several professors; about whether students are encouraged to do their own research or to work only on faculty's research; about funding; and about average time to graduation. Many students also ask about the relative ease or difficulty of access to populations for research or clinical training as well as for a social life. We at the University of California—Los Angeles, have several major advantages because of our location, including the size and the racial and ethnic diversity of the population as well as the fact that we have established working relationships with community agencies that serve as resources for research participants and as clinical training sites. Thus students who gain admission to our graduate programs are likely to find whatever they need for both their personal and their professional lives in Los Angeles, although it might take some effort to locate and gain access to the community or resource agency they are interested in. That said, Los Angeles poses some challenges that applicants need to be aware of, including the high cost of living and traffic congestion. The point is that the more questions applicants have, the greater the likelihood that they will get the information they need to make an informed choice if they are offered admission.

Admissions interviews also provide applicants with the opportunity to get to know faculty and graduate students and to tour the campus. Many programs have interview weekends that allow applicants to meet faculty and graduate students, both formally and informally. Applicants can meet faculty other than those with whom they interview and might work with. They also can meet graduate students and find out what it's really like to be a student in the program and in the department or school and to experience the social climate in vivo.

Interviews also allow applicants the opportunity to elaborate on their experiences beyond the page limits imposed in most applications as well as to clarify any problems or weaknesses in their record. For example, many talented students have excellent grades but weak GRE scores, or vice versa. If they are not screened out early and get the opportunity to be interviewed, the interview will offer a chance to explain why they think they did not do as well on the GRE or received a less than desirable grade in a particular course. Perhaps issues or events can put this blot on their record in perspective (e.g., having to work, loss of a close relative before the exam). Caution should be exercised in dealing with weaknesses in the record, however, because this is not an opportunity to try to gain sympathy. I say more about this a little later.

Even if they do not receive an offer to join the program, the interview can afford applicants the opportunity to get feedback about whether they should pursue admission to the graduate program and what they need to do to make themselves more competitive next time. Although this is not a very pleasant experience for either the faculty or the applicant, we sometimes find ourselves in situations when we have to let applicants know that they are not qualified for admissions to our graduate program(s). Despite the unpleasantness, however, this is still an opportunity for applicants to obtain valuable information about their weaknesses, whether they have chosen the wrong program or need more experience and training, and, if possible, what corrective steps they might take to improve their future chances. Not every faculty member will take the time to provide this feedback, but you never know until you ask. However, if you ask, then you need to be prepared to receive honest feedback, no matter how painful it might be.

WHAT YOU SHOULD AND SHOULDN'T DO IN ADMISSIONS INTERVIEWS

As noted earlier, admissions interviews should be considered opportunities for mutual assessment. Careful preparation is important, but avoid overrehearsal and the preparation of packaged answers. Be yourself! I remember interviewing a very talented applicant several years ago who had an excellent academic record but who was so well rehearsed and packaged that she even had a list of notes that she consulted in answering my questions. In fact, rather than being a conversation, the interview felt more like I was speaking with an automaton who could not or would not engage me and show me who she was. Therefore, even though she clearly had the requisite academic credentials to be very competitive for admission to our program, her interpersonal style was so stilted as to make her an undesirable candidate.

However, it is also a mistake to be too casual or to answer questions off the cuff with little thought. Think about what is being asked, take your time, and give the most thoughtful answer you can.

It goes without saying, but appropriate professional dress and behavior are expected, even when being interviewed by graduate students or postdoctoral fellows. They may not be faculty, but if you are scheduled to meet with them, then it is a formal interview that is part of the admissions process, and their impression of you will be taken seriously.

Regardless of who is interviewing you, give honest answers; be as clear and specific as possible about your background and experiences. Do not exaggerate your accomplishments in course work, research, clinically relevant experiences, teaching, or volunteer activities. By the same token, don't let false modesty undervalue or downplay your accomplishments either. The interviewers are very interested in knowing what you have accomplished to this point.

All interviewees experience some anxiety and nervousness, which is both understandable and expected. What is important is how you handle the stress, which provides faculty members with some indication of how you are likely to cope with the range of pressures that you will face in graduate school. A quick trip to the bathroom to freshen up and compose yourself before your next interview can be helpful.

Some candidates are so concerned with impressing the faculty and graduate student interviewers that they appear to be compelled to talk about themselves and all of the great things they have done. Although discussing one's experiences is an important focus of the interview, it is important to match the focus and pace of the interviewer. Overtalking conveys anxiety and may be interpreted as an excessive desire to impress or even narcissism. The latter is especially likely if the reports appear a bit exaggerated.

As I noted previously, great care should be taken in disclosing personal information (e.g., life hardships) because doing so may be premature and inappropriate, especially if the information is not directly pertinent to the issues being discussed. For example, a recent applicant disclosed that he had experienced some psychological difficulties and had gone for therapy. He did this apparently in an effort to convey the message that he was open and nondefensive. However, the disclosure was inappropriate and instead raised some concerns about his judgment. The same is true about explaining problems in the record (e.g., weak grades, marginal GRE scores). Placing such experiences in perspective can be very useful, especially if applicants can point to strengths in the record that compensate for the weakness (e.g., strong performance in math and statistics courses that demonstrate that they have the quantitative skills for graduate school despite a marginal score on the quantitative section of the GRE). What is important is to avoid the appearance that one is trying to engender sympathy and to excuse or ignore a significant weakness in one's preparation. It would be better to acknowledge the weakness and to discuss what has been done or is being done to correct it.

Finally, as stated earlier, because graduate admissions interviews should be considered opportunities for mutual evaluation, applicants should take full advantage of this opportunity to get as much information about the program as possible. Remember, graduate education is an arduous process that requires complete dedication. Therefore, you want to make sure that you go to a program that will prepare you for your future career in a climate that is as supportive as possible.

I have shared some thoughts about coping with the challenge of graduate admissions interviews, and I hope that these thoughts will prove helpful to you as you prepare for the graduate school admissions process.

Amanda C. Kracen

Fielding Offers and Making a Final Decision

8

From: Sycamore, IL

Area of study: Counseling Psychology, Virginia Commonwealth University, Richmond

Previous degree(s): BA in sociology from Brown University, Providence, RI

Career before graduate school: Public relations executive; small business owner; researcher in a university counseling service

Number of graduate schools applied to: 12

Age when started this graduate program: 27

Professional interests: Health psychology, behavioral medicine, group therapy, and international psychology

Career aspirations: Academic position that involves research, clinical work, teaching, and mentoring

lthough the shortest path anywhere is a straight line, my path to discovering psychology resembles the spiral of an ice cream cone . . . literally. After graduating from Brown University in 1998, I was certain that some day my studies would continue, but only after clarifying my interests. As I was unsure of a satisfying occupation, I decided instead to pursue a challenge. I moved to Ireland and started the country's first homemade ice cream business. With much hard work, I made the company profitable and expansion was the next step. However, I missed academic intellectual stimulation and working with people. I sold the business, began taking university night classes in psychology, and looked for a job. I was delighted to be hired for a research position in the Student Counseling Service at Trinity College, Dublin. It has been an amazing experience that has helped me realize my wish to study and train to become a counseling psychologist.

This paragraph was the opening of my personal statement for the 12 graduate schools to which I applied. I hoped to distinguish myself from the hundreds of other applicants who were competing for coveted graduate school slots. Therefore, in the rest of the essay, I shared my unusual history, explaining how the skills that I had learned in the ice cream industry could be used in academia. I sought to convince application committee members that I could be a successful graduate student.

Although the essay was definitely not flawless, I think it left an impression. When I spoke with interviewers during the application process, they remembered me as the "ice cream woman." I stood out in their minds, amid the stacks of applications they received. Once the admissions process was over, I was very grateful to have been accepted to five doctoral programs. I share these details to give you the context in which I made a final choice of graduate school. Because each program was unique and located in different states across the United States, the decision was difficult.

You may also face tough but exciting choices in your graduate school search. You might wonder exactly how to make such a momentous decision and how to seal the deal. Therefore, in this chapter, I review how offers are extended and suggest factors to consider when evaluating programs. I highlight the importance of talking with other people during the decision-making process and share recommendations about how to accept and decline offers. In addition, I walk you through my decision-making process. Although my approach was definitely not the only way, and the information presented here is not absolute or appropriate for every individual, I think it can be helpful to see how someone else navigated the major steps of the process. I hope this chapter will help you accept an offer at a graduate school that is the best "fit" for you.

I never took a psychology class as an undergraduate student at Brown University. Brown allows students to develop their own curriculum with no required classes outside the chosen *concentration* (Brown's term for one's major)—a policy that is both a blessing and a curse. In my first semester, I enrolled in a sociology class entitled Perceptions of Mental Illness. I decided to major in sociology after enjoying this one class, and I felt good that I, a naive student, had discovered my destiny: to be a sociologist. In hindsight, I realize that I should have explored more options before quickly committing to a concentration; I especially wish I had taken Psychology 101. I like to believe that there are only a few students who know what career they want when they enter college; the rest of us have to cope with ambiguity. If you are still searching and considering psychology as a career, please do not feel weighed down by uncertainty: instead, try reframing this mind-set as a strength: You are open to life and the many options it presents to you. Just as it took me and Dr. Baumeister (who penned the essay at the end of this chapter) a few years to "find" psychology, you too might slowly discover your occupational interests.

Although I enjoyed my sociology studies in college, I always felt that the classes and research were too removed from the people we studied. I was not passionate about continuing in the field, so I discontinued my studies after graduation. However, I experienced that common malaise that seems to affect many of us college graduates: having no clue about what I wanted to do for the rest of my life. Therefore, as I described in my application essay, I decided to pursue a challenge that seemed much more fun and meaningful than taking one of the well-paying but soul-numbing consulting jobs for which I had interviewed. Therefore, after college graduation, I returned to Ireland, the country where I studied abroad during junior year, where I had many friends, where I had fallen in love with my now-husband, and where there was no homemade ice cream!

To condense a long story of the trials and tribulations of opening an ice cream business, let me just say that I opened a company and was able to make good ice cream thanks to the great Irish dairy products that are available (and yes, I did make a Guinness flavor). However, a few years into business, I was unsatisfied. I was spending 70+ hours a week making ice cream, delivering it in a little truck, and sending and paying invoices. It was a lonely gig. I missed working with people, and this realization came about one night in an "aha" moment. I was at an Irish friend's wedding and spent much of the night chatting with her work colleagues. They were a lovely bunch of social workers, and I found myself asking numerous questions about their jobs and clients. I was fascinated; something clicked inside me. As I headed home to the bed-and-breakfast in the early hours of the morning, I remember saying, "Right, it's time to make a change. I want to be a social worker."

Now, I actually did not want to be a social worker, but this epiphany was the impetus to begin looking into related careers, particularly psychology. I spent the next 3 years researching degrees and careers in psychology, taking night classes in psychology, bombarding the few psychologists I knew in Ireland with countless questions, and wishing I had a book like this one. During this time, I also was fortunate to have someone purchase my business and even luckier to be hired at the Student Counseling Service at Trinity College, Dublin, to do research about college student suicide. Although I wanted to get on with my life and attend graduate school immediately, I realized how competitive the application process was, so I spent those years getting as much experience as possible to bolster my application. I wanted to be a strong candidate when I applied.

When I sent in my applications, I truly believed it was a long shot for me to get accepted into even one graduate program, especially because I was applying from abroad and did not understand the intricacies of the application process. I was pleased to be accepted at a handful of programs and to have the opportunity to choose among graduate schools. As I said, these decisions were difficult. Thus, let me share more information with you about fielding offers and making a final decision and, I hope, demystify the process so that you can make informed choices when it's your turn to decide.

Relevant Deadlines

Before I go further, let me provide a brief overview of the psychology graduate application process as it relates to getting offers and making a final decision. Most programs have application deadlines between November 1 and March 1. Once applications arrive, they are evaluated by applications committees. Interviews are usually held, and then offers are made to chosen applicants. Programs often extend offers to top applicants as soon as possible; admissions committees are aware that people apply to many programs and impressive applicants will most likely be in demand at multiple schools. Thus, it is in a program's best interest to make offers as early as possible.

It is important to know that once offers are made most graduate programs do not require a final decision from applicants until April 15. This deadline exists to ensure that applicants are not pressured into making hasty or premature decisions. As an applicant, you must realize that the deadline exists to protect your decision-making process and give you time to consider your options. Nevertheless, it is important that you respect the April 15 deadline. In addition, for each offer that an applicant sits on, there is a spot that cannot be offered to someone else. For more information about considering offers, you might want to check out the American Psychological Association's Rules for Acceptance of Offers for Admission and Financial Aid (see http://www.apa.org/ed/accept.html).

Receiving Offers

To give you more insight into the practicalities of how offers are made, accepted, and declined, let me explain how the process went for me. After doing my first interview by phone with a professor at a large university one January evening, I was shocked to receive an offer early the next morning via e-mail. I later learned that such a prompt offer is unusual, but that's what happened. I was excited; after months of worrying about getting declined at all schools, with this offer, I was at least assured of attending graduate school. After celebrating, I started to wonder whether I really wanted to enroll at that school. Because of the rural location, it had always been a second-tier option for me. However, I was definitely going to hang on to the acceptance until I heard from other programs. After I received a few "encouraging" (read: pressuring) e-mails from the professor to accept her offer, I e-mailed her, saying, "I am delighted to have received the offer because I am very interested in the program, but as it is early in the decision-making process, I need to hear from other schools before making a final decision." I was deliberately polite and positive, because if I were not accepted elsewhere, she would be my new advisor. However, I was firm when I stated that I needed a bit of time to evaluate my needs.

Between late January and mid April, I was contacted by other graduate programs, conducted numerous phone interviews, interviewed in person at one school, and heard the outcomes regarding my applications. I usually was notified regarding acceptance or rejection by the director of the program or the staff member in charge of organizing the applicant search. The process varied a great deal among university programs as to how and when I received information. Sometimes I was e-mailed, other times I received a phone call, and my rejections were typically letters sent in the mail. The timing differed quite a bit. The first offer of acceptance I received was an aberration. It was more common to be notified of the outcome via e-mail or phone a few days or weeks after the interview and then to have the electronic or verbal offer followed by a formal letter in the mail.

As soon as I was notified that I was accepted into a program, I immediately e-mailed the person who contacted me. Figure 8.1 is an example of an e-mail that I sent. I believe this is a good opportunity to acknowledge the offer and express your enthusiasm for the program. In addition, if you have been accepted to other programs, this is a tactful way to share this information with a program. It may help to let programs know that you are in demand. In any communication, be genuine. If you are quite certain you will not accept the offer, avoid gushing about the program. However, if you are considering the university as a viable option, share your excitement. In addition, I think it helps to let them know that you will get back to them with an answer in a timely manner.

Declining Offers

As you are accepted into or rejected by programs, it is helpful to constantly reevaluate your situation. If you have been accepted to at least

FIGURE 8.1

Dear Dr. Gimon:

I am thrilled to hear that I have been offered a position in the counseling psychology graduate program at First Choice University. It has always been a top choice because I have been very impressed with the program and the faculty. I plan to speak with some of your current students and gather more information. I have been accepted to a few other programs, so I need some time to consider my options and make a final decision. I will get back to you as soon as possible.

Thanks again for notifying me with this great news.

Kind regards,

Amanda C. Kracen

Sample e-mail for accepting an offer.

one of your first-tier programs, then you may want to decline offers from the programs you have designated as second-tier choices. When considering your options, always put your needs first, because you deserve the time and space to make this important decision. However, if you know you definitely will not attend a school, it is important to decline as soon as possible so the admissions committee can extend an offer to another applicant.

I believe that declining an offer is a privilege and requires some thought. It can be done numerous ways, but I think it is best to do it in writing, and because time is an issue, e-mail is the quickest option. It is critical to remember that the people you are responding to have offered you a coveted position in their program. In addition, people on the admissions committee may be potential bosses, colleagues, or supervisors whom you may encounter in the future. The psychology community is surprisingly small, so it helps to be professional and maintain relationships. Therefore, before declining an offer, I drafted a standard e-mail (see Figure 8.2), put it aside, and revised it the following day after thinking about what I had written. I suggest responding directly to the person who extended the offer to you and, if applicable to your situation, copying the professor with whom you may have been matched. In addition, I suggest that you print a copy of the e-mail to keep for your files.

FIGURE 8.2

Dear Dr. Deller:

Thank you for your recent offer to join the counseling psychology program at Second Choice University. I have been impressed with the program and enjoyed talking with Drs. Premkumar and Ufferman. I spoke with a few students, specifically Emma, Roberta, and Neha, and they had very positive things to say about their experiences. It has been a difficult decision for me, but I have decided not to accept the position at Second Choice University.

Thanks so much for your kindness and support throughout the application process. I hope our paths cross in the future, possibly at a conference or other professional event. Thanks again.

Kind regards,

Amanda C. Kracen

Sample e-mail for declining an offer.

Declining Interviews

One quick note before moving on: In addition to declining a slot in graduate school, you may also be in a position in which you might consider turning down an invitation to interview at a school. There are many reasons you may do so. Perhaps you've decided the school isn't a good fit, or you've already been accepted at a top-choice school. I was fortunate to be accepted into my top-choice school quite early in the process, so I declined interviews with a few schools that were second-tier options. If you are in a similar situation, I suggest formally declining in writing (e.g., via e-mail) in a courteous and professional manner.

Decision Time

Before commencing your decision making, you may want to touch base once again with each graduate program that you are considering. Although you do not want to inundate them with e-mails or phone calls, I think admissions committees appreciate knowing where applicants are in their decision-making processes. This can also be a good opportunity to ask any last questions that will inform your decisions. Therefore, in early to mid March, I once again e-mailed the contact person at each school. I reiterated that I was seriously considering the program and weighing my options among three schools. I gave them a general time frame for my decision, saying that I would get back to them within 2 weeks.

It was decision time for me. My choice came down to three schools, each with different qualities. I was thrilled with the realization that my dream of attending graduate school in psychology was coming true, and it was exciting to think that within a year, I would be at one of the three universities. I also felt some anxiety because this was a momentous decision. It was time for me to reevaluate my priorities and consult with others—steps that I highly recommend you take as well.

Pros and Cons

Making a final decision about graduate school is an individual process. However, in questioning a few graduate school classmates, I found that most of us resorted to the old pros and cons list. See Table 8.1 (pp. 182–183) for a list of the major factors that I considered and evaluated. Let me emphasize that I am including this list as an example to give readers insight into my decision-making process. I am not suggesting that these factors are better than others. A pros and cons list will vary for every person because of individual values and circumstances. I do suggest developing your own list, as it is a very helpful exercise.

As you can see, certain factors were important to me: academic issues, fit with advisor, job possibilities for my husband, people at the university, the financial package, location, and the weather. Because I was returning to education at the age of 27 and had a partner, quality of life in general was important to me. I suggest being very honest with yourself and evaluating your priorities. What do you want from life and from your graduate school experience? What are you willing to sacrifice to attend school? You will be spending several years (2–5 or more) at the university, so think realistically about what factors will make you happy. I believe that you are more likely to succeed as a graduate student if you are content with other aspects in your life. Exhibit 8.1 lists some factors you might consider.

Talking With Others

If you have a partner (or loved one) who will be affected by your decision or who is planning to move with you, I highly recommend includ-

---

EXHIBIT 8.1

Factors to Consider When Evaluating Graduate Programs

University: size, location, reputation, resources available

Location: urban/rural, weather, proximity to family and friends, geographic location

Program:
   General: number of credits or hours required for degree, number of students, diversity of students and faculty, flexibility in the program for personal interests, number of faculty with similar interests
   Specific to clinical, counseling, and school applicants: accreditation by the American Psychological Association or the Canadian Psychological Association, balance of research and practice training, theoretical orientation, typical practicum sites, rates of students who secure preferred internship sites

Advisor: academic interests, stage of career, publication record, grant funding, personal style, interest in mentoring, mentoring style, opinions of current students

Finances: assistantship and fellowship availability, number of work hours required to receive tuition remission, in/out-of-state tuition costs, cost of living in the area

---

ing him or her in your decision-making process. Not only will you learn about your partner's priorities, but you can incorporate these needs in your decision. As a newly married woman who was asking her Irish husband to move to the United States for the first time, I saw my husband's needs as being very important. I actively involved him in discussions regarding the universities; we constantly talked through the benefits and drawbacks of each school. For instance, although he encouraged me to make the final decision about which program to select, he definitely preferred to live on the East Coast. He liked the idea that with fewer airplane transfers it would be easier for us to return to Ireland and more convenient for family and friends to visit us. Now, a few years later, I can report that our choice in cities has been very popular with family and friends. We joke that we ought to hang a bed-and-breakfast shingle, as we have been pleasantly inundated with visitors.

   In addition to my husband, I also consulted with other people about my decision, including my parents, mentors, and current students at the three schools I was considering. I talked with them at length, using them as a sounding board to help clarify my priorities. When you are at this point, you are making a big decision—where to live and study for the next few years—so I suggest not taking it lightly. Do your research about

T A B L E   8 . 1

Factors I Considered for My Top Three Choices for Graduate School

Factors I Considered	School A (VCU)[a]	School B[b]	School C[a]
Academic issues	Counseling psychology program is located in the psychology department. Program has a strong health psychology emphasis. Accessible to a nearby medical school for potential research and clinical opportunities. Have never heard of the university until now?!	Counseling psychology program is located in the education department. No medical school, which might limit my research opportunities. Big program with many graduate students— could be good or bad?!	Counseling psychology program is located in the education department. Medical school is located in another city, which might limit my research opportunities. Well-known university
Fit with advisor	Impressed with and really liked my potential advisor. Potential advisor is a health psychologist with a strong history of grant funding. Potential advisor has joint appointments in psychology department and at the teaching hospital, which probably means greater access to health research but also that she will be extra busy. Potential advisor's current students are very enthusiastic about working with her.	My potential advisor seems kind but somewhat dry. Potential advisor is a well-known psychologist. Potential advisor has a strong history of grant funding.	My potential advisor seems like a lovely woman. Potential advisor's research interests do not exactly fit with my interests. Potential advisor's current students are very enthusiastic about working with her.

Job possibilities for husband	Favorable	Not great	Decent
Other people	I'm impressed with the program director and the two other faculty members with whom I talked— all very encouraging and supportive. Most faculty have some health psychology interests. Students are friendly and happy to answer all my questions.	I'm impressed with the five faculty members I met. I like the diversity of the grad students. I met a current graduate student at a conference who raves about the program and opportunities.	Although I did not speak with them, a few other faculty members do research that interests me. Students are friendly and happy to answer all my questions.
Finances	Low cost of living in the area Adequate assistantship ($10,000), with the possibility of being awarded a fellowship for 1st year ($13,000).	Low cost of living in the area Program is unsure of financial support that will be available.	Moderate cost of living in the area Best stipend ($16,000) Assured an assistantship in 1st year; however, I must secure my own assistantship in later years.
Location	Located in Richmond, and I've always wanted to live in the South. Located on the East Coast, which is near my sister and friends.	Located 2 hours from my mother's home. Best friend lives in the city. The city is comfortable and convenient.	Located in a city with a great reputation, but far from family and friends.
Weather	Seasonal but without extremes	Warm and dry	Warm and dry

Note. VCU = Virginia Commonwealth University.
[a]phone interview. [b]in-person interview.

all aspects of the school and get a sense of what your life will be like there. I found that current graduate students at the school are a superb resource. If you can, go visit and stay with a student. If not, arrange a phone chat with at least one graduate student, ideally someone who works with your potential advisor. Draw up a list of questions you may have and ask the student's opinion. In addition to asking questions about the school and the program, do not forget to ask about the city, neighborhoods where students tend to live, cost of living, students' social lives, and whether there are any online resources (e.g., local newspapers). In addition to graduate students, electronic mailing lists are useful for seeking ideas and opinions to help you evaluate your choices. You can develop and expand personal contacts via e-mail, but just make sure to seek e-lists that are managed by responsible parties (see Recommended Resources at the end of this volume).

Making My Decision

When applying to schools, I always had a top-ranked program as my dream school (School B on my list). It was located in the same state in which my mother resides, and after living in Ireland, I really wanted to live near my family. However, after doing my interviews, I was more impressed with Virginia Commonwealth University (VCU; School A on my list), a school that I had not seriously considered previously. However, it seemed to have nearly everything I wanted. I was very impressed with my potential advisor's research and qualifications; plus, she was warm and personable during my phone interview. Although it was not feasible to fly from Ireland to meet her in person, I felt that we fit well together. I also had good phone conversations with two graduate students and three other faculty members. In fact, if the relationship did not work out with my future advisor for any reason, I felt like I would enjoy working with the other faculty members as well. This is an important consideration, because as Dr. Baumeister points out in his essay, faculty members can change jobs and institutions. I am glad I considered this because my beloved advisor passed away unexpectedly in my 2nd year of graduate school. I had to select a new advisor in the program; I now work with one of the faculty members with whom I talked during the decision-making process.

In drawing up my list, VCU seemed to have the most positive qualities of the three schools. However, I was not yet convinced, so I bought a travel guide to Virginia. I read it from cover to cover and got excited. Although we had never visited, Richmond seemed like a good place to call home for the next 5 years. My gut was saying "VCU is the place for me." However, I needed to deal with one hang-up that I had: I had never heard of VCU until I began researching graduate schools!

Thoughts on Reputation

I am going to be honest here and admit my naive snobbishness because I think this is a common issue for many applicants (Dr. Baumeister also addresses the issue of reputation in his essay). I attended public school through high school and had always dreamed of going to an Ivy League university; my dream school was Brown. I was fortunate to be accepted and able to enroll. In addition to the stellar education I received, attending such a reputable school with a strong alumni association has since presented me with many opportunities. Therefore, when I began researching psychology graduate programs, I immediately looked at the universities with big reputations (e.g., Brown, Harvard, Yale, Stanford). However, most of them did not have the type of psychology program that I wanted: a counseling program with equal emphases on research and clinical training. In fact, most of the psychology programs that interested me were not at smaller, private schools but rather at large state schools. This required a major shift in my thinking.

It took a long time for me to realize what I now understand fully. Earning a graduate degree is a much different ballgame than is getting an undergraduate degree. You have to weigh the importance of the school's reputation with the other opportunities available to you at a school, such as working with a specific faculty member, pursuing a unique area of study, or engaging in a distinctive clinical training experience. At research-oriented programs, it is essential to consider the mentor who you will be working with while in graduate school because it is equally, if not more, important than the university you attend. Please read the previous sentence again and once again, because it is crucial!

I struggled with accepting an offer from a university that neither I nor my family and friends had ever heard of before my graduate school search. Ever the nerd, I investigated the university. I read everything I could about its history, scrutinized the university president's long-term goals for the institution, and checked rates of publication by members of the psychology department. I was reassured by everything I discovered. More important, my future advisor was very well respected in her field and had significant grant funding and connections with major research institutions. I decided that it was more important for me to get a good education that would be recognized within the field of psychology than worry about the "wow" factor of the university's name.

Accepting an Offer

With my internal struggle resolved, I decided to accept my place at VCU. I believe that, as with a job, a window of opportunity exists between the time you are offered a position by a university and the moment you accept. This is your one chance to *possibly* negotiate any perks. These extras could be related to finances, working with a specific faculty member, getting a specific assistantship, and so on. That said, be aware that many psychology programs either cannot or will not grant specific requests. However, I think that it never hurts to ask, if you can do it professionally and tactfully, so before accepting the offer from VCU, I e-mailed my future advisor and said that I was planning on accepting their offer but was concerned about the finances. I explained honestly that another school was offering more funding and asked whether VCU could add any more money to my offer. Unfortunately, she politely responded by saying, "Nope, we have nothing else to offer" but that as my advisor she would work with me to pursue additional funding in the future.

Nevertheless, I was glad that I asked. First, this was the only opportunity that I had to ask. I would have regretted passing it by if, when attending graduate school, I heard that another student was receiving more funding just because she had had the courage to ask. Second, it communicated to my future advisor that finances are a concern for me and I would like to be considered for funding if available. My tale has a happy ending. Out of the blue, 2 months later, I was notified that I had received a fellowship that provided me with more funding and relieved me of having to take on a 20-hour-per-week assistantship. I wonder whether part of the reason I was considered for the fellowship was because I pushed the envelope a bit.

I finally accepted my place at VCU via e-mail. I wrote an e-mail expressing my enthusiasm for joining the program and asking about the next steps in the acceptance process. I sent the e-mail to the program director, because she had extended the offer, and I copied my future advisor and the program administrator. I waited until I received written confirmation from the program director before declining offers from the other two universities that I was considering. I highly recommend waiting to receive this confirmation in writing before declining other schools, just in case there is a mix-up or some unforeseen snafu.

Before I move on, let me just say a quick word here about accepting an offer at a graduate school program. Unless extreme circumstances exist, I suggest that you do not change your mind once you have accepted a place. Not only is this annoying and frustrating for folks at the graduate program, but it is unprofessional. I have also heard from professors that it can affect your reputation and hamper your chances of getting in elsewhere.

Celebrating and Thanking Others

I was finally going to graduate school—and I knew where I would be living! After the ambiguity of the previous few months—not knowing whether and where my new life was to begin—I finally had the answers. And I really was going to become a psychologist. After 3 years of dreaming, it felt so satisfying to have some answers.

My next piece of advice is the easiest to follow: Celebrate! When you have made a final decision and accepted a place in a graduate program, you have successfully completed a very difficult process. Therefore, it is time to enjoy yourself. Interpret this advice however you want, but just do something that is fun for you! On the day I accepted my offer, I shared my news with friends and invited them out for a night on the town. During the previous few months, my husband and friends had put up with me as I plodded through application forms, discussed the pros and cons of every decision, and waited anxiously for the application process to conclude. It was only fitting to celebrate with them.

Regardless of what your final decision is, I highly recommend that you acknowledge the people who helped you throughout the process. Most will probably appreciate hearing your news and receiving your thanks. I contacted everyone (e.g., professors, bosses, mentors) who had been involved in helping me apply to graduate schools. I shared the news that I was going to attend VCU and thanked them for their assistance and support.

Conclusion

I hope this chapter helps you consider the intricacies of fielding offers from graduate programs and sheds light on how to make a final decision. To recap, in this chapter I shared how offers are often extended to applicants and suggested issues to consider when evaluating programs. I also encouraged you to talk with other people as you make decisions and provided tips for accepting and declining offers. I drew on my experience of making a final decision among graduate programs to illuminate how one might navigate the major steps of the decision-making process. That said, please let me reiterate that my path and process is not the right or ideal way of making a decision, it was just my way. What I hope is that by reading this chapter you come away feeling more empowered to make informed choices and ultimately select a graduate school that is a good fit for you.

I wish you all the best in your decision-making process. Although selecting a school may be stressful and overwhelming, be grateful if you have a choice to make. Many other well-qualified applicants will be disappointed not to get into graduate school, so please always remember how lucky we are to have the decisions to make. I suggest doing as much research as you possibly can and then listening to your heart. Wishing you the luck of the Irish (in Gaelic) with your graduate school decisions and future study, ádh mór ort!

Practical Tips

1. **Plan ahead.** Consider your long-term plans before submitting applications. Do you want to do extensive international traveling, have kids, or realize some other goal before graduate school, or are you willing to wait until after you graduate? Although any of these can be done while in school, you will be pretty busy, and faculty sometimes frown on students diverting their attention from academic and professional activities.

2. **Be professional.** Above all else, remember that graduate school in psychology is a professional endeavor; therefore, develop and maintain a professional identity throughout the application process. Each and every interaction that you have with people impacts their perception of you; thus, demonstrate that you are professional.

3. **Enjoy the entire application process.** Think of it as a game, albeit a serious one, with strategies and rules. Then play to win. I truly enjoyed the process once I framed it this way.

4. **Two heads are better than one.** Find one or two good mentors (e.g., professors, graduate students) and avail yourself of their wisdom during the application process. Bounce ideas off of them, ask them to read over essays, and so on; just be sure to do it politely and at a time that is convenient for them. Also, thank them for their help by sending them a handwritten note, gift certificate for a bookstore, or some other small token of appreciation.

5. **Market yourself aggressively.** Be careful to walk the line between being assertive and sounding obnoxious, but do not be afraid to state *why* you are an ideal candidate for admission to a graduate program.

6. **Be true to yourself in interviews.** Women, wear that engagement ring; men, keep the ponytail. At the same time, do give some thought as to how the individuals on the application committee may perceive you.

7. **Understand the costs involved at each program.** Before you accept an offer, ask detailed questions about funding sources and tuition requirements, particularly if state residency issues are relevant. I wish I had asked more of these questions.

Essay 8
Making Decisions: My
Reflections on Graduate
School and Career Choices
Roy F. Baumeister

I love my career. There's nothing in the world as interesting as people, and I get to spend most of my workday observing people, thinking about them, and testing the theories about people to find out which ones are correct. Reading the social psychology literature offers new insights about why people do the sometimes sensible and sometimes crazy things they do. My appreciation of movies, sports, and reality shows on television is enriched by what psychology has taught me about people. Knowledge of social psychology even sometimes comes in handy for understanding my friends, colleagues, and loved ones.

I didn't always love psychology this much. It is something of an accident that I am in this field at all. I went to Princeton intending to be a math major because I had been good at math in high school. When higher math turned out to be increasingly weird and boring, I decided that philosophy would be the right field for studying the ultimate questions about human meaning and life. When my parents refused to pay for a philosophy education, saying (with some justification) that it was a field with very few jobs and low-paying ones at that, I considered several other possible occupations, such as being a lawyer.

I settled on psychology partly because it seemed to promise an exciting way to resolve some of the philosophical questions that had interested me. For example, philosophers debate what is right and wrong. They have no solid way of agreeing on an answer. I remember being excited to read Freud's approach. He rejected the philosophical approach of analyzing the concepts of right and wrong from the lofty heights of spiritual wisdom and logical reasoning. Instead, he said, let's look at how ordinary people actually learn their concepts of right and wrong, and let's look at how these concepts actually emerged in human history. The idea that we could observe people and use those observations to test our theories, thereby confirming some and rejecting others, seemed a welcome improvement over the endless conceptual debates in philosophy.

Even so, my entry into psychology was not entirely auspicious. I recall my father's first reaction when I suggested that I would major in psychology: "You'd be wasting your brain," he said firmly. He thought no intelligent person should go into such a mess of a field. But then he checked into it. As it happened, there were some psychologists working at the same company he did who earned a higher salary than he, which to him was the ultimate test of whether a certain career was a good idea. And so he somewhat reluctantly agreed to pay my tuition as a psychology major.

I had spent my 2nd year of college in foreign study in Germany. I returned to Princeton for my 3rd year, having declared myself a psychology major without ever having taken an actual psychology course. In Germany, which featured a different education system, I had taken no tests and gotten no grades, but I knew that graduate school was a must for a psychology career, and I had to buckle down and get good grades. This was a period (the early 1970s) when psychology enrollments were rising rapidly, and competition for spots in graduate school was very tough.

Most of the people I met in psychology classes wanted to go into clinical psychology. I thought I did too. After all, Freud had been my initial inspiration, so I thought I should pursue a career like his. The professors told us that getting into graduate school in clinical psychology would be very difficult—often 700 applicants competed for four to six openings. Not liking those odds, I cast about for an alternative, and a couple inspiring professors turned me on to social psychology. I was really more interested in ideas than in treating people with mental illness anyhow (as was Freud!), so research sounded good.

Applying to graduate school was a strange experience. The odds of acceptance were much better in social psychology than in clinical (although this may not be as true nowadays). Several of my close friends applied to two or three dozen clinical programs and went through a long depressing season of being rejected by one after another (in some cases, by all of them). I applied to only seven social psychology programs and was accepted by all of them. I felt I had to keep my good news a secret because of the contrast with my friends' disappointments.

I've heard that many students with multiple offers choose their schools on the basis of which one offers them the most financial aid. I knew early on that this is a mistake, unless perhaps the differences are extreme. For one thing, the cost of living can be very different in different places; you can probably afford a nicer apartment and life in many small university towns than in New York or Los Angeles, even if the stipend is higher in those big cities. Even more important, a couple thousand dollars one way or another is trivial in the long run. What matters is to find a place where you will like your work (including liking the faculty and students you will work with) and where you can be productive. The only case in which I would recommend choosing on the basis of money is if you are deciding between a program that would require you to incur a large debt and a program for which you would not have to borrow much (or any) money. Leaving graduate school with a huge debt that will take a decade to pay off will put a crimp in your life afterward, especially if you have an alternative offer that will let you start your postgraduate-school life without such a debt. I had to live very cheaply in graduate school, but I was happy to start my job as a professor with no debts to pay.

For me, the big issue in my decision about graduate school was choosing between the person and the institution. I had several good offers. Was it more important to have a famous university name or a famous professor's name? I heard differing opinions. The issue was further complicated by the fact that some universities were known to have a great psychology department but others had a better overall university name. For example, most educated people all over the world respect the Ivy League universities, but not all of those schools will necessarily be top-notch in your specialty at all times. Other universities might have a better psychology department at the time but not have the great name.

Almost everyone told me it is important to consider who your advisor will be. This is tricky too, though, because people can move around. So you might choose a graduate program to work with Dr. Wonderful, only to find that Dr. Wonderful soon gets an attractive offer from another university and leaves. If you want to work with a particular advisor, ask him or her what would happen to you if a better job offer came along.

I didn't ask this question, but I should have. I went to Duke University, which seemed to have the right mix of a good social psychology program, a nice place to live, a well-respected university name (though turning down offers from Harvard and Yale still made me squirm), and the rest. Two famous social psychologists were on the faculty there. During my 1st year, one of them (i.e., Jack Brehm) accepted an offer elsewhere and left. During my 2nd year, the other one (i.e., Edward E. Jones, my advisor) told me he also would be leaving. Fortunately, he took me along (back to Princeton, as it happened), or else I would have been left in a program without any major social psychologists.

Working with a famous person in the field had costs and benefits too. On the plus side, Jones knew how to do experiments and publish research, and although we certainly had to battle with some rejections, he was able to teach me how to do the work and play the game. On the minus side, he no longer felt he had much to prove, and so he was content to work at a slow, thoughtful pace, which meant we did not get as many studies done or papers published as I would have liked. If you want to achieve a lot in graduate school, find a professor who is publishing at least half a dozen papers every year.

After graduate school, my association with the great man continued to have an effect. It is hard for young professors to get anyone to pay attention to their work, but having been Jones's student helped prompt people to give me a second look. For some of my peers, these effects were substantial. Every few years, Jones would decide that one of his current graduate students was the best student he ever had, and he would write great recommendation letters and do other things to promote that student's career. Having a famous person promote you in this way is a terrific boost. Unfortunately for me, I wasn't one of Jones's chosen favorites, and I think the fact that he was calling attention to other students reflected badly on me and possibly even made it more difficult for me to earn respect in the field. Later, as I started to do well on my own, he began to show more interest in me, but tragically he died from a heart attack while still in his mid-60s. His fame and influence live on, but I do occasionally regret that I didn't get the chance to show him I could be a better psychologist than he had seemed to think.

Where you went to graduate school ceases to have much effect on your career after a few years. Thus, there are two and a half main things you want from graduate school, at least if you want an academic career. First, you want to be able to conduct and publish plenty of research, because this is mainly what gets you a job. Second, it's important to work with professors who are either famous and respected or highly productive, because their recommendations will carry more weight. The half is to have some courses, especially in statistics, that will give you the knowledge and skills you will use in your work. I list this as "half" because most programs offer something along those lines, and no academic jobs will ask you what courses you took in graduate school.

Choosing a graduate school is a tough and momentous decision. These days I spend a fair amount of time and energy on the other side of the issue, that is, deciding which of the many interesting applicants should receive offers of admission. One thing remains the same: Not enough information is readily available to assist prospective graduate students in making wise, correct choices. But knowing what to look for and what questions to ask can help you make a more informed decision. There will often be unforeseen consequences or aspects. But that is part of what makes life interesting. Enjoy the process!

Frank J. Corigliano

What Happens If . . . : Alternatives for Unsuccessful Applicants

9

From: Bradenton, FL

Area of study: Clinical Psychology, St. John's University, New York, NY

Previous degree(s): BA in psychology from Baruch College, City University of New York, New York, NY; MA in psychology and education from Teachers College, Columbia University, New York, NY

Career before graduate school: International travel consultant

Number of graduate schools applied to: First time—15, second time—12

Age when started this graduate program: 32

Professional interests: The media and body image in males, body image and relationships, same-sex couples and depression, implicit discrimination toward older adults

Career aspirations: Blending clinical, teaching, and research components of past training

R ejection can be difficult. Rejection, in one form or another, is commonly experienced in graduate school and can feel particularly painful. However, rejection sometimes provides an opportunity for our greatest development. Much like the soreness after an especially challenging workout or fatigue after a comprehensive exam in a difficult course, pain is often a necessary precursor to growth.

I would like to thank all who continue to support and encourage me, especially Roni Beth Tower for her consistent, nurturing, and challenging approach to mentoring.

This chapter is intended primarily for applicants who are not pleased with the outcome of their initial application process. It opens with my story, followed by a brief pep talk.

As a student who was rejected and then successfully repeated the application process, I have much to share. After the pep talk, I discuss developing a plan for the future. I also suggest ways to evaluate your strengths and weaknesses and help you decide whether to reapply to graduate school. If you think that you need a new direction, I discuss some alternative paths. Finally, should you choose to reapply, I review ways to improve your application.

I took a nontraditional route to psychology. I was a bookish kid from Florida who, after high school, moved to New York City. I had visions of culture, travel, and a supportive environment for someone like myself. You see, not only was I a bit of a nerd, but I was beginning to discover that I was gay. In New York, I fell in love for the first time, married a man whom I adored, and set off to see the world while working in the travel industry. Fast-forward 10 years, and I was newly single and ready for change. Then I met my second partner. He encouraged me to return to my bookish strengths and attend college. As a first-generation college student, I had few role models who attended college, so I started out slowly. I took a couple of courses at New York University over the summer and discovered that I enjoyed the challenge of returning to school. The following year, I enrolled full-time at Baruch College, City University of New York, and happily studied psychology.

While an undergraduate student, I was a practicum student at Bellevue Hospital Center, one of the country's premier psychiatric facilities. This practicum inspired me to pursue a career in the field of psychology. I decided that, after earning my BA, I would apply to doctoral programs in clinical psychology. To stand out in this highly competitive applicant pool I wanted to do something that would help to distinguish me as a serious academic. To this end, I applied to and was accepted to study abroad for a semester at Hertford College, Oxford University. After returning from England, I graduated from Baruch with an undergraduate degree in psychology and a minor in business.

Although my path may seem like a privileged journey, I had many obstacles to overcome. I often felt I was taking a great risk by spending so much time and money on my education, which was funded largely with student loans. However, I was investing in my career and future, which Dr. Prochaska, in his essay at the end of this chapter, encourages us to do when we are not fulfilled. Toward the end of my time as an undergraduate, I was in high spirits, having discovered psychology as a passion. Looking ahead, I worried that the graduate school application process was going to be a formidable challenge.

I wanted to attend a clinical psychology PhD program, but knowing they are generally the most competitive programs, I was uncertain whether I would get in, especially on my first attempt. Some of these programs receive as many as 350 applications for a mere 6 to 12 slots. So to cover my bases, I applied to a range of programs, such as PhD, PsyD, and terminal master's programs at public and private universities. I also applied to "reach" and "safety" programs. I was offered admission into several MA programs, a PsyD program, and a PhD program. I was thrilled to receive these offers. However, I was not accepted to my top choice— one of the very few clinical psychology PhD programs in New York City. I decided to accept an offer to earn a terminal master's degree at Teachers College, Columbia University, and subsequently reapply to doctoral programs. Similar to Dr. Prochaska's taking one step back to take two steps forward, I took one step to the side. I made use of this time at Columbia to bolster my strengths and address my weaknesses as an applicant. After improving my application, I reapplied and accepted an offer to pursue a doctorate at my top choice: St. John's University. As someone who has overcome rejection and setbacks to attain his goals, I share information, thoughts, and encouragement in case you should find yourself in a similar situation.

A Brief Pep Talk

So what does it really mean to be an "unsuccessful applicant"? It may mean not getting any offers the first time around. It may also mean not getting offers from the first-tier schools, not getting into your preferred degree program, or not receiving the financial aid package you need. Whatever your definition, rejection of any application in which you invested a great deal of time, emotion, and money can be very difficult and may shake your confidence. I know that with each rejection, I felt depressed, agitated, and frustrated; it felt like a personal rejection of me, not just my application. If you find yourself in this position, first take a breath. Give yourself credit for all the work you did during the application process. It is important to come to terms with the feelings associated with rejection. Next, I suggest you think of something fun and completely irreverent to do with your rejection letters. You can laminate them like I did—they make great coasters. A colleague of mine compiled her letters into a coffee-table book. It is important to maintain hope and humor. Remember, you still have options. Stay motivated, and get ready for the steps ahead: deciding whether, when, and how you will reapply.

All too often I doubt myself and wonder whether my abilities or my personal resources are sufficient to accomplish a goal. I have come to the realization that at times, yes, I will occasionally fail, sometimes not be perfect, or even need to change direction completely. Although I previously felt paralyzed by the fear of making mistakes, I now see challenges as opportunities for growth and learning. I have developed an attitude that I may fall, but I will fall forward. I had to call on this attitude when I applied to Ivy League universities. As a student from a city university, I believed that getting into an Ivy League graduate program was quite a lofty ambition. Now I recognize that had I not taken the risk of applying, I would not have earned my master's degree from Columbia University or be where I am today. I encourage you to not underestimate what might be waiting for you in your future. Take a chance and leave the results up to the powers that be; don't count yourself out before even trying.

The Reevaluation Period

After being rejected, cursing the very idea of going to graduate school, and making some new laminated coasters, I was ready for the next step: a reevaluation period. During this period, it is necessary to examine how and why you were not successful so you can learn from the experience. You will want to review a number of variables, as I outline later, in an objective manner to accurately assess your suitability for graduate school. Some aspects of an application are under your control and can be improved, whereas other factors are beyond your control. The process of reevaluating yourself is a valuable one that will help you make informed decisions about future plans.

ACKNOWLEDGE EXTERNAL FACTORS

Consider that some things might be beyond your control when applying to graduate school, things that in no way reflect on your qualification as an applicant or a future professional. For instance, you might not be accepted because the professor you want to work with may not be taking a student that year. Or a decline in funding can reduce the number of students who are offered admission to a program. Situations like these may have nothing to do with you but can make or break your chances for acceptance. These factors tend to vary over time, so if possible, do your best to be aware of them before applying by talking with people in the program. Perhaps the next time you apply, circumstances may change and be in your favor.

FIGURE 9.1

Dear Dr. Kim:

Thank you for taking the time to consider my application to the clinical psychology program at First Choice University (FCU). I understand you receive many competitive applications and have limited space for each year's cohort. Although I was not accepted this year, I remain hopeful of attending FCU in the future. With this goal in mind, I would appreciate any feedback you can offer at this time, or I would welcome an opportunity to discuss how I can improve my application.

Best,

Frank J. Corigliano

Sample e-mail for requesting feedback in response to not being accepted to a graduate program.

SEEK FEEDBACK FROM PROGRAMS

It can be difficult to hear your application was less than perfect; however, feedback is generally very helpful. I suggest e-mailing or calling each program to which you were not accepted and inquiring about what you can do to develop a more competitive application. For example, I sent the e-mail in Figure 9.1 to several faculty members at different programs. A few responded and offered useful advice about augmenting my research experience, increasing my Graduate Record Examinations (GRE) scores, and refining my personal statement, all of which I did prior to my second round of applications.

REEVALUATE YOUR STRENGTHS AND WEAKNESSES

Before making major decisions about reapplying to graduate school, conduct a sober review of your application in its entirety. Start with the program requirements such as GRE scores and grade point average, letters of recommendation, and research and clinical experience. Then, take into account the feedback that you received from faculty members. Next, take a long, hard look at the gaps between what they wanted and what your application offered. Once you have identified weaknesses, you can address and improve them. You might consider organizing yourself by creating a table of your strengths and weaknesses. Include a list of program requirements and identify an action for how you might address each weakness. Table 9.1 is an example of such a list.

CONSIDER ALTERNATIVE AVENUES

You may want to explore other academic and career options. First, you may want to look at a broader array of psychology programs, locations, or faculty. You might also think about pursuing a degree in a related field (e.g., MSW, RN, MD) or a different, possibly less competitive degree in psychology. You might investigate careers that are attainable with your current education: Is there a job you are qualified for now that could satisfy your occupational goals? I encourage you to reflect on what you really want for your future, because reapplying to graduate school will likely involve a great deal of work, time, and expense.

Second, you might want to contemplate getting a job. Life experience, especially a position that adds to your research, clinical, teaching, or related skills, can be an asset to your application. Institutions such as universities, hospitals, and community agencies often have openings for people with a bachelor's or master's degree. Jobs such as research assistants or entry-level psychology technicians can place you in the center of the action, preparing you for that next step up the ladder of academia. Furthermore, working at a university can give you exposure to research, faculty, grants, and other inside information that can help you in the future. For instance, a friend who was not accepted into her preferred program worked as a research assistant for a couple of years. She credits the valuable experience as the reason she was successful when she reapplied.

Third, if finances permit, you may want to take time off and maybe even travel. Throughout my life, I've found that traveling helps clear my head. There is nothing like a 6-week trip across the Australian outback to put things into perspective! You could visit or even volunteer in a place where you might want to work someday or that is related to your academic interests. A colleague of mine took a year off after college, lived in Puerto Rico, and learned Spanish. That year was the impetus for her to decide she wanted to work with Spanish-speaking populations and provided her with interesting content for her personal statement.

TALK WITH OTHERS

Do not attempt to do the evaluation process in isolation; you are making major decisions and probably need the perspectives of others. If possible, discuss your thoughts and feelings throughout the reevaluation process with people who can give you constructive feedback. It can help to talk with advisors, graduate students, friends, and family. They can help you

TABLE 9.1

Sample List of Strengths and Weaknesses

Areas	Strengths	Weaknesses	Action (if reapplying)
Undergraduate degree/course work in psychology	Many psychology courses	Never took abnormal and social psychology classes.	Consider taking during the summer.
Research methods/ statistics courses	Got an A in Statistics 101	Few under-graduate statistics courses	Emphasize interest in statistical methods in personal statement; take additional courses in a terminal master's program.
GPA	Very high GPA	No weaknesses in the GPA	Emphasize academic success in personal statement and awards/distinctions earned.
GRE scores	High verbal and quantitative scores	Average analytical writing score	Consider submitting an alternative writing sample.
Clinical experience	Volunteered at crisis hotline	Limited clinical experience	Highlight volunteer work and career goals in personal statement; spend more time volunteering in a clinical setting.
Research experience	Presented posters	No published research	Highlight presentations in personal statement; seek out more research experience with established professor.
Letters of recommendation	Several strong letters	No weaknesses in this area	Keep in touch with letter writers and update them on accomplishments.
Personal statement	Well-written	Lacked detail on research interests	Update and strengthen personal statement; focus research interests.
Personal visit/interview	Experience from applying once already	Tendency to be nervous	Practice mock interviews with friends, professors, and supervisors.

Note. GPA = grade point average; GRE = Graduate Record Examinations.

clarify your goals and future plans. After consulting with others, I realized that many applicants experience rejection; in fact, it is a common outcome of the process. Being reminded of this encouraged me to dedicate the time to bolster my application and reapply.

ADDRESS YOUR APPLICATION WEAKNESSES OR FIND AN ALTERNATE PATH

After getting feedback, objectively evaluating yourself as an applicant, considering alternative options, and talking with others, you need to decide whether you are going to reapply. It is time for soul searching. In my case, I concluded that I wanted to pursue a PhD. I realized I was qualified enough to be admitted to some doctoral programs in clinical psychology, but I still needed to work on a few core areas to be accepted to my top-choice schools. I chose to enroll in a terminal master's program because I knew I would have the opportunity to develop professionally and address the weaknesses in my application.

DEVELOP GOALS

Now that you have made an informed decision about your future plans, it is time for the action stage. Clear and measurable goals can help you be focused and motivated. Whichever path you choose, it helps to list specific actions you can take to improve your situation.

Reapplying to Graduate School

If you are committed to reapplying to graduate school in psychology, I suggest you dedicate yourself to improving your application. Addressing my weaknesses meant retaking the GRE, gaining research and clinical experience, honing my interviewing skills, and editing old personal statements. I was able to do each of these while completing a terminal master's program. I briefly share my experiences to help you think about practical ways to increase the likelihood of being accepted to a graduate program. Of course, tailor these suggestions to your unique situation and goals. For more ideas on strengthening your application, you may also want to reread chapter 6. Also, before moving on I must share that I often found it useful to keep in mind that even psychologists who are leaders in the field (such as Dr. Prochaska) occasionally must overcome barriers in their professional development. If they can do it, so can you; reapplying is just another barrier to overcome.

CONSIDER RETAKING THE GRE

Because GRE scores generally are quite important, allocate resources (i.e., time, money, and energy) to preparing. Think about studying more, or in a different way. I took the GRE a second time and increased my score significantly. However, if you do not think (on the basis of practice tests results) that you can raise your scores substantially by retaking the exams, then you may have reached your ceiling. We all have limitations. Knowing the difference between the things I could change and the things I could not change freed me to focus on the things I could do something about.

On the basis of my experience with the GRE, I offer one hint: If the cost of preparation courses or materials is truly out of your reach, ask for a discount. Because of my financial hardship, Kaplan gave me a generous 50% discount on a test-prep class. Don't forget, it never hurts to ask. And, in general, be resourceful when seeking to enhance your application (e.g., trade services with a friend for tutoring sessions, obtain used test materials online and from friends or the library).

GAIN (MORE) RESEARCH AND CLINICAL EXPERIENCE

Many programs consider research and clinical experiences essential features of a strong application. Even if you are applying to a more practice-oriented program or degree, such as a PsyD or MA, research experience (e.g., working with a research team, presenting at conferences) demonstrates involvement in the scientific process and an ability to think critically. I sought out research experiences during my master's program and gained valuable skills, which I could write about in my personal statement when I reapplied. Similarly, clinical experience, even if you are applying to a more research-oriented program, can inform your understanding of the population you want to research and the variables that should be investigated. Furthermore, it shows that you are interested in people beyond just using them as research participants. Volunteering at an eating disorder unit indicated that I was committed to developing my clinical skills and that I cared about the patients with whom I conducted research.

DEVELOP BETTER INTERVIEWING SKILLS

The field of psychology often requires frequent interviews: We interview for graduate school, externships, internships, and jobs. Therefore, it is critical to polish your interviewing acumen. To improve in this area, I reviewed books on effective interviewing, practiced introducing myself to strangers, and watched a videotape of myself doing mock interviews. Better skills helped me stand out as a confident and well-prepared applicant.

IMPROVE YOUR PERSONAL STATEMENT OR WRITE A NEW ONE

Like your wardrobe, a personal statement must stay fresh and up-to-date. If you are reapplying, you have had at least a year to develop and grow. Therefore, you need to update your old personal statement or write a new one. What have you accomplished since the first time you applied? How are you different from the person whose application was not accepted previously? If you applied to the same program before and were rejected, be sure to let readers on the admissions committee know what you did during the interim to become a stronger applicant.

UPDATE YOUR CURRICULUM VITAE AND LETTERS OF RECOMMENDATION

Before reapplying, don't forget to amend your curriculum vitae (CV) to reflect your latest achievements. In addition, provide this updated CV to your letter writers, either the same people or new ones, so that they can revise and improve your letters of recommendation. If you have taken the time to make yourself a more competitive candidate, you definitely want your strengths communicated in these components of your application.

Conclusion

As I said initially, rejection can be very difficult. However, every setback offers new opportunities to fall forward. I hope you were inspired, or at least encouraged, by my pep talk and my personal experiences to recognize that unsuccessful applicants can often become incredibly successful applicants. I encourage you to use the information I shared in this chapter to find your own path, and I look forward to one day reading *your* success story.

Practical Tips

1. **Be an academic entrepreneur.** My parents did not earn college degrees. They built businesses and fostered an environment in which I learned the importance of creating my own opportunities. I have transferred this mentality to academia, whereby I create opportunities by being independent, assertive, and involved.

2. **Make certain that faculty members know you.** Be sure they know you by name and are aware that you plan to apply to graduate school. If they know you, they are more likely to involve you when opportunities arise (e.g., to work in a lab, to join a project).

3. **Attend psychology conventions.** The American Psychological Association and your state psychological association provide many opportunities, such as conferences, to learn and network with leaders in the field. Also, attending conferences will allow you to see what topics professionals in the field are currently researching, the methods they use, how they recruit populations, and where the research dollars are going.

4. **Join psychology clubs at your school or start your own.** Some friends and I founded a club, PSYCHSoc, with the primary goal of hosting a research conference. The conference was an opportunity to present our research in a peer-reviewed setting and learn from others.

5. **Set priorities.** I found I can do it all, but not all at once! Find a way to balance your responsibilities as you move through your day and your career. At times, I am very busy with research or patients, whereas at other times I am obsessed with writing or submitting proposals to conferences. When you apply to graduate school, juggle the tasks, get them done, and keep your priorities in mind.

6. **Nurture a supportive network.** Years of studying and sacrifice have been made easier because I have a partner who encourages me, family who look out for me, and friends to whom I can (and do!) complain. They are the ones on whom you will rely when the rejection letters come in, when you are feeling stressed, or when you are celebrating the achievement of your goals.

Essay 9
My Journey Overcoming
Barriers: Identifying
Alternatives and
Pursuing Passions
James O. Prochaska

I learned at a young age that barriers at times can get the best of us and at other times can inspire us. I watched my father struggle with his demons of depression, alcohol, and violence and tragically they got the best of him. I felt depressed by my inability to help him. Now I know that his struggles were the inspiration for my becoming a psychologist, to discover how people can overcome chronic conditions and how I can help those who are not ready to change.

However, I didn't feel ready to apply for graduate school because I became a psychology major late in my junior year. I had anxieties about the Psychology section of the GRE, did not know professors very well for recommendations, and did not have clarity about what type of graduate program would be best for me.

Nevertheless, I had a strong conviction that I could make a difference as a psychologist. I also had a strong grade point average and confidence in my ability to write an engaging essay. So I focused on those parts of the application process that were under my control, including reading a leading Introduction to Psychology text for the GRE and producing an inspired statement about myself and my mission as a psychologist.

Fortunately, as a senior graduating from Wayne State University, I found myself blessed with wonderful choices of PhD programs in clinical psychology, including Harvard University and Clark University. One of my professors received his PhD from Clark and claimed that it was to psychology what Paris was to art. So I matriculated there and got depressed.

I didn't know how to paint. That is, I didn't know how to do psychology. However, at the end of the first semester our class was required to present an original research project to the entire department. The faculty tried to help by tossing out research topics in each class. But I had such a need to be independent that I tossed out their ideas in favor of my own. The problem was that my project became so confounded that it was not interpretable. I remember sitting catatonically at my desk, totally unable to write because my science made no sense.

Night after night I sat without a sentence to show for my time. I told my roommate to reserve me a room at the Worcester State Hospital. How awful it felt to be falling apart when I was supposed to become a clinical psychologist.

In the midst of my despair, I somehow came up with a therapeutic solution. If I wrote my research presentation using the most complex vocabulary possible, no one would be able to decipher what I was saying. Brilliant! I took out my thesaurus and wrote my report in one evening, and no one could tell whether my presentation was their problem or mine.

At least my presentation fulfilled the requirements for this ungraded assignment. This was one of those projects in which I could not be both satisfied and finished, so I just had to be satisfied that I was finished. Lessons learned: (a) Don't be more independent than you are ready to be, and (b) even when you feel most helpless there can be creative ways to cope. However, I had to deal with my depression and my dependence. I went back home for the holidays and asked the love of my life, "If I were a carpenter, would you marry me anyway?" Jan said, "no"! Lesson learned: Don't expect a lover to be a therapist.

But Jan was right. She knew I would never be fulfilled unless I became a psychologist. Besides, I could not hammer a nail.

I dealt with my dependence by transferring back home to Wayne State, taking one step back to take two steps forward. And I went into therapy.

I remember moaning to my therapist, "I should have gone to Harvard. I will never be able to do anything great!"

All he said was, "Why not?"

So I got un-depressed and went on to learn a good deal about how to do psychology as a therapist and a scientist. I was planning for a full-time clinical career until I did a full-time clinical internship. Then I realized I was not prepared for a structured position that involved working from 8 a.m. to 5 p.m. My love of autonomy and creativity makes me averse to positions that lack flexibility. I need to be able to read or write until late into the night.

In my 5th year of graduate school, I changed my career plans and decided that I really wanted the autonomy of academia. Fortunately, it was 1969, and there were plenty of opportunities. I accepted a position at the University of Rhode Island without a single publication. I didn't even wait for an offer from Penn State and cancelled my visit to the University of Colorado. Today I wouldn't be seriously considered for a starting position at any of these universities without a growing series of publications. How fortunate I feel that in my day I could be given excellent opportunities even though I was a slow starter as an undergraduate and graduate student.

I joined a department that was just starting PhD programs in clinical, school, and experimental psychology. My colleagues were supportive;

the students were stimulating; my part-time practice was rewarding. I received tenure and promotion to full professor within 7 years.

My love life was wonderful: I had a wife who was a terrific social worker and mother and a son and daughter who were such joys. We lived on eight acres in the woods with ponds and stone walls and the beauty of nature.

In spite of such an idyllic life, I got depressed. Again. I was not making much of a creative contribution to psychology. I was not fulfilling my potential as a psychologist. Once again, I was a slow starter.

I remember moaning to myself, "I should have gone to Penn State. I will never be able to do anything great!"

Then I heard my therapist within say, "Why not?"

So I went running—but not from myself. I was trying to discover where I went wrong. As I jogged, I recalled one of the lessons I learned as a graduate student reading a book about the personal knowledge of scientists. Scientists must be passionate about their search. However, most of the time my teachers taught me that scientists have to be objective.

I have come to believe that scientists, on the one hand, cannot and do not need to be objective. Science, on the other hand, can and needs to be objective. Like most of us, scientists make their best contributions when they are passionate about their work. I committed myself to pursuing my passions wherever they led, and it has made all the difference since.

After this transformation, my reward and grant productivity increased by 1,000%. I was recognized as one of the five most influential authors in psychology. Most important, I have been able to help many more people than I ever imagined possible.

The gist of it is this: Same person. Same position. Same psychologist. Different pursuit. Plenty of perspiration. And help from a lot of people.

Lessons I've learned are (a) don't plan a career for a lifetime—plan a career for as long as your passion for it lasts, and then change; (b) if your environment doesn't permit you to fulfill your potential, leave or transcend your environment; (c) don't put pressure on yourself to make your best contributions at a young age—psychologists make their most important contributions after age 40; and (d) self-actualization is not something you can do at one time—it is something that takes a lifetime.

Recommended Resources

This list of resources includes some of the many books and Web sites that are available and relevant for applicants. Please be aware that such resources often change and can become outdated.

Books

American Psychological Association. (2007). *Getting in: A step-by-step plan for gaining admission to graduate school in psychology* (2nd ed.). Washington, DC: Author.

American Psychological Association. (2008). *Graduate study in psychology*. Washington, DC: Author.

Bracken, S. J., Allen, J. K., & Dean, D. R. (2006). *The balancing act: Gendered perspectives in faculty roles and work lives*. Sterling, VA: Stylus Publishing.

Buskist, W., & Burke, C. H. (2006). *Preparing for graduate study in psychology: 101 questions and answers* (2nd ed.). Boston: Blackwell Publishing.

Castellanos, J., Gloria, A. M., & Kamimura, M. (2005). *The Latina/o pathway to the Ph.D.: Abriendo caminos*. Sterling, VA: Stylus Publishing.

Cone, J. D., & Foster, S. L. (2006). *Dissertations and theses from start to finish: Psychology and related fields* (2nd ed.). Washington, DC: American Psychological Association.

Green, A. L., & Scott, L. V. (2003). *Journey to the Ph.D.: How to navigate the process as African Americans.* Sterling, VA: Stylus Publishing.

Hasan, N. T., Fouad, N. A., & Williams-Nickelson, C. (2008). *Studying psychology in the United States: Expert guidance for international students.* Washington, DC: American Psychological Association.

Jacobs, L., Cintrón, J., & Canton, C. E. (Eds.). (2002). *The politics of survival in academia: Narratives of inequity, resilience, and success.* Lanham, MD: Rowman & Littlefield.

Keith-Spiegel, P., & Weiderman, M. W. (2000). *Complete guide to graduate school admission: Psychology, counseling, and related professions* (2nd ed.). Mahwah, NJ: Erlbaum.

Knight, A. (2002). *How to become a clinical psychologist: Getting a foot in the door.* New York: Brunner-Routledge.

Kuther, T. L. (2008). *Surviving graduate school in psychology: A pocket mentor.* Washington, DC: American Psychological Association.

Li, G., & Beckett, G. H. (2006). *Strangers of the academy: Asian women scholars in higher education.* Sterling, VA: Stylus Publishing.

Matthews, J. R., & Walker, C. E. (Eds.). (2005). *Your practicum in psychology: A guide for maximizing knowledge and competence.* Washington, DC: American Psychological Association.

Mayne, T. J., Norcross, J. C., & Sayette, M. A. (2006). *Insider's guide to graduate programs in clinical and counseling psychology: 2006/2007 edition.* New York: Guilford Press.

Morgan, B. L., & Korschgen, A. J. (2005). *Majoring in psych? Career options for psychology undergraduates* (3rd ed.). Boston: Allyn & Bacon.

O'Hara, S. (2005). *What can you do with a major in psychology?* Hoboken, NJ: Cliff Notes.

Peterson's. (2003). *Graduate programs in psychology* (4th ed.). Lawrenceville, NJ: Author.

Princeton Review. (2007). *Cracking the GRE psychology subject test* (7th ed.). New York: Author.

Sternberg, R. J. (2007). *Career paths in psychology: Where your degree can take you* (2nd ed.). Washington, DC: American Psychological Association.

Walfish, S., & Hess, A. K. (Eds.). (2001). *Succeeding in graduate school: The career guide for psychology students.* Mahwah, NJ: Erlbaum.

Williams-Nickelson, C., Mitchell J., & Prinstein, M. J. (Eds.). (2007). *Internships in psychology: The APAGS workbook for writing successful applications and finding the right match: 2007–2008 edition.* Washington, DC: American Psychological Association.

Web Sites

AllPsych ONLINE: http://www.allpsych.com

American Psychological Association (APA): http://www.apa.org

American Psychological Association of Graduate Students: http://www.apa.org/apags

APA Divisions: http://www.apa.org/about/division.html

APA Education Directorate: http://www.apa.org/ed

APA Office of Program Consultation and Accreditation: http://www.apa.org/ed/accreditation

APA Rules for Acceptance of Offers for Admission and Financial Aid: http://www.apa.org/ed/accept.html

Association of Psychology Postdoctoral and Internship Centers: http://www.appic.org

Association of State and Provincial Psychology Boards: http://www.asppb.org

Athabasca University Psychology Resources: http://psych.athabascau.ca/html/aupr/psycres.shtml

Canadian Psychological Association: http://www.cpa.ca

Committee on Institutional Cooperation: http://www.cic.uiuc.edu

Computer Retrieval of Information on Scientific Projects: http://crisp.cit.nih.gov

Educational Testing Service's Graduate Record Examinations: http://www.gre.org

Educational Testing Service's Test of English as a Foreign Language: http://www.toefl.org

Encyclopedia of Psychology: http://www.psychology.org

gradPSYCH: http://gradpsych.apags.org

GradSchools.com: http://www.gradschools.com

Graduate Study in Psychology: http://www.geocities.com/Heartland/Flats/5353/classes/graduatestudy.html

National Science Foundation: http://www.nsf.gov

National Science Foundation's Research Experiences for Undergraduates: http://www.nsf.gov/funding/pgm_summ.jsp?pims_id=5517

Project 1000: http://mati.eas.asu.edu:8421/p1000

Psi Chi: http://www.psichi.org

Psych Central: http://psychcentral.com

Psych Web: http://www.psywww.com

PsycNET: http://psycinfo.apa.org

Psychology Today: http://www.psychologytoday.com

PubMed: http://www.ncbi.nlm.nih.gov/entrez

Social Psychology Network: http://www.socialpsychology.org

U.S. Department of Education's Free Application for Federal Student Aid: http://www.fafsa.ed.gov

U.S. Department of Labor Bureau of Labor Statistics: http://stats.bls.gov/oco/ocos056.htm

Glossary

Christina M. Grange

ACCREDITATION: A designation granted by the American Psychological Association and the Canadian Psychological Association to clinical, counseling, and school psychology doctoral programs and internships. It assures the educational community and general public that a doctoral program has met a rigorous set of standards for training students.

ADVISOR: A faculty member who is generally responsible for consulting with a student regarding academic matters, research, and professional development. In psychology programs, the advisor generally serves as the chairperson for thesis and dissertation research.

AMERICAN BOARD OF PROFESSIONAL PSYCHOLOGY (ABPP; HTTP://WWW.ABPP.ORG): An organization that certifies specialists in psychology to practice (i.e., provide mental health services) in private or public sectors. Certification involves individuals submitting to a peer review that involves an assessment of whether they meet the standards and demonstrate the competencies required in the specialty.

AMERICAN PSYCHOLOGICAL ASSOCIATION (APA; HTTP://WWW.APA.ORG): A scientific and professional organization that represents psychology in the United States. With more than 150,000 members, APA is the largest association of psychologists worldwide.

AMERICAN PSYCHOLOGICAL ASSOCIATION OF GRADUATE STUDENTS (APAGS; HTTP://
WWW.APA.ORG/APAGS): The official graduate student association for APA that
represents graduate students' interests and promotes professional development.

ASSISTANTSHIP: Funding awarded to graduate students as they work to obtain their graduate degree. Assistantships generally require individuals
to work for a specified number of hours (usually 10–20) to receive a
stipend. In addition to the stipend, an assistantship sometimes covers the
cost of tuition (i.e., tuition remission). There are three common types of
assistantships:

> ADMINISTRATIVE ASSISTANTSHIP: Responsibilities may include working in a
> university office to provide support (e.g., serve as an undergradu-
> ate advisor, work as an assistant to a graduate program director).
> RESEARCH ASSISTANTSHIP (RA): Responsibilities may include working on
> a single research project or on a program of research. These posi-
> tions are usually available because a faculty member has received
> grant funding.
> TEACHING ASSISTANTSHIP (TA): Responsibilities may include teaching an
> undergraduate or graduate course or assisting a professor who is
> teaching a course.

BOULDER MODEL: A model for training psychologists that was born out of
the first national training conference on clinical psychology, which was
held in 1949 in Boulder, Colorado. Participants at the conference agreed
that the PhD would be the degree necessary to qualify as a psychologist.
Participants also decided that the ideal training model would be the
scientist–practitioner model, which prepares students to work as researchers and clinicians.

CANADIAN PSYCHOLOGICAL ASSOCIATION (CPA; HTTP://WWW.CPA.CA): A scientific
and professional organization that represents psychology in Canada.

CLINICAL SUPERVISOR: A senior therapist who is responsible, both ethically
and legally, for the clinical activities of a supervisee (i.e., often a graduate
student in training). A supervisor typically provides support, facilitates
learning, offers feedback, and evaluates a supervisee's progress and development.

CLINICAL WORK: A broad term used to describe the many forms of direct
service to clients and patients (e.g., psychotherapy, assessment, case management). Clinical work is a required training component of doctoral
programs in clinical, counseling, and school psychology.

CONFERENCES: Professional meetings specific to disciplines or topics. Research conferences serve as a venue for issues to be discussed and for

new research to be disseminated through poster presentations, paper presentations, or symposiums (e.g., panel discussion).

Curriculum vitae (CV): A written description of one's work experience, educational background, skills, and publications. It is generally more detailed than a résumé.

Dissertation: A doctoral-level research requirement that represents all components of formal, original research conducted by a graduate student with the support of a panel of university faculty. It is usually the culmination of a student's training and research experience while in graduate school.

Doctor of philosophy (PhD): A research degree—the highest awarded by a college or university in a specified discipline—received after an individual has met program requirements.

Doctor of psychology (PsyD): A professional degree—the highest awarded by a college or university in applied psychology—received after an individual has met program requirements. This degree emphasizes clinical practice and the application of research rather than the conducting of original research.

Experimental psychology: A general category of psychology subfields that focus on basic research. Among these subfields are cognitive, developmental, social, and biological psychology.

Externship: A training experience in which students provide psychological services to clients or patients in settings beyond a school or university (also referred to as *external practicum*).

Fellowship: An award, similar to a scholarship, that is given to support research or teaching and provides financial support. Fellowships are often awarded by a college or university (or sometimes by a larger agency, such as the National Institutes of Health). They may have departmental or academic responsibilities associated with them.

Graduate Record Examinations (GRE) General Test (http://www.ets.org): A standardized test that is required for admittance to most graduate programs that consists of three sections: Verbal Reasoning, Quantitative Reasoning, and Analytical Writing.

Graduate Record Examinations (GRE) Subject Test (http://www.ets.org): A standardized test that is required for admission to some graduate programs. Scores help graduate school admission committees assess students' knowledge of a specific subject matter. Subject tests are offered in a variety of fields, including psychology.

Grant: Funding awarded to individuals for a proposed project. In psychology departments, faculty members typically submit research proposals specific to their particular areas of interest. Funding sources may include large agencies (e.g., National Institutes of Health) or smaller institutions (e.g., universities, private sources). Graduate students often serve as assistants on grants awarded to faculty members and may receive tuition, stipend payments, or supplementary funding for this work. In addition, graduate students can apply for grants to support their research.

INTERNSHIP: A training experience, usually of a 1-year duration, that is generally the final clinical requirement for doctoral candidates in clinical, counseling, and school psychology programs. It involves an application process facilitated by the Association of Psychology Postdoctoral and Internship Centers (APPIC; http://www.appic.org).

MASTER OF ARTS (MA): A degree, typically without a strong research focus, usually awarded for the completion of a postgraduate course of 1 or 2 years in duration.

MASTER OF SCIENCE (MS): A degree, typically featuring a strong research focus, awarded for the completion of a postgraduate course of 1 or 2 years in duration.

MASTER OF SOCIAL WORK (MSW): A professional degree that prepares an individual to practice social work (i.e., a discipline that uses a social systems approach to create social change for individuals, groups, and communities).

PEER REVIEW: The process wherein scholars critique proposed research articles before they are accepted for publication in a peer-reviewed journal.

PEER-REVIEWED JOURNALS: Scholarly publications in which new research is shared with the wider scientific community.

POSTDOCTORAL TRAINING (POSTDOC): A specialized training opportunity that individuals who have earned their doctorate can apply for; it does not result in another degree, but it is considered to be valuable supplemental experience. Postdoctoral opportunities may focus on research or clinical training or both and are usually 1 to 2 years long.

PRACTICUM: A general term to describe training experiences in which students provide psychological services to clients and patients in a variety of settings.

PROFESSIONAL SCHOOL: An educational body that grants only graduate degrees and may be either affiliated with a university or a freestanding institution.

PSI CHI (HTTP://WWW.PSICHI.ORG): A national honor society in psychology that promotes scholarship and the advancement of the science of psychology. Membership is open to undergraduate and graduate students who meet academic qualifications. Students become members by joining the chapter at the school in which they are enrolled.

PSYCHIATRIST: A physician (i.e., doctor of medicine) who treats patients with mental disorders and is licensed to prescribe medication.

PSYCHOLOGIST: The professional title of someone with a doctoral degree in psychology (i.e., a PhD or PsyD) and who is trained in the behavior, thoughts, and emotions of individuals or groups. He or she often works as an academic, clinician, researcher, or consultant, but many other career paths are possible. The legal definition of *psychologist* may differ by state.

PSYCHOLOGY SUBFIELDS:

ABNORMAL PSYCHOLOGY: Focuses on maladaptive or deviant behavior and psychopathology.

BIOLOGICAL PSYCHOLOGY: Focuses on the physiological processes that influence thoughts, feelings, and behavior.

CHILD AND ADOLESCENT PSYCHOLOGY: Focuses on the psychology of children and adolescents, particularly the biological, psychological, and social aspects of their development.

CLINICAL PSYCHOLOGY: Focuses on the assessment and treatment of mental and physical health problems. This field has traditionally differed from counseling psychology because of its emphasis on psychopathology. Over the years, differences between clinical and counseling psychology have become less noticeable.

COGNITIVE PSYCHOLOGY: Focuses on thought processes and how people process, store, and retrieve information.

COMMUNITY PSYCHOLOGY: Focuses on improving the well-being of people and their communities through the understanding of how individuals operate in social systems.

COMPARATIVE PSYCHOLOGY: Focuses on the behavior and mental processes of animals in order to better understand human experiences.

COUNSELING PSYCHOLOGY: Focuses on the assessment and treatment of mental and physical health problems. This field has traditionally differed from clinical psychology because it is less concerned with psychopathology but addresses personal and interpersonal development across the life span. Over the years, differences between clinical and counseling psychology have become less noticeable.

DEVELOPMENTAL PSYCHOLOGY: Focuses on growth and change across the life span.

EDUCATIONAL PSYCHOLOGY: Focuses on how humans learn best in educational settings. Educational psychologists typically are researchers, whereas school psychologists are practitioners.

EVOLUTIONARY PSYCHOLOGY: Focuses on the inherited genetic qualities that influence thoughts, feelings, and behavior.

FAMILY PSYCHOLOGY: Focuses on growth and change within the family system.

FORENSIC PSYCHOLOGY: Focuses on legal issues and criminal behavior.

HEALTH PSYCHOLOGY: Focuses on the interrelationship between psychological processes and physical well-being.

INDUSTRIAL/ORGANIZATIONAL PSYCHOLOGY: Focuses on individual and group performance at work and other aspects of the workplace.

PERSONALITY PSYCHOLOGY: Focuses on patterns of personal characteristics and individual differences.

PSYCHOMETRICS: Focuses on the measurement principles and techniques used in the study of psychology.

QUANTITATIVE PSYCHOLOGY: Focuses on the development and use of statistical analyses and procedures.

REHABILITATION PSYCHOLOGY: Focuses on the application of psychological principles to improve the well-being of individuals with disabilities.

SCHOOL PSYCHOLOGY: Focuses on the assessment and treatment of academic, social, and emotional factors that affect students' performance in school. School psychologists are practitioners, whereas educational psychologists typically are researchers.

SOCIAL PSYCHOLOGY: Focuses on how relationships and social conditions affect individuals and groups.

SPORT AND EXERCISE PSYCHOLOGY: Focuses on the enhancement of athletic performance and exercise for individuals and teams.

PSYCHOTHERAPY: The treatment of mental and emotional problems using psychological methods. The approach generally involves verbal interactions between a therapist and a client or patient, development of an interpersonal relationship, and implementation of strategies to address a client's or patient's concerns.

STIPEND: Type of salary for graduate students that typically requires them to work. Stipends are funded by departments, fellowships, or grants, and duties often include serving as a research, teaching, or administrative assistant.

TENURE: A status earned by faculty members at universities that ensures academic freedom and job security.

TERMINAL MASTER'S DEGREE: A degree that is considered an end in itself and that is awarded when students have completed master's-level requirements for a specific graduate program. In contrast, many doctoral programs in psychology are organized for students to acquire a master's degree as they complete requirements for the doctoral degree. Students may apply to a doctoral program after acquiring a terminal master's degree.

THESIS: A document that describes a master's-level research project and its findings. It is often required by psychology graduate programs.

TRANSCRIPT: A document listing a student's academic performance at an educational institution; it often includes the following: name of school, major and minor, courses completed, grade for each course, and grade point average.

> OFFICIAL TRANSCRIPT: A transcript from the school registrar that is usually stamped with the school seal and provided in a sealed envelope. At least one official transcript is generally required for graduate school applications. At some universities, there is a fee for official transcripts.
>
> UNOFFICIAL TRANSCRIPT: A transcript that is not sealed in an envelope and often is obtained from a school registrar or from a school's Web site. This document is useful to review but is not generally accepted as part of graduate school applications.

TUITION REMISSION: A benefit offered by some graduate programs whereby tuition is waived partially or fully. Tuition remission may be awarded in conjunction with an assistantship.

VAIL MODEL: A model for training psychologists that originated at a national training conference in Vail, Colorado, in 1973. In this model, students earn a PsyD (i.e., doctor of psychology) degree as an alternative to the traditional PhD (i.e., doctor of philosophy) degree. The professional PsyD degree was designed to provide specialized training as a scholar–professional, which prepares students to work primarily as clinicians. This model has a lesser degree of training and focus on research skills than does the traditional PhD training model.

WAIT-LISTED: A status for applicants who have not been rejected from nor accepted to a graduate program and therefore been placed on hold. They may be invited to attend at a later date.

Index

About the Editors

Amanda C. Kracen, MS, is a 5th-year doctoral student in counseling psychology at Virginia Commonwealth University in Richmond and specializes in health psychology and behavioral medicine. Prior to graduate school, Ms. Kracen earned a BA from Brown University and worked as a researcher at Trinity College, Dublin, in Ireland. Her clinical work and research focus on the health and well-being of health care professionals and how these factors affect patient care. She is an active member of Divisions 17 (Society of Counseling Psychology), 38 (Health Psychology), and 52 (International Psychology) of the American Psychological Association (APA). She has won awards for her research and service, including the Award for Extraordinary Service from APA Division 52 in 2006.

Ian J. Wallace, MA, MS, is a 5th-year doctoral student in counseling psychology at Virginia Commonwealth University in Richmond, specializing in health psychology and sport psychology. Mr. Wallace earned a BA in psychology from The College of New Jersey and an MA in clinical psychology from Pepperdine University, while working full-time as a case manager at an inpatient psychiatric facility. His research focuses on the mechanisms of health behavior change in youth and adolescents; he served as the data manager for a grant-funded, multisite community intervention study that promoted preventive behavior among teenagers. As a clinician, he most enjoys working with athletes and couples.

DEMCO